ANNA LEE

ANNA LEE

Memoir of a Career on *General Hospital* and in Film

by Anna Lee

with Barbara Roisman Cooper

FOREWORD BY MAUREEN O'HARA

McFarland & Company, Inc., Publishers

Jefferson, North Carolina, and London

Unless otherwise noted, all photographs
are from the collection of Anna Lee.

LIBRARY OF CONGRESS CATALOGUING-IN-PUBLICATION DATA

Lee, Anna, 1914–2004.
    Anna Lee : memoir of a career on General hospital and in film /
by Anna Lee, with Barbara Roisman Cooper ; foreword by
Maureen O'Hara.
        p.   cm.
    Includes index.

    ISBN-13: 978-0-7864-3161-8
    softcover : 50# alkaline paper ∞

    1. Lee, Anna, 1914–2004.   2. Actors—Great Britain—Biography.
3. Actors—United States—Biography.   I. Roisman Cooper,
Barbara, 1941–   II. Title.
PN2598.L37A3   2007
792.02'8092—dc22
[B]   2007013508

British Library cataloguing data are available

On the cover: Anna Lee in a publicity photograph from General
Hospital in 1988 (©ABC Photo Archives)

Manufactured in the United States of America

McFarland & Company, Inc., Publishers
  Box 611, Jefferson, North Carolina 28640
    www.mcfarlandpub.com

*Anna Lee passed away before she completed her autobiography.
Her son, Jeffrey Byron, offers this dedication in her name,
as it expresses her wishes for the book:*

To my children,
Venetia, Caroline, Stephen, and Jeffrey,
my grandchildren, my great-grandchildren,
and, of course,
fans and colleagues of
General Hospital
so they will know the whole story
—Anna Lee

Her co-author offers this dedication:

For my husband, Martin,
for all the good things he is to me

and

in memory of my parents,
Helen and Isadore Roisman

—Barbara Roisman Cooper

Acknowledgments

by Barbara Roisman Cooper

Without Anna Lee, all the memories would have faded to black. So, most of all, Anna, thank you for living a life worth sharing.

A very special thank you to Maureen O'Hara for the touching words about her long-time friend and co-star.

The inspiration and assistance from Anna Lee's *General Hospital* family, their insights about this lovely lady, and their anecdotes about her life on the set gave meaning to her last quarter century. The love and admiration of the cast, crew, and executives of *General Hospital* make her story possible. A special bow to Leslie Charleson, who was instrumental in organizing her colleagues for interviews between takes and whose personal regard and devotion to her television "Mummie" went beyond the camera. Also, I appreciate insights from other *General Hospital* associates in front of and behind the camera: Joe Behar, Shelley Curtis, Stuart Damon, Jane Elliot, Jo Ann Emmerich, Anthony Geary, John Ingle, Francesca James, Wally Kurth, Anne Jeffreys, Bill Ludel, Brad Maule, Lenny Marcus, Donna Messina, Wendy Pennington-Holz, Wendy Riche, Constance Towers, and Dale Walsh.

Anna's great friend, Patricia Barry, offered details about a particularly difficult time in Anna's life. Patricia Crowley, who played a lengthy personal and professional role in Anna's life, shared her memories of early television; so did her sister, Ann Crowley Jones.

Anna Lee's children supplied memories of what it was like to live with an actress. Her youngest son, Jeffrey Byron, actively supported this project from day one, urging his mother to continue even through her great personal and physical pain. Thanks also to daughters Caroline Stevenson and Venetia Stevenson, and son Stephen Stafford.

Anna's only surviving sibling, Ruth Winnifrith Wood, regaled me with wistful stories about the early days of the Winnifrith family and her sister, who, to this day, she still calls Joan.

There was always encouragement—and a red pen—from my husband Martin. My cousins, Kathy Keane and Howie Fishman, kept smiling and nodding, even when they heard the same story for the umpteenth time.

Others who provided details, details and more details: Leslie Charleson's personal assistant, Krista Dragna, who knows more about *General Hospital* than anyone; Janice Headland, Materials Officer, Films, British Film Institute, who provided names and dates; Kate Edelman Johnson, who remembers some of the trying times; June Parker Beck, editor and designer of the Maureen O'Hara website; Joyce Howard; Jean Simmons; Tommy Garrett; Mitchell Messinger, Director, Media and Talent Relations, ABC Daytime Television, who coordinated interviews; Coral Petretti, Supervisor, Photography, Disney/ABC Television Group, for assisting with photograph selections; John Oddy, Executive Director, Royal Oak Foundation; Wheeler Winston Dixon, University of Nebraska, Lincoln; Buddy Weiss and Ronald Mandelbaum at Photofest; and Robert Osborne, Turner Classic Movies on-air host and *The Hollywood Reporter* columnist.

Thanks also to the Academy of Motion Picture Arts & Sciences' Margaret Herrick Library staff.

Because of the contribution of all these people, Anna Lee's colorful life will never fade.

Contents

Foreword
by Maureen O'Hara

When I first met Anna Lee, it was on the set of *How Green Was My Valley*. I was immediately impressed by her smile, and the sweetness of her nature. She had a great sense of humor, which brought a lovely element of fun to the shooting of the movie. I will always remember how kind and considerate she was to everyone. We became good friends on and off the set and could sit and gossip for hours about our personal lives.

In fact, I admired her so much that when I gave birth to a daughter I named her Bronwyn for Anna Lee. I didn't care for the name Anna and said as much to her. I told her I would name my child Bronwyn for the role she played in *How Green Was My Valley*. She was thrilled that I thought enough of her to do that.

There are some people in life who are destined to remain forever friends. That was the case with Anna, Roddy McDowall, and me. The three of us called each other on a regular basis and met as often as possible for dinner—many times at Anna's home. She was a wonderful hostess, and I have fond memories of many great meals and conversations at her table, in her home with Robert Nathan.

I was so happy when she met Robert and their relationship developed into a wonderful marriage. It was a marriage of love and mutual respect, something Anna so yearned for and deserved. We were also happy for Robert that he found Anna at that hour of his life and received such devotion from her.

Before Robert, Anna went through so much unhappiness in her personal life. Whenever I would hear of her problems, it would make me feel

1

so sad for her, and I tried to keep in touch and offer as much support as possible, as did Roddy McDowall and so many other great friends in quiet ways.

In spite of her misfortunes, Anna was always courageous and considerate of all of us. Even in her last years with pain and suffering this remained the case.

My last memory of her when visiting at her home not long before she died was sad because she was quite sick, and I knew her end was near. She died soon after. I pray she has found the peace that she deserves with Robert, her last love, and all of her family and friends who loved her and have gone before her. I'm so happy she was able to tell her story her way, and hope you all enjoy the journey she has chosen to share.

Co. Cork, Ireland
December 2006

Preface

by Barbara Roisman Cooper

John Wayne, Marlene Dietrich, Bette Davis, Joan Crawford, Boris Karloff—and a drooling camel. These are just a few of the actors with whom Anna Lee shared the screen over a remarkable career spanning 70 years.

From the early days of British film, through key roles in numerous American pictures and as the "First Lady of Television," Anna Lee's career culminated in a starring role in the most famous of all daytime soap operas, *General Hospital*.

Life took her from a childhood in England spinning tales about fairies while sitting on the lap of Sherlock Holmes' creator, Arthur Conan Doyle, to starring in Hollywood as Lila Quartermaine, doyenne of TV daytime dramas, for 25 years. In between, she shared the world's stage with a broad array of friends, lovers, and acquaintances: General George S. Patton, Howard Hughes, John Ford, Jack Benny, and many more.

The daughter of a rural Anglican clergyman, Anna Lee went from stage to film to television, with stops along the way as a star of World War II USO shows in the Persian Gulf, a Montana rancher, and a Beverly Hills store clerk. She fell in—and out of—love with many a uniformed serviceman and endured poverty and abuse along the path of a truly unique life. Her three husbands—two of them famous—shaped her adult life in ways wonderful and wicked.

Anna Lee places stardom in perspective and reveals how she overcame her greatest challenge: two decades in a wheelchair while television cameras captured her every expression.

Her life is a testament to a woman who lived her 91 years to the fullest.

I first met Anna Lee while researching my book *Straight from the Horse's Mouth*—the story of Ronald Neame, director of the original *The Poseidon Adventure*, *The Prime of Miss Jean Brodie*, and many more noteworthy films. He and Anna had both a professional and highly personal relationship.

I worked with Anna Lee for five years, first in the sunny living room of her charming Beverly Hills cottage, with her beloved Great Dane, Hugo, sitting next to her wheelchair. Here she recounted to me a life of romance, rags, and riches, one that befitted the soap opera icon she had become. Then, during the last year, as her health deteriorated, I sat beside her bed, and we watched her films, and she would laugh as she told me about her acting colleagues, her costume fittings, and the premieres she attended.

Anna Lee generously gave me access to her personal scrapbooks and correspondence, and I spent time at both the Margaret Herrick Library of the Academy of Motion Picture Arts and Sciences in Los Angeles and the British Film Institute Library in London researching the details of her career. I also interviewed more than three dozen people who worked, played, loved, and traveled with Anna Lee. Some of their anecdotes and remembrances are quoted in this book. I never found a single person who spoke ill of her.

It was a privilege to know this brave, talented woman. Doing her life justice has not been an easy task; I hope I have been up to it.

Introduction

Written by Anna Lee in 2003. She died on May 14, 2004.

This has not been an easy story to write. My memory is still reasonably good at 90, but so often I find people and places disappear in the shadows of my mind. Sometimes I cannot remember where the real story begins and where my imagination takes over.

My late husband, novelist and poet Robert Nathan, describes this in a poem, which appears as a frontispiece in his novel, *The Summer Meadows*.

> ...Behind, in summer meadows,
> The live, bright figures come and go. They are far away
> Smaller and smaller, seen for a moment and lost again,
> Golden, tiny creatures, in and out of the sun, ourselves
>   Among them,
> Leaping and darting, dancing in butterfly clusters,
> Singing of love, singing of youth eternal.
>   It was all there once.
> It is all there still.
>   We go forward into the forest.
> We can never go back to join them. We can never return there.

Sometimes fact seems entwined with fantasy. There are times when I doubt my own memory. Did I actually see those fairies so long ago? During World War I, did I really wade into the English Channel and plan to swim over to the Continent and kill the Kaiser to save King and Country? Was it really General George S. Patton who gave me an award for entertaining the troops during World War II?

Did I really share the screen with the super-sized American John Wayne,

charming Ronald Colman, tough guy Edward G. Robinson, henpecked Paul
Muni, mysterious Conrad Veidt, poetry-loving Boris Karloff, and gorgeous
Marlene Dietrich?

Although the events and people are, alas, gone, they still "leap and
dart" in and out of my memory.

This memoir is partly due to the encouragement and sometimes more-
than-gentle persuasion from my colleagues on *General Hospital*, the daytime
soap series on which I have appeared for 25 years, including Leslie Charleson,
Stuart Damon, and Wendy Riche. They're amazed at my longevity and the
fact that even being wheelchair-bound, I still work two or three or four days
a week.

My life has been long and filled with events, small triumphs, many dis-
appointments, moments of great happiness and deep sorrow. They flicker
clearly—and then they are lost again.

I write this before the colors fade entirely.

So, fact or fantasy—or a little of both—this is my story.

1

Early Memories

Ightham is a village nestled in the foothills of Kent, certainly the most beautiful of the English counties. There are beechwood trees; bluebells carpet the meadows in summer; soft green hills rise in the north; and gray marshes slope to the sea.

Some days after my birth on January 2, 1913, my father, the Reverend Bertram Thomas Winnifrith, baptized me at his church, St. Peter's. I was named Joan Boniface. Boniface was the saint from whom the Winnifrith family was descended. Although I am the namesake of a saint, I fear I did not inherit his virtuous traits!

The year after I was born, war broke out. "The Great War" it was called, then "The War to End All Wars."

I have only a few memories of those years. One I especially recall is my father carrying me downstairs one night out onto the front lawn to see a Zeppelin in flames slowly floating downward. It crashed several miles away.

And then there was the terrifying incident with the mule, which belonged to the Horse Gunners who were stationed nearby. The animal broke away from its barn and ran into our kitchen garden where I was playing. I ran down the path to the greenhouse with the mule in hot pursuit. I crouched behind a large rhubarb jar while the terrified animal tried to back its way out into the garden. As I knelt, frozen with fear, its enormous hooves clattered up and down within a few inches of my face. I don't know who was more frightened, the mule or me. Finally after what seemed hours, two soldiers rushed in. As one of them calmed the beast and led it away, the other picked me up and carried me, sobbing, back to the house.

That was, I think, the first of many times that I would be in the arms of a man in uniform. But more of that later!

There was another story that I heard repeated over and over again, until it became embedded in my memory. One of the kitchen servants asked another, "Did you hear how Miss Joan tried to swim across the Channel to kill the Kaiser?"

It was true that I hated the Kaiser. A picture of him hung on the nursery wall next to a photograph of Kitchener, the hero of Khartoum. The Kaiser was wearing a helmet with a point at the top and had a horrible sneer on his mustachioed face. My nurse used him to threaten me. "Eat your porridge, Joan, or the Kaiser will get you!" she'd say. Adding, "If you don't behave yourself, I will tell the Kaiser!"

I must have been about four years old when my mother took my nurse and me down to Hythe, a seaside town in the southeast of Kent on the English Channel. On a clear day the coast of France is actually visible in the distance.

Seated on the beach one sunny afternoon, I was happily playing with pebbles when I heard a great booming sound and saw great clouds of smoke rising from the distant coast.

My nurse seemed unperturbed by the sounds. I ran to her, demanding to know what the noise was.

"Them's those Huns shooting at our boys!" she replied. "Someone should kill that Kaiser!" she added angrily. Perhaps her fellow was over there.

I returned to playing with the pebbles, but an idea began to form in my mind. "Why not *me?*" I thought. I was convinced that I could do my duty for King and Country!

As soon as my nurse was asleep, I took off my shoes and socks and made my way down to the water's edge. Without a moment's hesitation, I strode, fully dressed, into the sea. I waded forward until I was up to my chin in the water, ready to face the Kaiser.

All of a sudden, I felt two strong arms gather me up and pull me from the water.

As he carried me to the beach, he asked, "What on earth were you up to, young lady?" he asked.

"I was going to France to kill the Kaiser," I replied matter of factly.

"A jolly good idea," he said, "but I think we had better get you into some dry clothes first, or you'll catch cold."

I pointed out my nurse, who was still asleep. He awakened her, and admonished her: "You should take better care of your charge. She could have been drowned, and then where would you be?"

I wish I could remember the face of the man who rescued me. But I do remember he wore a Harris tweed jacket, and he had a moustache.

The memory of that day remains faint, obscured by years, but there are still times when I smell damp Harris tweed, tobacco, and Bay Rum Hair Tonic, and I remember!

All in all I had a wonderfully happy childhood. Long, tranquil days, seemingly never-ending summers filled with the scent of new-mown hay and the warm, sweet fragrance of the yellow forsythia and climbing roses that grew beneath the nursery window.

I have always believed in fairies. I still do. As a child, I knew that they were in the woods at Ightham. They left trails of tiny white mushrooms beneath the trees and "fairy rings" in the meadows. They danced among the flowers in the Rectory garden. If I knelt down and closed my eyes and stayed very still, I could hear a very faint murmuring sound and a rustle, which meant that they were present.

One day, when I was sitting among the flowers, a lovely little creature of translucent green appeared, climbing up a stem of a foxglove. Its wings were transparent and webbed, like those of a butterfly.

My new governess, whom we called "Dai-Dai," was sitting nearby.

"Dai-Dai," I whispered. "Come quickly and see this fairy."

"That's not a fairy, dear," she said. "That's a dragonfly. A great many of them fly around here, especially in the hot weather."

I looked again at the little creature on the foxglove. It fluttered its wings and flew away. It certainly *did* look like a dragonfly, I thought. But I was convinced it was really a fairy!

My best friend, Francesca Bowra, lived close to the Rectory. I don't know if she really believed in fairies, but when I told her of my plan to look for them on the Enchanted Isle, she agreed to come along.

Shortly after dawn one morning, I slipped out of bed. Unfortunately, my clothes were all in the next room where Dai-Dai was sleeping. I knew there were some warm coats in the hall closet downstairs so I put on my party shoes—bronze leather with elastic bands that criss-crossed around the ankles—and tiptoed down stairs. I found my mother's black velvet opera cloak in the closet and flung it over my flannel nightdress. I opened one of the large windows in the dining room and climbed out.

In the east, the sky was just turning pink. I ran up Rectory Lane to Francesca's house. I climbed up the vine, which grew on the side of the house, and tapped gently on her bedroom window. Francesca was too scared to climb down the vine, so we quietly went down the staircase, carefully unlatched the front door, and slipped out into the cool of the dawn.

The Bowra house was on the corner of Rectory Lane and the Tonbridge Road, which led down a hill toward the village. We had not gone far when we heard the sounds of a horse and cart coming toward us. We pressed ourselves into the hedge on the opposite side of the road, hoping not to be seen. It was the milkman, making his early morning rounds. He saw us! He waved. We smiled and waved back. What must he have thought?

A quarter of a mile down the hill, we turned onto Busty Lane, which led past the meadow on which the island was situated. We climbed over the fence and made our way down to the little stream. I waded across, my clothes were now sopping wet and dragged heavily behind me. My mother's opera cloak left a wide swath in the grass and mud.

Francesca complained that she was exhausted after the long walk. She sat down, ate a chocolate egg from the provisions we had brought along, and promptly fell asleep.

I sat with my back against a large tree, closed my eyes, and listened intently for the sound that would mean the fairies were present. I heard it: a faint rustling. As I opened my eyes, I could see movement in the tall grass that grew at the edge of the stream. As I watched, the grasses parted, and a fairy appeared. It was larger than I expected, almost three inches tall and dressed in green.

I crept closer, trying to see it more clearly. Then, looking directly at me, it raised its arm and pointed upward to the tree, as if to show me where to find more fairies. I looked up and saw several small forms swinging in the branches. Then I looked back toward the first fairy, but it had disappeared. I tried to climb the tree, but my limbs would not move. Suddenly I felt completely exhausted, and, like my friend, fell asleep.

I later found out there was pandemonium at the Rectory when Dai-Dai found that I was not in my room and had discovered the open dining room window. She had run in terror to my father who sent someone down to the village to alert the police and the Boy Scouts. The Bowras had found that Francesca was also missing. The entire neighborhood was scoured, and within a couple of hours we were found and brought home... in disgrace.

My father was furious. I had never seen him so angry. "You are a wicked little girl," he said. He didn't shout; he never did, but his words were loud enough. He took a deep breath. Then, "Go to your room and stay there until I can decide on a suitable punishment. I am expecting a visitor. So I will see you when he leaves."

Dai-Dai took me upstairs, and I got into bed and lay there, waiting for my sentencing.

My father's visitor was an old friend whose son was enrolled in the Rectory school. He must have inquired about me, and my father must have told him what I had done.

"Some nonsense about looking for fairies," my father told him, probably embarrassed.

"No, Bertram. It's not nonsense," said the visitor. "Fairies are real! I believe in them. In fact, I have just finished writing a book about two young girls from Yorkshire who actually took photographs of the fairies they saw. The book will be published quite soon." He asked, "If you don't mind, may I speak to Joan and hear what she saw this morning?"

I was brought downstairs in my dressing gown and climbed into the visitor's lap. He was a giant of a man; his large moustache tickled my cheek as we talked.

He wanted to know what the fairies I had seen were like, what they were doing, and anything else I could recall. I told him everything I could remember; including the "fairy music" I had heard. What a pleasant feeling to know that a grownup believed in fairies as I did.

He was most attentive during my tale and promised to send me a copy of the book he had just written.

True to his word, *The Coming of the Fairies* arrived months later, and he had inscribed it to me! The photographs taken by the two girls were wonderful, and I believe even the hardiest of skeptics could not have failed to have been impressed.

It was not until some time later that I learned that the visitor's name: Sir Arthur Conan Doyle, creator of Sherlock Holmes!

To me, Sir Arthur will always remain a dear and good friend... and the friend who saved me from my father's wrath.

Winter brought so many exciting activities—snow and sledding and children's parties. The owners of the big houses gave parties for children at Christmastime. Every year, the faces were the same. There was John Watney from Ivy Hatch, whose father owned Watney's Ale. There were the Wedgwood children of the famed porcelain family. Their mother kept her husband's sword hanging over her bed, a memento of his death in the Great War, which I thought so sadly romantic! The Wedgwoods started my love for china and porcelain. Randolph Churchill and his sister Sarah were sometimes at the parties. Randolph was a horrid little boy; he was very conceited, and he pulled my hair!

The party that I will always remember was given at Fairlawne, one of the most beautiful houses in Kent and was home to the Cazelets.

At this particular Christmas party, I was sitting with Dai-Dai watching the other children when I became aware of a small boy with whom I became instantly infatuated. I ran forward and flung my arms around him, kissing him soundly on the mouth! He didn't like it, and he wriggled himself free and shouted, "Take this nasty little girl away!"

He was Peter Cazelet. I was five years old at the time, and he was seven. I left the party in disgrace, but I never forgot Peter.

He later made his name as the trainer of horses for Queen Elizabeth

The Queen Mother for her entries in the Derby and Grand National. There is now a Cazelet Handicap Chase. His elder brother, Col. Victor Cazelet, was killed on July 4, 1943, in a helicopter crash on Gibraltar.

During one of my visits home years later, I telephoned Peter. "This is the nasty little girl who kissed you at your party so long ago," I reminded him. Although I don't think he remembered me, he invited me to Fairlawne. Unfortunately, I was unable to go because I was returning to America the following day.

I never saw him again.

Planning for Christmas was always the most wonderful time at the Rectory. Preparations began in November with the making of the Christmas pudding on "Stir-up Sunday," so called because the Church of England collects requests to the Lord to "Stir up the wills of His faithful people that they may bring forth the fruit of good works."

We would all stand around the kitchen table while our mother mixed a large bowl of flour, suet, eggs, currants, and spices, topping it off with a liberal amount of cooking brandy. Each of us took turns stirring it with a wooden spoon. Then, several silver charms were dropped into the mixture, including a wedding ring, a thimble, a sixpence, and a three-penny bit. The legend was that when the pudding was served on Christmas Day, whoever received the slice containing the ring would be married within the year; the person who received the thimble was destined to become a spinster or bachelor. Of course, the money represented riches.

A few days before Christmas, a large pine tree from the neighboring woods was cut down and brought to the Rectory on a farm cart and placed in the hall near the front door. Then my mother and the older children decorated it with beautiful glass ornaments. There was no electricity at the Rectory, so to light up the tree, they placed many small while candles into metal containers and clamped them to the branches. This, of course, was a terrible fire hazard, and when the candles were lit on Christmas Eve, my father stood by with a bucket of water.

Every room in the house was decorated with pine boughs, holly, and mistletoe. How lovely it all looked! I still try to retain some of that feeling today when I decorate for Christmas in California.

Carolers would come round, usually a group of choirboys and villagers, who walked from house to house. We would invite them in for something to drink: mugs of hot cocoa for the youngsters and hot toddies for the grownups.

We did not hang up stockings in the traditional way. Instead, we were given pillowcases, which we placed by the fireplace. On Christmas morning, they miraculously appeared at the foot of our beds, bulging with gifts.

After church on Christmas, we opened our presents. There might be a doll or toys or books. I always wanted a scooter, but my father, being a practical man, would not hear of it because, he said, "One shoe will be scuffed and worn, and the other will be like new." I received a hoop and stick, so both shoes were equally scuffed.

Christmas dinner was either roast goose or duck and was served as soon as my father returned home after the evening service.

Then came the moment we had all been waiting for: the Christmas pudding. We closed the curtains so that the room would be dark. Then, the cook poured brandy over the pudding, and set it ablaze.

Mummie would slice the pudding, making sure that the piece containing the ring went to my oldest sister Margaret, who was sure she would be an old maid.

The following day was Boxing Day, when the householders present gift boxes to their employees.

The presents that I gave at Christmas were all homemade. I started in October, knitting scarves and making pincushions and calendars. I stitched away, hemming handkerchiefs and making something called "modesty vests," small squares of material trimmed with lace and embroidery to be placed in a lady's neckline to conceal immodest cleavage.

The colors of these past events and people are sharper than some more recent events. While they are still relatively bright and clear, I shall start from the beginning.

Family History
and a Maternal Mystery

Before becoming Rector of St. Peter's in Ightham, my father, Bertram Thomas Winnifrith, had been headmaster of Prospect House Academy, a school in Hythe founded by his father. He lived there with his first wife, Emily Denny. Their daughter, Mary, was born in 1892, but Emily died shortly after. Mary went to live with her maternal grandparents until she emigrated to Canada where she married. She died there at the age of 92.

In 1897, my father met the young woman who would become my mother, 22-year-old Edith Maude Digby-Roper. It was love at first sight for both of them, and they were married within a few weeks. The Winnifrith parents disapproved, especially my paternal grandmother. Edith, she said, was "too upper crust to make a good poor man's wife." How wrong she was!

Soon after their wedding, my parents bought a home in Hythe called Marlborough House, which faced the sea. How they paid for it on a school-master's salary, I do not know. Almost certainly, the money came from my mother. They established a boarding school at Beaconsfield House, which was flourishing by the time they left in 1907.

Their first child, Berenice, died tragically in 1901 at the age of 16 months. The story is that the nurse placed her on a greatly over-heated chamber pot, and Berenice died of shock.

My father had obtained his M.A. from Oriel College, Oxford, and at the same time continued to pursue his ambition to be ordained. He was instructed by the Archbishop of Canterbury, and in 1904, attained his goal. He became curate of two local parishes in Kent—Cherton and Saltwood—and continued his work as headmaster.

There was just enough income from the parishes and the school to enable the little family to live comfortably. My father was ambitious and was looking for a parish of his own, preferably one where he could establish a school and augment his meager income as a Church of England clergyman.

An advertisement for the sale of an advowson—when someone nominates a rector or vicar of a vacant parish—in Ightham appeared in a local paper. With a handsome yearly income and a Georgian house large enough to house 15 to 20 boarders, it seemed ideal. Ellen Macfarlane, my mother's guardian, nominated my father, and more than likely paid the purchase price, an enormous sum: 3,000 pounds. The Bishop of Rochester accepted him. Bertram Winnifrith was instituted as rector in 1907.

My father came from a long line of clergy. As far back as A.D. 680, there was a Benedictine monk named Winifried, or Winfrith, from Devonshire, who was consecrated Archbishop of Mainz in A.D. 711 Later, he was formally given the name "Boniface." He served for many years as a missionary throughout Europe and was canonized several years after his death.

My grandfather, the Reverend Alfred Winnifrith, was Rector of Mariansleigh, a parish in Devonshire. During the First World War, he looked after Belgian refugees, for which he was awarded the Medaille du Roi Albert by the King of Belgium, an honor he greatly prized.

My father's two brothers had also been ordained. Uncle Douglas took his Orders in 1900. While living in Devonshire with his father, he joined the Volunteer Battalion of the Devon Regiment. After serving two curacies, he became an Army chaplain, serving in the Great War. He was twice mentioned in dispatches for his service in the Marne, Aisne, and Armentiers campaigns. Quite an honor!

In 1928, he retired and served as a vicar of Four Elms, Kent. He and Aunt Margaret had one child, a daughter, Patricia, who was always ill. Since she was close to my age, I was often asked to stay at Four Elms for days at a time and was expected to play with her and to keep her amused. I behaved very badly on those occasions. I did not like Pat, teased her, called her "Seedy Pat," and generally made her life miserable. Years later, when she died, I had pangs of remorse. After Aunt Margaret died in 1947, Uncle Douglas spent his remaining years in a nursing home.

Then there was Uncle Alfred. He was involved in a notorious divorce scandal and was defrocked, but that was much before my time. Although my brothers and sisters and I were not supposed to know anything about the case, we discovered old newspaper clippings in the desk drawers in the Rectory study, which told the whole story. We devoured every word, amid whispers and giggles.

Apparently, Alfred had fallen in love with one of his parishioners, a married lady named Rose Miller. He had been named co-respondent in the divorce suit that followed. During the trial, Alfred contended that there had been no adultery, and Grandfather Winnifrith rallied to his son's defense. The court found against him, and a *decree nisi* was granted. Alfred was obliged to relinquish his Holy Orders.

Worse followed. The King's Proctor unearthed evidence that Alfred and Rose had co-habited during the six-week *decree nisi* period. Rose had hidden love letters under the stair carpet in her lodgings. They were both convicted of perjury and sent to prison. He served his sentence in the notorious Wormwood Scrubs; she served in Holloway. The public disgrace was a blow to the family's reputation and prestige.

Upon their release, Alfred and Rose married. I remember them as a dear and loving couple and spent many happy times at their home in Clapham where Uncle Alfred founded a private school for boys. Aunt Rose was an exceptionally beautiful woman and a wonderful cook. I especially recall her banana custard pudding.

They had a daughter, Alfreda, whom we called Freda, but she too had a tragic life and died at the age of 12. Uncle Alfred died in 1950, followed a few months later by his beloved Rose.

My mother's genealogy is shrouded in mystery and conjecture. Although as a child I was not interested in her family history, I do remember asking her why we had no grandparents on her side of the family. She dismissed our queries with the explanation that her father had been drowned at sea, and her mother died shortly afterwards of a broken heart.

When she became a bit nostalgic, she showed us photographs of Sherborne Castle in Dorsetshire in a worn leather album. She pointed to pictures and said, "This is where I lived when I was a girl. I left there when my mother died and went to live in Bath with John and Ellen Macfarlane."

The mystery deepened about 1920 or '21 when two of my mother's friends, the Voysey sisters, probably relatives of the famous architect Charles Francis Annesley Voysey, were visiting. As they chatted over tea, they were thumbing through a current issue of *The Tatler*, a society magazine of the day. I was playing with my dolls on the other side of the room.

Suddenly, one of the visitors let out a cry. "Maude, look! He's the very image of Joan!" They spread out the magazine and were peering at a photograph.

Hearing my name, I ran over to see who was the image of me! Staring back from the page was a picture of a little boy about my age seated on a pony and wearing the classic hunting habit. The caption read: "Simon Wingfield Digby, eldest son of Col. Frederic Wingfield Digby of Sherborne Castle, Dorset."

"Who is he, Mummie?" I asked.

"Oh, that's a cousin of yours, but we don't talk about him," she replied and abruptly closed the magazine, tucked it under her arm, and she walked out of the room. The visitors followed close behind.

"A mystery cousin. How wonderful," I thought. "And one we're not supposed to talk about." What could be more intriguing? But as with all children, I forgot about it after a while.

Until 1929.

I was performing in a play for The Footlights, the Cambridge University Dramatic Club. One afternoon following a rehearsal, I was seated in a teashop when I noticed a young man at the table next to me. I particularly noticed his hands: he had filbert-shaped fingernails just like mine. I knew this was an inherited trait from my mother's side.

I asked his name.

"Simon Wingfield Digby," he responded.

"Oh, my. You must be my long-lost cousin I'm not supposed to talk about!" I laughed. Simon and his brother, George, were both at Trinity College and were pleased at the idea of meeting a cousin whom they had no idea existed.

Simon invited me to Sherborne to meet his parents when I finished my engagement a few days later. Of course, I had to ask my mother's permission.

"I don't mind *you* going, but I *never* want to see those people," she said. "They were very unkind to your father."

I remember that Mummie had told me that at the time she met Daddy, she was engaged to a Wingfield Digby, and when she broke it off, they were very angry.

I drove down to Sherborne with Simon. I had seen photographs of the Castle in my mother's album, but none of them did justice to its beauty. A large park filled with grazing deer surrounded the Castle, and in the distance, I could see the ruins of the old castle built by Sir Walter Raleigh in 1590. The park, with its fifty-acre man-made lake, was designed in 1756 by Lancelot "Capability" Brown, the renowned landscape gardener. A charming Georgian bridge spans the lake at the far eastern corner of the deer park.

The interior of the Castle was magnificent. Room after room was filled with exquisite antique furniture and precious porcelain; portraits by Gainsborough and Van Dyck lined the walls.

History was around every corner.

I was shown to a bedroom that had belonged to Admiral Robert Digby, who was Admiral Nelson's commander-in-chief. I especially remember the bathroom with its large fireplace.

It was a magical few days. The Wingfield Digbys were very kind to me. I was quite sure they knew what my mother's relationship was to the family, but their lips were sealed.

One evening after dinner, Colonel Wingfield Digby showed me the family portraits. He pointed to one, a man dressed all in black, John Digby Wingfield Digby, (yes, a double Digby), the Rector of Coleshill. "He is the great-great grandfather that you and Simon have in common," he explained. So there *was* a connection.

Simon was as curious as I was to discover the identity of my mysterious maternal grandmother. During subsequent visits to the Castle, we pored over dusty books and scanned the huge family tree that was painted on the wall for clues.

Finally, we came to a conclusion: there is only one person who could possibly be my grandmother. She was one of the daughters of the man whose portrait I had seen that first weekend. One of his five daughters (there were also three sons) was our candidate: his youngest daughter, Edith Henrietta Georgina, Simon's Great Aunt Edie.

She became pregnant in 1875, the story goes, and her father left his parish and took her away from Sherborne to escape the embarrassing situation. Where they went is not known, but they lived for a time in Bournemouth.

After her father's death, we learned, she founded a home for unwed mothers. Simon and I went to see the home in Bournemouth. Hanging in the hall was a picture of Edith Wingfield Digby.

By the time we finished our investigation, we were convinced: Edith Wingfield Digby was my maternal grandmother.

I would probably have let the matter rest had it not been for my brother, John. When he and Lesbia Cochrane became engaged in 1935, his future father-in-law wanted information about our family. Sir Arthur Cochrane, Clarenceux King of Arms, was the number two-person in the hierarchy of the Royal College of Arms, and he wanted to trace the heritage of his future son-in-law.

The Winnifrith family tree was easily documented, but when Sir Arthur inquired about my mother's parents, John gave him the "official" family biography.

However, Sir Arthur didn't stop at that. Delving into the Admiralty records for 1875, he found that my mother's father, Captain Henry Blaker, R.N., did not exist. He requested a copy of my mother's birth certificate and showed it to John. It was a forgery. The record shows that Edith Maude Blaker was born on August 1, 1875 at Horfield, near Bristol. The father was listed as Henry Blaker, seaman, Merchant Service; the mother's name was Ellen Blaker.

The signature was actually that of Ellen Jane Macfarlane, our Aunt Ellen, who we called Auntie Nellie.

In a letter to me, John wrote, "I visited Auntie Nellie in Bath. I did my best to quiz her about our mother's early life. I got absolutely nothing out of her. She shut up like a clam, and I was left in no doubt that she regarded this a closed subject, and all she would tell me was that she brought up our mother."

We were back to the beginning. Together John and I did our best to sort through the pieces of the puzzle. What we discovered was that Edith, having given birth to a daughter, found it increasingly difficult to deal with the gossip that arose about the little girl. The presence of an illegitimate child was a problem, so she decided to put her up for adoption. A suitable candidate, Ellen Jane Blaker, was located, probably with the help of the servants.

Ellen lived in Bath with her common-law husband, John Henry Macfarlane. Ellen evidently received a considerable sum of money from the Wingfield Digbys and was persuaded to record the child's birth as her own. On the certificate, she gave herself a false maiden name, Wilton, and a fictitious husband in the Merchant Navy. The new "mother" was evidently told that there would be more money forthcoming to enable her to raise the child in comfortable surroundings and pay for her education.

Legal adoption seemed out of the question. The story the Macfarlanes told everyone was that Edith Maude Blaker was their "niece." Mummie always referred to them as her "guardians."

John Henry called himself Colonel Macfarlane, as he had held the rank of Lieutenant Colonel in the Royal Gloucestershire Engineers. He was an excellent musician and a Fellow of the Royal College of Organists. Before meeting Auntie Nellie, he had been quite a womanizer and had been married three times. Uncle Jack was a keen horseman would take her riding with him on the top of Landsdown. Years later, Mummie told us what a Tartar he was about horsemanship in particular and discipline in general. She told us how he would make her walk in front of him with a stout cane between her elbows, forcing her shoulders back. The result was that for the rest of her long life, she carried herself magnificently, back straight, chin up. But she seemed to have been happy with the Macfarlanes.

Since Auntie Nellie had taken it upon herself to promote Edith's "father" to the rank of Captain and changed his service association to the Royal Navy, the local paper at Hythe that covered the wedding reception of Mr. And Mrs. Bertram Winnifrith, quite naturally describe the bride as "the only child of the late Captain Henry Digby Blaker, R.N." The deception continued.

Further research revealed that the Digby connection was, as we said in those days, "on the wrong side of the blanket."

On one of my visits to Sherborne, Simon suggested that we visit the only Digby aunt who was still alive and lived just a short distance from the Castle. She was a dear old lady of 90 years with white hair and a charming smile. Oddly, she did not invite us into the house. Instead, we all stood by Simon's car and talked for some minutes. We asked questions about Great Aunt Edie.

The old lady began to giggle. "Oh, dear, we're not supposed to talk about *that*! We promised we wouldn't!" No amount of flattery or cajoling could get anything more out of her. We were sure she knew the truth though.

John, Simon, and I collected enough evidence to be virtually certain that our material grandmother was Edith Henrietta Georgina Wingfield Digby, and our great-great-grandfather was The Reverend John Digby Wingfield Digby. We based our conclusion several points: Edith was not a Winnifrith or Macfarlane name; it was a Wingfield Digby name. My brother John was baptized with "Digby" as his middle name. Mummie kept those albums with pictures of Sherborne Castle and reminisced about living there. The money to pay for the house in Hythe and to purchase the advowson for my father could not have come from the Macfarlanes or the Winnifriths; they didn't have that kind of money either. But the Wingfield Digbys did.

Unfortunately, Sir Arthur's probe into my mother's past reached her. Over the years, she had so carefully cultivated the story that was now being proven false. She was angry and hurt by the thought of anyone prying into her secrets.

One day, years later, my sister Ruth found her in the living room of her London flat tearing up letters, documents, and photographs and tossing the scraps in the fire. Turning to Ruth, she cried triumphantly, "I have destroyed it all. Now no one will ever know."

When John and Lesbia married, Mummie attended the wedding but refused to speak to Sir Arthur.

The story continued. In March 1935 when I was living with her in London, she announced that she was going to Bournemouth to visit a sick friend. She returned later in the day carrying a small attaché case, which she took to her room. When I came in, the case was open on the bed. What I saw was a surprise: the case was stuffed with bundles of bank notes in 50 and 100-pound denominations. Mummie noticed my look of astonishment and was quick to explain, "It is a legacy from an old friend."

A few days later, Simon called to say that Great Aunt Edie had died.

Putting these incidents together, we concluded that Edith, knowing that she was dying, felt a sudden need to see the daughter she had abandoned long ago. Filled with guilt, she was anxious to include her as a beneficiary in her will but realized that any mention of a daughter would give away all the secrets that the Wingfield Digbys had taken so much trouble to hide. Checks would also expose the secret. The only solution was cash. She also gave my mother a gold and pearl brooch, which Mummie wore constantly.

We never did solve the mystery of our maternal grandfather, and it will probably always remain just that... a mystery.

Uncle Jack died about 1916, so I never really knew him, but I visited Auntie Nellie quite often at her home at 6 Beaufort West, Bath.

During her marriage to my father, my mother was often away several days at a time attending to her duties as Vice President of the Mothers' Union of Kent. She traveled to towns and villages to promote the organization's message that "marriage is at the heart of Christian family life."

I find it amusing that some time in the mid–1930s, she was asked by the Union to visit the Windmill Theatre, a theatre in London run by Laura Henderson. Variety acts performed, while nude girls stood absolutely still at the sides in *tableaux vivantes*. Mummie was asked to see if she thought this was a negative influence on the girls who performed there. Off she went, and, surprisingly, she enjoyed the performance. She spoke with the girls and reported to the Union that she saw no negative influence on them by appearing in such a show.

In the years following my father's death, my mother had several offers of marriage. Her most persistent suitor was Hewlett Johnson, the Dean of Canterbury, known as "The Red Dean" for his enthusiastic admiration of Communism. With any offer of marriage, she said, "Your father was my one and only love, and I shall remain faithful to his memory until the day I die."

More Family
and a Local Murder

When my mother was away, I would tiptoe into my father's study and curl up on the floor and watch him as he wrote his sermons or answered letters. He was a quiet, soft-spoken man with dark hair and blue eyes and a mouth that turned up on only one side when he smiled. This gave him a lopsided but endearing look. He had a high, broad forehead, a feature all the children inherited. He was a great lover of cricket, and I remember a large color picture of cricketer W. G. Grace hanging on the wall.

While he worked, I made paper spills, folded pieces of newspaper, which are twisted into long, thin strips, and then I popped them into the holder that hung by the fireplace. He used these to light his favorite clay pipe.

My father's church, St. Peter's, still stands on a little hill overlooking the village where it has been for more than 800 years. The heavy oak entrance door dates back to 1552. Several years after my father became Rector, he noticed a crack in the plaster ceiling above. He had the roof taken down and found that it concealed a magnificent 15th century roof. He had it restored, and it is now one of the finest roofs in the county. He also had a new organ installed.

Inside the church are many medieval monuments, which always fascinated me as a child. One especially interesting one is that of Dame Dorothy Selby, who was supposed to have discovered the November 1605 Gunpowder Plot and disclosed it in her needlework. According to Edward Bowra, Francesca's father and the local historian, the legend is fabrication, probably due to a misinterpretation of words on her epitaph: "...whose art disclosed that plot."

My gentle, scholarly father could certainly rail against his parishioners when he felt strongly about an issue. One of these incidents occurred in 1908, and the villagers were still talking about it when I was very young.

A murder, which has become part of Ightham legend, had occurred in August 1908. Major-General Charles Luard, late of the Indian Army, and his wife, went for a walk through a private wood near their home, which was not far from the Rectory. Mrs. Luard decided not to accompany her husband to the golf club.

When the General returned home and his wife was not there as expected, he retraced his earlier steps. He found her at The Casa, dead from a shot in the head. The local constabulary called in Scotland Yard. There were clues and sightings of a supposed culprit. Mrs. Luard was buried in St. Peter's churchyard with the service read by my father.

The inquest into the murder was adjourned. With the absence of any evidence to the contrary, suspicion began to fall on the General himself.

According to my father's Tythe Book, a diary in which he recounted the activities of the parish:

> ...cruel and idle gossip had been at work and in the absence of any evidence to the contrary—suspicion began to attach itself to the General himself, nor did it end here. He was the recipient of hundreds of vile effusions accusing him of the crime and wherever he went he was ogled by an idle and cruel world. When one remembered how he and his wife were all in all to each other ... these horrid suggestions were all the more cruel.... One could see that the poor old man was becoming broken and his mind becoming unhinged. I was not, therefore, surprised when I heard that he had committed suicide [by throwing himself in front of a train].... On the following Sunday I preached [about the] terrible want of charity which had been shown by the many in the case of General Luard. I said his wife had been cruelly murdered but he had been doubly so—by the cruel tongues of slanderous people....

Despite many parishioners objecting to a suicide being buried in consecrated ground, my father stood firm, and today, because of his staunch commitment to what he thought was right and just, the General and Mrs. Luard lie side by side.

The murder is unsolved to this day.

As serious as he was in this instance, my father had another side, a more playful one. Like many clergymen, he loved performing. I remember his booming baritone voice singing secular songs at the Village Hall. Because I was always showing off—or "pulling faces," as he called it—and was the most uninhibited of the family, he encouraged me to become an actress.

Considering the reputation actresses had at the time, I find it strange that he had no objections.

He didn't live to see me achieve success in the profession he foresaw for me, but he was able to see my first public appearance. I performed before an audience of about 70 villagers in a one-act play called *Mechanical Jane*. I played the title role, a robot-like character who did the housework for two maiden ladies who think this "automatic domestic servant" will take care of all their chores. My sister, Margaret, played one of the other characters.

The first performance on January 26, 1923, was such a success that it had to be repeated the following Saturday, much to my father's delight. I still have the review from the local newspaper, *The Chronicle and the Courier* which reads:

> ...Miss Joan Winnifrith ... gave a good enough account of herself to ensure the immediate success of the piece, and her marvelously accurate representation was made all the more noteworthy by reason of its obvious difficulties...

When Margaret and I were leaving the Hall after the second performance, the village policeman approached us. He congratulated Margaret. Then he added, "Mark my words, Miss Winnifrith, we 'aven't 'eard the last of Miss Joan."

My father was delighted. He hugged me and said, "Well done, Joan! I knew you could do it! Now this is just the beginning."

Although Margaret disapproved of acting, this sort of amateur theatrical was acceptable because it was local, we were also doing it for a worthy cause, and we didn't receive any pay—that would have been the ultimate sin.

I remember my father often rode his bicycle back and forth to the church from home, and we were one of the first people in Kent to have a touring car, a 1921 or '22 yellow Darraq, rather racy for a rector's car. We also had a Daimler that we used as the parish car.

There were the special days that I spent with my father. He would bring Tommy, our pony, and trap, a small carriage, around to the front door. "Come along, Joan," he would say. "Let's go visiting."

By "visiting," he meant calling on the sick, which he did two or three times a week, as part of his parish duties. At first I rather dreaded seeing these old and infirm parishioners in the hospital and cottages in the village. I soon became used to it—and rather enjoyed it.

The best time of all was when our duties were finished. My father would often let me take the reins and away we'd go. I can still hear Tommy's even paced trit-trot, trit-trot down the country lanes as we spent the remainder of the afternoon driving about the neighborhood.

Besides being the Rector of St. Peter's in Ightham, my father was the headmaster of a preparatory school for boys. The Rectory was large enough to house twelve to fifteen boarders and a resident tutor. An advertisement in a catalog from Gabbitas and Thring, the school agents, read:

Ightham Rectory Preparatory School
For backward or delicate boys and those
whose parents are residing abroad.
Specialised coaching for boys wishing
to enter Public Schools. Outdoor sports,
including cricket and football.

When I was seven, I was allowed to take lessons with the boys in the large schoolroom in the stable yard. I remember my delight at having my own desk on which I carved my initials with a penknife. I studied Latin and Greek as well as history, geography, French, and literature. The only subject I was never able to master was mathematics. To this day, the very sight of figures gives me a headache.

By the time my parents moved to the Rectory, there were two children: Margaret, born in 1902, and Cyril, born in 1904. Both arrived while my parents were living at Hythe. John, Ruth, and I were born at Ightham Rectory and were known as "The Rectory Children."

Margaret, the eldest daughter, had long, golden hair that reached below her waist. I was always envious of that beautiful hair. As a young woman, she had been engaged to a young man who had gone out to Africa on safari and was eaten by a lion. Poor Margaret was in shock for quite some time and became very saintly, giving all her money to missionaries. I remember sharing her bedroom for a few days while the nursery was being painted. She spent most of the time together beseeching me to give up the idea of becoming an actress.

"They are sinful people, Joan," she said. "They will lead you into evil ways."

Margaret taught English literature to the boys in Ightham School. She was a wonderful teacher, and I shall always be grateful to her for opening up the magical realms of literature for me, especially *Wind in the Willows*, *At the Back of the North Wind*, and *Tanglewood Tales*. But it was poetry that I really loved: Chaucer, Shelley, Keats, Wordsworth, Rupert Brooke. Because of her, I have always loved poetry with a passion.

Margaret eventually married a clergyman who was twenty years her senior, but he died shortly afterwards. Several years later, she fell in love with yet another clergyman, this one ten years her junior. They married and lived happily until her death at the age of 81 in 1983.

Cyril had a tragic life. When he was eighteen months old, a careless nurse accidentally tipped him out of the perambulator. He fell on his head and remained unconscious for several hours. The doctor was sent for and, after examining Cyril, told my mother that he had suffered a severe concussion, but there did not appear to be any further damage. The following day, Cyril was taken to London to see a specialist who also assured my mother that no real harm had been done.

He seemed to make a complete recovery. As a youngster, he showed great talent at games and lessons. He had a beautiful treble voice, which won him a place in the Cathedral Choir School at Christ Church, Oxford. Just as he was about to assume the prestigious place as Solo Boy, he developed fainting spells known as *petit mal*. He was obliged to leave Oxford and come home. His illness took a turn for the worse: epilepsy. Years later, when my mother had to leave Ightham, there was no one to care for Cyril. It was clear that his condition was so severe that he could not remain with us. Finding a place where he could be looked after was not easy. Eventually, we located the David Lewis Colony of Epileptics in Cheshire. But before we sent Cyril there, we wanted to explore every medical possibility.

Sir Hugh Cairns, a neurosurgeon and one of the greatest authorities on the brain, had successfully operated on patients with epilepsy. (Sir Hugh was one of the doctors who attended to T.E. Lawrence after his fatal motorcycle accident and was instrumental in making crash helmets compulsory.) We took my brother to him for an examination. My mother and I sat in the doctor's Harley Street office waiting for the results of the tests.

Sir Hugh assured us that Cyril's illness was indeed caused by the injury from his fall as an infant. An operation *could* be performed, and the chances were good that he would be cured. However, the area upon which he would operate was the speech center of the brain. There was a risk that following the surgery Cyril would be deaf or mute.

We left the choice to Cyril. It did not take long for him to decide: the operation would not take place. The following day he left for the David Lewis Colony where he would spend the rest of his life.

The next few years were full of frustration for Cyril. He was good looking, a fine athlete, and he longed for freedom. There were consolations, however. He could visit us for limited periods, and we all took turns driving to Cheshire to spend time with him. He enjoyed the company of his fellow patients and the nursing staff. He watched cricket and tennis on television and kept up with the news on the radio. We kept him supplied with tobacco for his pipe and tins of his favorite biscuits.

On February 17, 1988, I received the news that Cyril had reached the end of his long journey, and, at 84, had died peacefully in his sleep. His ashes now rest in the family grave at St. Peter's.

My brother John was the first of the Winnifrith children to be born at Ightham Rectory. He was five years old when he was told that he had a new sister who was to be called "Joan," Joan being the feminine version of John. My father told him that he must be my protector and look after me, which he did ever after.

Our father told us that we must try to be Spartans. I was not sure what a Spartan was, but John explained that we must never show any fear or cry. In order to practice, we would stick needles into our arms and legs and try not to utter a single cry. I sometimes wonder if this accounts for the fact that throughout my life I have been able to stand a considerable amount of pain.

John and I played tennis and croquet and had tea in the garden beneath the arbutus tree. We'd feast on strawberries from the kitchen garden, jam sandwiches, and cake. The only thing I didn't like were the wasps that buzzed around the ham. Once, I was stung on the face, and I remember my mother saying, "If a wasp ever gets into your mouth and stings you, beg, borrow, or steal a raw onion and swallow it!" At the time, I thought, "How strange for a clergyman's wife to tell us to *steal*."

From his prep school at Eastbourne, John won a scholarship to Westminster, one of the most prominent schools in England. From there, he went up to Christ Church, Oxford, where he rowed with the College Eight. As a young man, he traveled widely on the Continent and learned enough Russian to use it as the language needed to pass into the Civil Service. He entered the Board of Trade, but was soon transferred to the Treasury Office. For a short time, he was Private Secretary to Sir John Simon, Chancellor of the Exchequer.

He and Lesbia had three children, two sons and a daughter.

In 1942, he became Assistant Secretary of the War Cabinet and was the civil servant in charge of Winston Churchill's wartime headquarters. After the War, he was appointed Permanent Secretary to the Ministry of Agriculture and Fisheries. His final, and most prestigious, appointment was as Director-General of the National Trust, a post he held from 1968 through 1971. He and his family moved to the National Trust house in Appledore, Kent.

In 1959, he was decorated with the Order of the Bath and knighted by Queen Elizabeth II, and became *Sir* John Digby Winnifrith.

Ruth was the youngest of the Rectory children. I remember April 23, 1917, the day she was born. I was playing in the nursery when I heard the crunch of wheels on the gravel driveway. I looked out and saw Dr. Walker, our family doctor, alighting from his carriage and walking up to the front door. I asked my nurse if someone was ill.

"Your mother has had a bad cold," she told me, "and the doctor is keeping her in bed for a few days."

The next morning my nurse told me to hurry and eat my breakfast. "Your mother wants to see you, Joan. She has a surprise for you."

A surprise! That meant only one thing: a present! Perhaps it would be the tricycle I had been begging for or a new paint box.

I crept into her bedroom. My mother was lying in bed holding—not a tricycle or a paint box—but a baby girl with a plump face and rosy cheeks. Once I got over my disappointment, I grew to love Ruth. Many years later, I learned that she was really a twin. My mother, on one of her visits to London, had fallen down the steps of St. Paul's Cathedral and had suffered a miscarriage. She lost one of the twins, but the other, Ruth, was born sound and healthy.

It is strange to think how little I remember of Ruth during those days when we lived at the Rectory. I suppose I was too busy climbing trees and playing with John or with the boys during school term to give her any thought.

Ruth doesn't remember an important incident in my young life, although she was there.

An early governess, appropriately named Miss Payne, insisted that I accompany her to Borogreen, a local village, one afternoon to do some shopping. I protested that it was too far to walk, but she was adamant. "It's less than a mile away. It will be good exercise, and you can help me push the baby's pram."

I walked along side her, scuffing up clouds of dust as we went. Ruth slept peacefully. It was a terribly uninteresting walk, and I was bored. In order to pass the time, I picked poppies and daisies growing in the roadside hedges.

"Something for Mummie," I thought.

We arrived at the village, and Miss Payne stopped outside a shop, carefully setting the brakes on the pram, telling me, "Now, Joan, look after the baby. Be sure no one touches the pram."

"But, Miss Payne," I whined, "I want to go to the sweet shop for some toffee."

"And with what would you buy the sweets?" she asked most unkindly. I had been naughty—again—and she knew that I had not received my six pence pocket money that week.

I was alone, penniless. I had nothing to look forward to except a dreary walk home. An idea occurred to me: I'll sell my flowers.

I stood at the end of the pavement, accosting anyone who passed by

At the Rectory, 1917. *Left to right:* me, my father, John (standing), Cyril, Mummie holding Ruth, and Margaret. (Collection of Venetia Stevenson)

with a pathetic, "Please, buy my flowers. Only six pence a bunch." Nobody stopped.

Then a nice looking gentleman approached. I pulled a long face. "Please, sir, my baby sister is very sick, and I have to get some milk," I moaned. "But I lost the money. Could you please give me six pence so that I can go to the dairy?"

What an act!

As if on cue, little Ruth awoke from her slumber and began to whimper.

The stranger looked at me. I returned his stare, unblinking. He looked into the pram where rosy-cheeked Ruth was again gurgling happily. She certainly did not act like a sickly baby.

I held out my wilting flowers.

"I can't take your flowers because I'm off to the train station. Take this and buy something for the baby." He handed me a shilling!

What would I tell Miss Payne?

As she exited the shop, I ran towards her and cried, "Look at my shilling. A kind gentleman gave it to me to buy some sweets."

Miss Payne turned scarlet with horror. "How many times have you been told never to talk to strangers, especially men?"

"But he was such a nice man," I said. Then I improvised. "He told me I reminded him of own little girl who died, and he wanted me to buy some caramels which were her favorite."

Whether she believed me or not, I don't know, but she reluctantly allowed me to buy some toffee.

Immediately upon our return home, Miss Payne told the story to my mother.

"Are you telling the truth, Joan?" Mummie asked.

My answer to my beloved mother was to haunt me for years. "Yes, Mummie."

One day I wandered into Miss Payne's room at the top of the stairs. I found her rouge and smeared it all over my face and over some of her things. To my horror, she returned to her room and found me. She was so angry that she got a stick—not a cane, but a stick with knobs on it—and thrashed me again and again.

Cook must have heard my cries because she came running. "Stop that this instant," she demanded. "I shall have to tell Mrs. Winnifrith."

Miss Payne was told to collect her things and leave immediately.

I saw very little of my sister during the early days of my career. When I left for America in 1939, Ruth joined the Women's Royal Navy Service— the WRENS—and was assigned to aerial photography. She met an RAF officer, Peter Wood, whom she married. They had three sons and lived in Kent, not far from where we grew up. Peter died in 2001. Ruth lived in their home in Sevenoaks until recently when she moved into a nearby flat.

Ruth and I are now the last of the Rectory children. Several thousand miles separate us. Since I can no longer travel, I telephone her every Sunday morning, and we talk about the past, the present, and what's left of the future.

Speaking with her makes the dimming colors brighter.

Life at the Rectory

Life at the Rectory was very comfortable. The house had seven bedrooms but *just one bathroom.*

There were banks of rhododendrons that bordered the driveway. The beautiful trees: a tulip tree that towered over the front law, a monkey puzzle tree—the only one I couldn't climb—that stood by the front gate, an arbutus tree, and my favorite tree of all, the giant cedar tree in the meadow, which I climbed when I had a problem.

My father had an income of 2,000 pounds a year, a huge sum in those days. We were able to afford a cook; a housemaid; a parlor maid; Lewis, the butler; Mr. Cant, the one-legged gardener, and his wife, who did the laundry; a stable boy; a man who came to wind the clocks; and one who came to tune my mother's Bechstein piano.

Our day—one without electricity or telephone—started early, about 6:30 in the morning. A maid came upstairs carrying a jug with hot water, which had been heated in the kitchen and brought up to the bedrooms. It was poured into the basin on the washstands in each of the bedrooms.

Dai-Dai came in and helped me wash my face and hands. This wasn't a proper bath. Bath time was Saturday night. We children shared the bath water; John bathed first and then me. I was well into my childhood before I had bathwater I could call my own.

After I dressed, I was escorted downstairs to the dining room where my father stood, prayer book in hand. The other members of the family were there too as were the cook, the upstairs maid, and Lewis. If it were term time, all the boys from the school who lived in the house would be there as well.

We knelt while my father read several prayers, including Psalm 23. He

31

would conclude in a loud, cheerful voice, "Good morning, everyone! Eat a good breakfast." Then he was off to attend to parish or school duties.

We children were not allowed to eat with the grownups until we were seven years old. So I ate alone in the nursery. My breakfast consisted of bread cut into squares; milk was poured over it. It was horrible. I detested it, and tried to spit it out.

Breakfast over, I was placed on a chamber pot and the order was given, "Now, Joan, do your duty." I did not understand why this task was given such a noble name. I visualized a dozen or more British sailors, bare-bottomed, squatting on china chamber pots in front of a large Union Jack emblazoned with the words, "England expects every man to do his duty!"

Finally, I could no longer bear the bread and milk. When my nurse went downstairs and I was alone in the nursery, I slipped out of my chair and carried the nasty stuff over to the bookcase that stood against the wall next to the fireplace. Spoonful by spoonful, I stuffed the contents of the bowl behind the bookcase. Flushed with victory, I returned to my chair and assumed an angelic countenance. I continued this process for several weeks.

The day of reckoning came during spring cleaning when the maids pulled all the furniture in the house away from the walls to dust and mop. That included the bookcase in the nursery. There they discovered lumps of moldy bread.

Of course the maids reported their find to my mother who was most distressed. "Oh, Joan, what a waste of food. Think of those poor, hungry children in India." I had heard so many times about those children that I tried to imagine what they looked like: dark skin, large reproachful eyes, turbans.

When I was allowed to eat with the grownups and the boarders, I met an Indian boy Sankaran Nair, one of the boarders; he and I became great friends.

I asked him, "Sankaran, you seem so happy. Were you ever one of those hungry children in India who I am always being told about?"

"Joan, I'm sorry to disappoint you," he laughed, "but I'm afraid I am not poor, and I have never been hungry. However," and his voice took on a serious tone, "there is a great deal of poverty in my country. Many children *are* starving, but it is something the government should take care of. That is why I intend to go into politics. The first thing I shall do is to see that a law is passed to make birth control available to everyone in India."

I had no idea what he was talking about, but he *did* go into politics and also fought with great distinction in World War II. We continued to write to each other through the years. The last letter I received from him was July 3, 1965. The letterhead read: Major-General Sankaran Nair, London. He wrote that he was leaving England for America on July 9 and would contact me on his arrival in New York.

He wrote, "I am very much under the order of my Government ... as regards the time I am allowed to spend overseas.... United Nations headquarters are arranging my accommodations in New York and Washington, but I shall look forward very much to seeing you." I was then living in Connecticut.

It was not to be. I never saw or heard from him again.

I can remember only a few of the boys' names now. One name I do remember, along with the face, was Malcolm Conan Doyle, Sir Arthur's son. He was plump and had dark, unpleasant eyes. Sir Arthur had placed him in my father's care, hoping that he could somehow teach him enough to pass into Harrow or even one of the minor public schools.

Malcolm, who later took Adrian as his first name, was a bully and unpopular with the other boys. I remember leaning out of a window overlooking the schoolyard to see Malcolm being stuffed head first into an empty water barrel. I screamed with delight, "Push him in! Further! Further!" One of the masters came into the yard and pulled him out, much to the annoyance of the other boys and me.

I wanted very much to look like the boys at school, so I appropriated John's cut-down gray flannel shorts and gray sweater. To complete the picture, I cut my hair as near to my head as I could with a pair of shears. There were, not unexpectedly, gasps from everyone when it was discovered that I had shorn my long hair. My mother was angry, but I wasn't punished. She whisked me off to the local barber to have it done properly.

Perhaps I tried to make myself as unattractive as possible because someone—I can't remember who—said, upon seeing me for the first time, "Oh, dear, she looks like a cracked egg."

My mother countered with, "Joan is not a pretty child, but she has a quaint face."

From that time on, I was called "The Ugly Duckling." I became rather proud of the name. Years later, I discovered an old exercise book in which I had inscribed, "Joan Boniface Winnifrith, U.D."

Dai-Dai felt that my being called "Ugly Duckling" would have a negative effect on my personality. She used to tell me that I was not ugly, but that I had a face "full of character."

She had a plan to change my feelings about myself.

The local artist, Cyril Chitty, lived with his mother in a house directly across the lane from the Rectory. Mrs. Chitty often invited me for tea. I loved going there because she served strawberries with clotted cream and Madeira cake. Dai-Dai visited with Cyril in his studio, just a short distance behind the house. It was here that she must have confided her anxiety about my self image. She probably suggested that he could be of help if he would ask to paint my portrait.

"I'm not beautiful enough for a portrait," I told him, when he did ask. "I'm an ugly duckling."

"Do you know the story of 'The Ugly Duckling'?" he inquired. I admitted that I did not. "Well, then, I shall tell you the story while I paint your portrait."

For the next several days, with Dai-Dai sitting nearby, he painted and told me the story of the duckling that grew up to be a beautiful swan, was admired by all, and, in the end, married a handsome prince.

It was a lovely story, but I realized that whoever wrote it must not have been a very good ornithologist, or he would have known that ducklings grew up to be ducks. Cygnets become swans.

The portrait showed a nice-looking girl with shoulder-length hair—it had grown out by then—and a good complexion. Mr. Chitty presented the picture to me, and for some time I tried to look less the ugly duckling. I washed my face in the morning dew and spread dandelion leaves over my face, which I had heard removed freckles. I even brushed my hair.

Years later, the painting hung in my Palestine, Texas, home, but when the house went up in flames, it went too.

I shall always be grateful to Mr. Chitty and to Dai-Dai for their concern.

It was Mr. Chitty who inspired me to take up painting, and I often slipped away to the summerhouse overlooking the tennis court, which I made into my "studio." I can't remember producing any masterpieces, but I did sit happily in front of a makeshift easel, dreaming up watercolor scenes of imaginary lands. It was my secret garden.

One of my father's friends, and a special friend of mine, was the Bishop of Rochester. He was a dear man and always found time for me when he visited. My father had instructed me to address him by his official title, "My Lord Bishop." I shortened it to "My Lord." One day I called him "Lordy" by mistake. I apologized, but he said he didn't mind. So from that day on that was how I addressed him. It was our secret.

I once asked him if he would like to see my studio. I was very particular who was allowed to visit. I took his hand and led him to the garden. Every year after that I painted him a picture for Christmas, a landscape or imaginary castle, pasted it on cardboard, and attached it to a calendar.

So many interesting people lived in Ightham when I was growing up.

Walter and Leslie Monckton lived in the village. Walter was the one I remember best. He was one of the Church Wardens. Tall and erect, he carried the silver offertory plate up the aisle, pausing at every pew to collect contributions. He endeared himself to me one Sunday when I realized with shame and horror that I had forgotten to bring my sixpence to donate. Walter handed me the plate. I flushed with embarrassment and shook my head. He quickly pulled a shilling from his pocket and handed it to me to put in the plate. Then he smiled at me and whispered, "Now God will bless us both!"

Walter was a promising young barrister who rose to great heights, finally becoming Attorney General to the Prince of Wales, later King Edward VIII, and became a well-known figure during the abdication proceedings in 1938. He was knighted, and in 1957, he was awarded the title Viscount Monckton of Brenchley.

Years later, I met Walter during a charity gathering at Ightham Mote. I asked him if he could obtain a signed photograph of the former king, now the Duke of Windsor. He promised he would, but said I must write to the Duke myself and added that I should also ask for a photograph of Mrs. Simpson, now the Duchess of Windsor, because that would please him.

A few months later, I received two photographs, one signed "Edward P and the other, "Wallis Windsor." I lost both of these treasures in that same Texas fire years later.

Another memorable character was John's godmother, Mrs. Wilkerson, who lived at Crown Point a few miles from Ightham. She had the distinction of owning a gruesome relic of England's past: the head of Oliver Cromwell, which, it was rumored, she kept in a velvet-lined hatbox under her bed. John and I were not allowed to see the head, of course, but we did try to sneak into her bedroom—without success. I heard that decades later a relative of hers donated the head to Sydney Sussex College at Cambridge University where it was buried in an unmarked grave.

My godmother was Winifred Goldsworthy, whom everyone in the family called "Auntie Winnie." She lived at Yaldham Manor, a lovely 15th century house a few miles from the Rectory. She lived there with her brother, Everard, a thoroughly unpleasant man.

Auntie Winnie was very wealthy. She had a lady's maid, a cook, and a chauffeur who had been her coachman. Apart from Yaldham Manor, she owned a country house near Sevenoaks, a house in Bexhill-by-the-Sea, and two flats in London, one in Queens Gate and the other in the Ladies' Park Club in South Kensington. Auntie Winnie had everything she wanted... except a child. Before long she would play an important and colorful role in my life.

I would often ride over to the Manor on my bicycle and sometimes spend the night there, not so much to visit my godmother as my mother thought. I wanted to see the Yaldham ghost.

The story went that at the stroke of midnight, a coach and pair, driven by a headless horseman, galloped down the drive to the Manor. With each visit, I waited for him to appear. Perhaps, I thought, I wasn't destined to see him. Then one winter's evening, I decided to return the Rectory in time for supper. My godmother offered to drive me, but I told her I would be quite safe.

It was dusk as I bade her goodbye. Fog was creeping in, making it difficult to see ahead more than a few feet. Suddenly, I heard the sound of galloping horses, and something dark moved out of the gloom. I flung myself into the ditch that ran alongside the road, pulling my bicycle in after me. I crouched there until the sound of coach and horses faded away.

When I returned to the Rectory, I was shaking with fear. I told my mother that I had encountered the Headless Horseman of Yaldham Manor.

"Nonsense, dear," she said. "It was probably Mr. Webster's horses that got loose from his stables and were enjoying a gallop down the road."

Another of the neighbors was Mrs. Newberry, wife of Percy Edward Newberry, who had accompanied the Earl of Carnarvon and Howard Carter to Egypt in November 1922. She was famous for her embroidery. In 1923, she was asked to repair some of the fabric found in Tutankhamun's tomb. Her handling of the King Tut fabric possibly contributed to the story that she died a mysterious death like so many others who were involved in the opening of the tomb.

One of the annual events that my father took part in was Armistice Day each November 11 at 11 in the morning to remember the end of World War I. The villagers assembled around the War Memorial, which stood on a hill facing the High Street. My father stood by the stone cross, his white surplice blowing in the wind. As the church clock chimed 11, everyone stood with bowed heads. For two minutes, there was complete silence. Drivers pulled their cars to the side of the road and stopped their engines. Even the birds in the trees stopped chirping. It was as though the entire world had stopped and was silent in honor of those who had died.

Then came the sound of a bugler playing the melancholy notes of "The Last Post." This was followed by my father leading the singing of the hymn, "Oh, God, Our Help in Ages Past."

When it was over, car engines roared again, birds chirped, and everyone went home for lunch.

Along with his parish obligations and supervising the boys' school, my father also participated in what were called *locum tenens*. These were two-week-long semi-holidays in which a clergyman from one parish would exchange duties with a clergyman from another. Our entire family would pile into our Darracq and head for various locations.

Among the *locums* that I remember was the one in which we stayed at a Georgian rectory near Southwold, close to Uggeshall. Another time we spent the time at Bosham, near Chichester. It was there that John and I took a walk, and I stumbled and fell—splat—into the mud. I was covered from head to toe in the brown muck. John made me walk behind him all the way to the rectory.

We had a variety of pets over the years. The first one I recall was a gray Persian cat that belonged to my mother. It was called by the clever name of "Kitty." When I was very little, the cat crawled into my pram and sat on my face. I could have smothered, but luckily someone pulled it off. To this day, I don't have a fear of cats; I just don't want to be near them.

The first pet of my own was Tommy the tortoise. One day he walked away—very slowly—and never came back. Then came Hector the rat, who was kept in a cage. I let him out to run about the garden. One day, he went up a tree. I never saw him again.

These halcyon days, full of colorful characters and events, came to an abrupt end for all of us when I was eleven years old.

5

The End of the Beginning

By 1922, it became obvious that my father's health was failing. He had always been plagued with bad digestion, and the strain of his religious duties, his large family (especially Cyril's health), the school, everything weighed heavily on him. Eventually it was too much, and he suffered a nervous breakdown. He was given a rest cure, which, in those days, was the only remedy.

He recovered sufficiently to resume his parish work. But in 1924, he had what we thought was a recurrence of the old trouble. It was diagnosed as peptic ulcers. Again, whatever the treatment was, it was ineffective.

One morning in July 1924, Dai-Dai came to get me from the nursery. She took me to the back door of the Rectory where my father was seated in the back of the car with my mother.

"Smile and wave goodbye to your father, Joan," directed Dai-Dai. "He's going off to a nursing home to get well."

I never saw him again.

He was taken to a nursing home outside of London. A few days later, he lapsed into a coma, and on July 30, 1924, he died. He was 56 years old.

Although the family story says that death was due to a peptic ulcer, it always sounded odd to me. According to the death certificate, which I obtained years later, the cause is listed as meningitis, which sounds more likely.

Even after almost 80 years, I can still clearly remember being told about his death. When Margaret broke the news to me, I rushed out of the house, and clamored up as high as I could go in my favorite cedar tree. I sat on one of the branches and gazed out over the meadows toward the hills.

I can't recall how long I sat there. In the distance, I heard the deep, muffled clang of the "passing bell" from St. Peter's. It tolled every two minutes. The sound reverberated throughout the area and my heart. It proclaimed to the villagers and the surrounding area that their beloved rector, my father, was dead.

It was a beautiful day, sunny and warm, but I was filled with an overwhelming sense of melancholy and despair, not just because of the death of my adored father, but also from a premonition that my childhood was over.

Two weeks later, August 15, the funeral was held at my father's church. Ruth and I wore pale gray linen dresses with black sashes; around our hats, we had black ribbons with streamers down the back. We rode to the church in a hired car which smelled of stale tobacco and decaying leather. Uncle Alfred and Aunt Rose accompanied us. When we arrived, I was astonished at the enormous crowd and the number of floral tributes. There were so many people who wanted to pay their respects to my father that the church could not accommodate them all. They stood on the hill outside the church gate, and even in the graveyard.

John, Ruth, and I sat with our mother in the family pew. My father's surplice and vestments were laid out over the chair on which he had sat for so many years. Throughout the entire service, I could see my mother, kneeling with her hands over her face, the tears streaming down her face.

Clergymen from a 20-mile radius came to pay their respects. I had never seen so many clerics in one place. The Bishop of Rochester read the service.

Besides the family and my father's religious colleagues, others who attended included my godmother, Winifred Goldsworthy; the Colyer-Fergusson family; the Moncktons; Mrs. Chitty; Mr. and Mrs. Bowra; members of the Mothers' Union; and so many other people who played a part in my early life. Ruth and I were taken home before the interment, but the other Rectory children remained with my mother. The Rectory felt cold and empty without the warmth and vibrancy of my father. He had brought such affection and humanity to our home and community.

A lengthy news article about the ceremony appeared the following day in *The Kent Messenger*, along with "An Appreciation of the Late Rector of Ightham." The author of the tribute summed up my father's life:

> He was honest, direct and straightforward in expressing his clear-cut views which he held; and it may truly be said of him that he tried by his life and doctrine to set forward the simple faith which he professed, not only with his lips by with his life.

Today the altar rails, a beautiful silver processional cross, and the restored St. Catherine's Chapel in the church commemorate my father.

Despite her grief, my mother, as "patron of the living," had to appoint a new rector, pay for what were called the "dilapidations of the Rectory," and prepare to move to a new home all within six weeks. Packing family possessions began immediately. Much of what we had accumulated over the years had to be disposed of. The "rag and bone" man came in, taking with him many of my dolls and toys, and my lovely rocking horse.

While my mother searched for a new home for us, Ruth and I were sent to my godmother's home at Bexhill-by-the-Sea. We suffered weeks of misery. Auntie Winnie was a great believer in exercise, and Ruth and I were required to trudge up and down Sutherland Avenue, rain or shine, twice a day. Perhaps in her way, she thought this might take our minds off our sorrow.

We were finally able to rejoin our mother at the house she found for us in Rochester. It was actually my father's dear friend, the Bishop of Rochester, who was able to secure Restoration House for us.

By the time she found our new home, paid the moving expenses, and settled the dilapidations bill, there was little left. She had to draw on her capital and reduce her income. She had about 800 pounds yearly, and there was additional income in the form of an honorarium as Secretary for the Diocese of Rochester from the Mothers' Union. My mother also had an uncanny knack of making money on the stock exchange. She even had dreams of winning the Derby and other races, but she would never follow up on this because, to her, gambling was wrong.

My father's will left one-third of his estate in trust for Cyril and the other two-thirds went to my mother.

Restoration House had been built in 1587 of red brick, the old narrow shape, which had mellowed to a warm pink over the previous centuries. Ivy and lichen crept up the walls. It was a magical house, filled with history, romance, and mystery.

In 1660, on his way from the Continent to London, Charles II supposedly used it as a half-way house after he was restored to the throne. He instructed the owner, Sir Francis Clark, an ardent Royalist, to "henceforth call this house Restoration House." It was rumored that he kept his mistresses there, but, of course, none of my family would believe this... except me. I had romantic dreams of seeing Nell Gwynn descending the staircase carrying a basket of oranges on her hip.

Charles Dickens had used the house as his inspiration for Miss Havisham's Satis House in *Great Expectations*. My mother's bedroom was supposedly the room where the formidable Miss Havisham laid out her wedding breakfast on the fateful day when the groom failed to arrive.

The house was fully furnished, and I remember a 12-foot-long oak refectory table that filled the paneled dining room. The table was so heavy that it supposedly hadn't been moved since Charles II's time.

The kitchen and pantry were below ground and could be entered by a stone staircase from the hallway. My imagination ran wild when I learned there was an underground passage leading down to the river from a trap door inside the brick bread oven. I could just see smugglers rolling barrels of rum up from the water's edge. Oh, how I wanted to go down those steps just once.

"Please! *Please!*" I begged my mother. "Let me go down there."

"Certainly not!" she replied each time. "You'd catch your death of cold. Besides," she added pragmatically, but not necessarily accurately, "it's been blocked up for years."

The best part of living at Restoration House was that it had a secret room upstairs and at least two ghosts.

As soon as John arrived home from school for the holidays, we began our search for the secret room.

"What makes you think there is one?" asked Margaret, always the practical, unromantic one.

"That's easy," I said. "Come into the garden, and I'll show you."

Reluctantly she followed me into the garden, and we stood on the lawn, gazing up at the north wing of the house.

Now, count the windows," I said. She counted.

There was one window that we could not account for. We never did find that room.

I had hoped that I would be the first to discover one of the ghosts, but it was my mother who did.

We heard about it the next morning as it happened in the middle of the night, of course. Mummie said she was awakened to the bleating of sheep, followed by a shriek, and then a thud. She threw on her dressing gown and went to her bedroom door. As she opened it, our dog, a little terrier named Scamp, followed her, all his hairs standing on end and his eyes wide with terror.

"Come along, Scamp," she commanded. "We're going to see what's happened." He wouldn't budge.

Mummie picked up him, shaking, and went all around the house. Her first stop was our rooms to see if perhaps we'd fallen out of bed. Then she proceeded to the lower part of Restoration House and bravely went through every room to see if someone had broken in. Nothing.

She returned to her room and remained alert for the rest of the night.

The next morning, she asked Uncle Alfred, who was staying with us, "Did you hear a strange noise in the night?"

"Why, yes, I did, Maude," he confirmed. "I heard a cry. I don't think it was of this world."

Some weeks later, Mummie spoke with the woman who owned the house and to whom she told the story of that night.

Rather chagrined, the elderly lady confessed, "Oh, my dear, that's the Restoration House ghost. I didn't tell you about it because we thought you'd be frightened. It isn't heard very often and has never hurt anyone."

She recounted this story to my mother: a previous owner, the mayor of Rochester, had a son of about 18 years of age, a rascal and ne'er-do-well, who was always trying to bait his father in some way. The boy was a drover of sheep, considered about the lowest form of work in those days, certainly not in keeping with his father's standing in the community. The son knew his father was giving a lavish party one evening. To anger and embarrass him, the young man arrived drunk at the house, drove his sheep into the house and up the grand staircase. The father was standing at the top of the stairs as the sheep clattered their way to the landing. He became so infuriated with his son that he struck him, knocking him over the banister to his death.

That explained the mysterious sounds in the night: the baaing of sheep, the scream, and the thud.

I did finally claim a ghost as my own. He was an elderly Benedictine monk who used to come out of the fireplace in my bedroom, watch me benignly, walk about the house, and then return to his resting place. This ghost was a kindly fellow, and he was mine.

John and I found a so-called "priest's hole," the hiding place used by wealthy Catholic families to hide a visiting priest because they were afraid the Roundheads would persecute him. We found a monk's robes and an empty wine bottle in the hiding place.

Rochester was a fascinating town, with a beautiful cathedral and the ruins of a 14th century castle.

Chatham, the neighboring town, had none of the charm of Rochester. It was loud and noisy. Sailors from the nearby dockyard caroused with the local girls, and I heard with the jingle of the trams and the hoot of the barges sailing up the Medway River all mingling together.

I saw my first motion picture at a theatre in Chatham High Street in about 1924. I had never been to a cinema before. One day, I walked from school to the town and boldly laid down my six pence admission on the counter of the Odeon Theatre.

"Wait a minute, dear," called the girl behind the window. "You must be accompanied by an adult."

"My governess will be along in just a moment," I fibbed and marched in. The film was *Forbidden Paradise* with the exotic Pola Negri. I remember a scene where she takes the man's hand and leads him into her bedroom.

That was the first time I felt a slight twinge of sexual excitement. I was 12 years old.

After the movie, I went to a fish and chips shop. That wonderful smell pervaded every corner of the town. I bought as many as I could carry, wrapped in newspaper and doused with vinegar, which is the traditional way to eat this delicacy. I then found a quiet place to sit and gorge myself. Over the years, I have tried fish and chips in many places, but none taste like the ones in Chatham. Perhaps it was the newspaper that gives the fish the distinctive taste; maybe it was the air itself.

My mother had Cyril come down from the home to Restoration House. Sadly, some six months later, my mother decided he was better off in Cheshire, and he returned to the home. It must have been an unbearably difficult decision for her. It was best for him and for us, though.

Smugglers, hidden rooms, ghosts, and the cinema had to be put aside when I was sent off to boarding school. Granville House, where Margaret had attended some years earlier and where Ruth would be sent after I left, seemed like a prison compared to my school days at the Rectory. I was only allowed to return home during the all-too-short holidays at Christmas, Easter, and summer to see my family—and my ghost.

Sir Arthur Conan Doyle's sister, Ida Foley, whom the girls fondly called "Fido," ran the school. She was kind and warmhearted, but she could be strict as well.

I had been given the usual tests for incoming pupils, but because my scores were higher than most of the girls my age, quite possibly because of the education I received at my father's school, it was decided that I should begin in the Fifth Form, with girls a few years older than I. This irritated my roommates who called me "Miss Know-It-All." They teased me mercilessly.

I remember one incident in particular. After the lights were out, the girls stuffed me into a wicker laundry hamper and locked the lid. There was no room to move. I could hardly breathe. I began to panic. I rocked the big hamper back and forth, back and forth, until finally it tipped over and hit the floor with a thud. The noise awakened the matron who slept next door. She rescued me, put me back to bed, and scolded the girls. Worst of all to my tormentors, she threatened to report them to Mrs. Foley.

There was another ghastly incident. One of the five girls who shared my dormitory room crept into my bed and placed her hands between my thighs.

"This will feel lovely," she whispered.

"Go away," I told her. "Leave me alone. I want to go to sleep."

"Oh, you're no fun," she said as she angrily left my bed.

At the beginning of my third term, I was moved into a three-bedded room with two girls my age. Everything changed for the better. Rutti Jamsidee Jeejeebhoy, from Calcutta, and Jean Conan Doyle, Sir Arthur's daughter, became roommates and great friends. During World War II, Jean was awarded a DBE and became Air Commandant Dame Jean Conan Doyle. She was appointed Director of the Women's Royal Air Force in 1965, and at the age of 53, she married Air Vice Marshal Sir Geoffrey Bromet, becoming, Lady Bromet. We corresponded for years and remained friends until her death in 1997.

Every week at Granville House, all the girls assembled for a Drawing Room Evening. While we embroidered, Mrs. Foley read aloud. I remember Fido reading Charles Dickens' A *Tale of Two Cities* and Sir Walter Scott's *Marmion*.

Fido and I had something in common: we both played the cello. My father had left me his cello, and I think it was for his sake that I did my best to master the instrument. I never learned to play very well. I played in school concerts with Mrs. Foley, sawing my way through Jacques Offenbach's "Barcarolle."

At school, we played hockey. How I hated that game. It was ridiculous to have a group of sweating girls hitting a ball around the field and falling all over each other. I would much rather have played cricket. That is an elegant game.

One afternoon about 1927, I sneaked out of school and went into town to the matinee of a play, *Her Cardboard Lover*, starring Tallulah Bankhead. (This wouldn't be the only time I would sneak away from school.) Seeing this performance convinced me that I wanted to go on the stage. Bankhead made theatrical history when she appeared in black satin cami-knickers on stage in that play. I raised a few eyebrows years later in a film, *Hangmen Also Die*, when I wore apple green cami-knickers (even though the film is in black and white).

Because my mother didn't object to my acting aspirations—she remembered how much it would have meant to my father—I asked if she would contact her friend, Mrs. Thorndike, mother of the great actress Sybil Thorndike, and arrange for an interview.

One summer afternoon, we went up to London to the Lyric Theatre in Hammersmith where Miss Thorndike was appearing in repertory with her husband, Lewis Casson.

I certainly didn't look the part of a budding actress. I was dressed in my school uniform of a navy dress and navy wool bloomers, my hair in

Opposite: **The school outfit I wore when I auditioned for Sybil Thorndike.**

braids. We arrived a few minutes before the curtain fell on the afternoon performance. The stage doorman was expecting us and said, "Come this way, please. Miss Thorndike would like you to wait in her dressing room."

We followed him to a small, untidy room. There were several costumes on a rack. Her dresser was busy stitching a hem on one of them. Her dressing table was covered with sticks of Leichner Grease Paint, and several telegrams were wedged into the mirror frame. In the corner, behind the jars of creams, lipsticks, and eye shadows was a framed photograph of her husband. "How romantic," I thought.

We heard applause and knew the matinee was over. Moments later the door opened, and Sybil Thorndike swept in, obviously exhilarated by her performance.

"Mrs. Winnifrith," she said as she stretched out her hand. "My mother told me you were coming. How nice to meet you." Then she turned to me. "This must be Joan," and she took my hand.

I'm not sure what took place during the next half hour. I was in such a daze. She chatted with my mother about this and that for several minutes. Then she turned to me.

"So," she began as she seated herself at her dressing table and looked intently at me, "you want to be an actress, do you?" Without waiting for me to reply, she continued. "At your age, so did I. I have never regretted it. It's not an easy life, and it's full of disappointment, rejection, and hardship. But if you can fight your way through them," at this point her eyes sparkled, "the rewards are immeasurable." Her voice was deep and resonant and filled with warmth.

I listened, hardly breathing. These were words I longed to hear.

"Once you set foot on that stage," she threw an arm toward the theatre, "it will dominate your life, perhaps even causing problems in your private life." Her advice continued to pour out. "You *must* master your craft. Some people think acting is easy. It's *not!*" When she enunciated the "t," in "not," a fine spray of saliva came from her mouth. "There is so much to learn, and one must never stop learning." She finally paused and asked, "How old are you, Joan?"

"Fourteen," I said, and then amended it hastily to, "almost fifteen."

"The first advice I am going to give you is to finish your education. Education is so important to an actor." I could see my mother nodding in agreement.

Then came the moment I was dreading. "Would you recite something for me? I'd like to hear the quality of your voice."

My mother had told me to prepare something to recite. I had thought of Keats or Wordsworth or a Shakespearean sonnet, but my mother suggested the poem by Rose Fyleman, "There Are Fairies at the Bottom of My Garden." There I stood in the famous actress' dressing room reciting the little poem about fairies.

I don't know how she kept a straight face, but the fairies must have brought me luck because when I had finished, she said, "Joan, I want you to study hard, and when you have passed your Senior Oxford examination and are ready to leave school, come back and see me. I will arrange for you to meet Elsie Fogerty, head of the Central School of Speech and Drama, by far the best dramatic school in England. I'll arrange an audition with Elsie, and I'll be there to give you moral support." She concluded with the advice, "Try to memorize one of Shakespeare's sonnets every week. It's good for the memory and keeps one alert."

Now, more than ever, I wanted to be an actress. Although I had never been an outstanding student, I now had an incentive. On one of my early report cards, I remember Mrs. Foley had written, "needs improvement" or "disappointing work," and also, "Joan's imagination is too vivid for her own good. She must learn to curb it, or it will lead her into trouble."

But now with Sybil Thorndike's offer, I studied and studied. Some nights, I studied in the bathroom or read with a flashlight under the covers of my bed way past lights out, determined to pass the Senior Oxford before I was 16. Somehow I did pass it, and true to her word, Miss Thorndike (she became Dame Sybil in 1931) took me to see Miss Fogerty.

At the time, the Central School's headquarters were in the Royal Albert Hall. My audition was held on the enormous stage of that auditorium, with the fearsome Elsie Fogerty and my mentor in attendance. I recited John Milton's *Sonnet 16*, which begins, "When I consider how my light is spent..." and concludes with one of the most famous lines in English poetry: "...They also serve who only stand and wait."

I must have impressed Miss Fogerty because I was accepted.

Miss Fogerty was a daunting personality and her nickname, "Fogie," reflected that. No sweet nicknames for her!

She founded the school in 1906, and decades later she could claim a number of theatrical legends as alumni. Peggy Ashcroft referred to her as "a brilliant, inscrutable woman whose influence on the theatre ... was lasting. [She was a] commanding, eccentric, and unique personality."

Miss Fogerty also had a unique appearance. She always wore a hat, and I cannot remember her in anything but a severe black dress, on which we could see the remnants of her breakfast. I think she was so totally absorbed in the school and her students that she didn't care about her appearance. Miss Fogerty—I doubt she ever married—was in her sixties when I attended.

In her resonant tones, she would tell us to repeat, "Around the ragged rock the ragged rascal ran." She would exhort us to "Roll those r's! Roll them 'til they roar like lions."

Once I was accepted, it was not possible for me to live at home. The commute was too long. Through the Mothers' Union, Mummie found a "respectable" lady for me to board with. On their recommendation and without my mother ever having met her, I moved into Mrs. Stanley Stubbs' home on Cromwell Road. Had my mother met her, I doubt she would have taken their suggestion. Her house smelled of liver and onions. My room at the top of the house was small, cramped, and cold, and I had to share it with the landlady's daughter. She smelled of licorice and snored at night. Mrs. Stubbs was less than hospitable. In short, I was miserable.

Fortunately, there was a lovely girl next door with whom I became acquainted. Veronica Butler, who was also a student at Central School, and I took the bus up Cromwell Road to Kensington, and then on to the Albert Hall. It was Veronica who introduced me to Gerald Cadiz, a young sub-lieutenant in the Royal Navy, who was stationed in Portsmouth on the submarine, the HMS *Serapis*. He took me to dinner at Quaglino's, and he kissed me on the way home in a taxi. It was the first time I had ever been kissed. I enjoyed it.

Love notwithstanding, I could no longer bear Mrs. Stubbs. I phoned my mother to say I was coming home, packed my things, and took the train from Victoria Station. She met me at the station in Rochester, and I explained how unhappy I was at the lodgings. She was most sympathetic and found me another room with a nice elderly lady in South Kensington.

Not long after I moved into my new quarters, Gerald told me he was about to be sent to Hong Kong. He told me he was in love with me and asked me to marry him. I said yes. I was 17; he was 21. It would be the first of several times that I would fall in love with a man in uniform. I've always wondered whether I was in love with the man or the uniform.

Now, I wondered, how would I tell Mummie?

I was very happy at the Central School where we studied everything that would aid us in a classical theatrical career: voice projection, mime, dancing, and fencing, among other classes. Miss Fogerty taught elocution and recitation, which were her academic fortes.

I was a model student, and with my recitation of "Beauty Was with Me Once" by John Masefield, I won the prestigious Dawson Milward Cup for Poetry. My classes at Central School were going well, and in another year, I would graduate.

Then I did something foolish.

I heard that a motion picture was in production at Elstree Studios, and extras—then known as "crowd players"—were being paid the grand sum of three pounds a day for work in a "quota film." These were films, shot in a matter of days, which were created to meet the government regulation that a percentage of all films playing in British cinemas had to be made in the United Kingdom. This was to counteract the huge influx and popularity of films from Hollywood. The law was supposedly a protective measure for the British film industry. It wasn't. It did, however, provide a training ground for many in front of and behind the camera.

So I skipped my classes, took a bus to the studio, and spent the day on the set pretending to be a customer in a teashop where two of the leading characters were playing a scene. It was not a leading role—or even a supporting one—but exciting, nevertheless. I enjoyed watching what was happening in front of and behind the camera and listening to the director shouting at the actors.

At the end of the day, I rode the bus back to London, proudly clutching my three one-pound notes.

Somehow word got back to Miss Fogerty, and the following day, she assembled the entire student body of about 40 on the stage at Albert Hall. She announced in a voice that made me shudder, "It grieves me to tell you that one of our finest pupils has seen fit to prostitute her art by working in pictures."

There was an audible gasp from the students—and me.

I was allowed to finish the term but was not asked to return. Thus ended my days at Central School, but, I hoped, not my career.

6

A Beginner Learns—
the Hard Way

I soon discovered that finding a job, either in the theatre or in films, wasn't going to be easy. Even with my two years of training at Central School behind me, I was inexperienced and painfully shy. I found it difficult to knock boldly on the doors of producers' offices.

Gerald was very supportive, but he was soon to be posted to Hong Kong.

When I told Mummie that I was engaged, she gave me a pat on the hand and said, "That's nice, dear" and carried on with what she was doing.

With Gerald leaving and a tentative acceptance from Mummie, I decided to move ahead with my career and find an agent. But who? Where and how would I find one?

I walked past theatre after theatre on Shaftesbury Avenue and around Leicester Square, hoping to see an announcement of a new play so I could ask for an audition. One day, as I again trudged down the now-familiar street, I spotted a small brass plate on a building I had passed many times: Bramlin's Theatrical Agency, Second Floor.

I climbed the dark stairs, took a deep breath, knocked at the door of the office, and walked in. A tall, thin man sat behind the desk. His hairline was receding and his skin was spotted. His voice was kind when he asked, "Yes, young lady, what can I do for you?"

"I'm an actress," I said. "I need an agent."

"Well, then, let's have a look at you. Pull up your skirt, dear."

"Why?" I asked rather indignantly.

"Legs are very important, so I want to see them," he said honestly.

I pulled up my skirt inch by inch by inch to just above my knees. The gentleman, evidently satisfied with my limbs, nodded, and I quickly dropped my skirt.

"Tell me what you've done, dear?" he continued.

I told him about my two years at Central School. He wasn't terribly impressed.

"I'll speak with Mr. Bramlin about you, but with no experience...." His voice trailed away. So concluded my first meeting with Eric Goodhead, who would later become my agent.

Nothing immediately came of that interview, but one morning I received a phone call. "Joan," said Mr. Goodhead, "I've been talking to a writer who has a play running in the West End. He's looking for an actress to understudy the lead when it goes on tour with the Southern Provincial Company. I think you should meet him."

Within the hour, I was in the Bramlin office. As I had never met a playwright before, I was sure they were all elderly gentlemen resembling George Bernard Shaw.

Did I receive a shock! Charles Bennett was an attractive young man with blond, wavy hair and a charming smile. He looked at me skeptically and said, "You're rather young, aren't you?"

"No," I replied, pulling myself up to my full five-foot-two-inches. "I'm almost 21." I lied. I wasn't yet 17. It wouldn't be the last time I lied about my age.

"*The Last Hour* has been running at the Comedy Theatre. I'm taking it on tour soon," he explained. "The part I want you to read for is Mary, who has hidden some important papers from the villain in order to save the life of the hero. The play is a thriller which takes place in the parlor of a bar in the Goat and Compass Inn in Devonshire."

With that, he handed me a script in which a scene was marked. "Take a look at the scene," he directed. "Read it over, and when you're ready, I'll listen to you."

Of all the plays and films in which I have had roles, I can barely remember a single word. But to this day, almost 75 years later, I can still recall the line I screamed in Bramlin's office. "Stop! Stop! I know where those papers are!"

I must have read the entire scene with great conviction because I got the part as the understudy for the character of Mary Tregellis. All that was left to do was to get Mummie's permission. That wasn't going to be easy.

She was immediately against the idea of touring. "You will be away a long time and in all those strange towns," she remonstrated. Once again, she decided to consult Sybil Thorndike's mother, who assured her that no harm would come to me, provided that I join the Actors' Church Union.

One of my early promotional stills, when I was still a brunette.

This would mean that in every town in which we performed—Portsmouth, Dover, Eastbourne, Chatham, Leytonstone, and Plymouth, among others— the local clergyman would visit me and make sure that no evil would befall me.

The visiting clerics were kindly, cheerful, and reassuring. However, one of them pinched my bottom, which I thought rather unseemly and not in keeping with his Holy Orders.

Touring was a new experience for me. The theatre train left the station early on a Sunday morning. The sets, lighting equipment, and wardrobe were loaded into its cars; we actors followed in another. As soon as we reached our destination, our first job was to find rooms, or "digs," for the week. Sometimes, if we were lucky, another actor who had used them before would recommend rooms, but I remember plodding up and down streets looking for a sign that read, "Room for rent." A room was usually a pound a week, which included breakfast of a kipper or a bowl of porridge and a cup of tea. No smoking or cooking was allowed in the room. Usually the sheets were clean, but once I found lice in the bed.

I never did get to go on as Mary; the leading lady was never indisposed. I did, however, have my moment on stage. One night, the actor who played the man who is burned alive got drunk in his dressing during the performance. In the last act, his burned body is supposed to be found in the fireplace, but by this time, the actor had passed out. In desperation, the stage manager dressed me in the "dead man's" clothes and laid me out in the fireplace. It was not a great part, but at least I was playing before an audience.

After several months, I returned to London and continued my stage work with the London Repertory Company at the Regent Theatre, King's Cross, where I played a variety of roles, including Tessa, my favorite stage role, in *The Constant Nymph*.

When I was living in Hollywood in the early '40s, director Edmund Goulding was casting the film, *The Constant Nymph*. I had met Goulding earlier and knew him well. I longed to play the role of Tessa, but he wanted me to read for another role, Florence. I wasn't interested. In the end, Joan Fontaine played Tessa for which she received an Academy Award nomination for Best Actress in a Leading Role, and Alexis Smith was Florence.

I also appeared on stage in *The Barretts of Wimpole Street* and in an adaptation of *Jane Eyre*. Bernard Lee was my co-star in several productions. He went on to play "M" in many of the James Bond films.

While I pursued my theatrical ambitions in 1930, I lived with Auntie Winnie, who had moved to her flat at the Ladies' Park Club in Knightsbridge. Despite her slightly indulgent attitude toward my theatrical proclivities, she was thoughtful and generous.

Also living at the Club was her cousin, the widow of Field Marshal Viscount Garnet Wolseley, one of the great Victorian military heroes; he had been sent to command an expedition to save General "Chinese" Gordon at Khartoum.

Lady Wolseley received a call from the American ambassador that a visiting American wanted to meet a proper young lady to dine and dance with him at the Savoy Grill. She asked my godmother if she would allow me to go. What could Auntie Winnie say! If the American ambassador referred him, he must have the appropriate credentials. So I was allowed to go. He would be the first American I had ever met. I wondered what he would be like; I'd heard so many tales.

The young man arrived at the Club in a taxi to collect me. He was tall and pleasant looking. He wore a dinner jacket, which would have been *de rigueur* for the time and place, but the surprise was that he was wearing black tennis shoes. I wore a new red velvet panne dress.

I was quite sure he was an impoverished student. I didn't want to embarrass him. So when we were seated at the table and I was handed the menu, I read it from right to left and deliberately ordered the cheapest items I could find. I also told him I did not drink wine.

Dinner was not exactly what I expected. He seemed rather deaf and conversation was difficult. Therefore, he did most of the talking. His topic of choice was airplanes, and he told me about a film he had just made in Hollywood, called *Hell's Angels*, which featured lots of flying. I told him I didn't know much about airplanes. I had only been up once and was sick afterwards.

He didn't seem impressed. Maybe he hadn't heard what I said.

While we were dining, I noticed there were three large chaps sitting at a nearby table; they never took their eyes off him. After dinner, we danced; he wasn't a bad dancer. Then he said he had some people coming up to his suite and asked me to join them.

"How," I asked myself on the way up in the lift, "could this young man afford to stay at the Savoy?" It was all very mysterious.

When we arrived at his suite, there was no one there. It was a put-up job! He grabbed me and tore the neckline of my dress trying to get at me.

I screamed, "I want to go home!" He immediately relented and called in one of the men I'd seen in the Grill. Only then did I realize they were his bodyguards. I was escorted downstairs where the doorman hailed a taxi, and I stumbled into it. The cabbie was paid and told to take me to the Club. I arrived home safely, but I was badly shaken.

The next morning, I received a box of flowers with a note: "Thank you for a delightful evening. I hope this will replace your evening gown." Tucked in with the roses was a 20-pound note.

The card was signed: Howard Hughes.

I didn't find out who he was until years later.

Auntie Winnie was incensed and harrumphed, "Those Americans!

They're all the same!" She was never keen on Americans. At that point, I wasn't sure I wanted to meet any others.

About the same time, Auntie Winnie announced that she wanted to have me presented at Court. Lady Wolseley consented to fulfill the role as presenter, perhaps to make amends for what had turned into an unpleasant experience for me.

I received instruction regarding the appropriate behavior, including how to curtsy. Auntie Winnie had a beautiful dress made for me; we purchased a pair of over-the-elbow white leather gloves—an absolute requirement for the ensemble—and two ostrich feathers to wear in my hair.

Although initially I wasn't interested in being presented, I finally decided it would be a once-in-a-lifetime event and looked forward to it. But, alas, three days before the ceremony, Lady Wolseley came down with some illness. My godmother could not act as a substitute presenter. In those days, only a married woman could do the honors. Auntie Winnie couldn't find anyone else at the last moment.

I was terribly disappointed, but I was left with a beautiful dress and gloves.

Finally, my association with the London Repertory Company came to an end, and I was again paying visits to Bramlin's.

Day after day, I was told there was "nothing."

Finally, I was scheduled for two "auditions," both of which I remember all too clearly.

Mr. Goodhead arranged for me to go down to a "producer's" country home. The gentleman greeted me at the door with a rifle in his hand, and told me we would talk shortly about the show he was planning. He then asked me to take off my shoes, a stylish pair of patent leather I had bought for the occasion.

"Throw one up in the air," he commanded.

I did as he asked. He fired at it, and shot the heel off—Annie Oakley style.

After some small talk, he told me to visit a shop in the Edgware Road and buy a pair of leather panties. When I had them, he instructed, I was to come back and see him. I can't believe that I actually went to the shop and looked at the garment.

I phoned Mr. Goodhead, told him what had occurred, and said that I wouldn't be returning to see the "producer," no matter what the role was.

Mr. Goodhead phoned again and said Douglas Fairbanks wanted to meet me about a film he was going to make. I knew that Fairbanks was an American film star, and I was flattered that he had heard of me. When I arrived at the appointed place, a young man of about 20 greeted me. Now I knew that Fairbanks was in his mid-forties by 1930, so who was this?

He introduced himself. "I'm sure you were expecting to see my father, but he is away scouting locations. I'm Douglas Fairbanks, Jr." He was effusive in his apologies, and said, "The least we can do is have something to eat. Please come in."

He ushered me into an office-like room with a view of Hyde Park. A log fire blazed. The furniture was mahogany, and the chairs were upholstered in chintz. Hunting prints hung on the wall, and over the fireplace was a large oil portrait of Fairbanks, Sr., as a pirate, probably from his 1926 film, *The Black Pirate.* An enormous white rug covered the hardwood floors.

"My father sends his apologies, but he has been delayed up North and won't be back until tomorrow. Meanwhile, he asked me to interview you." He gestured toward a chair. "Tell me what you've done."

I told him about Central School and about my tour with *The Last Hour.* He sat at the desk and wrote everything down. After some minutes, a butler brought in dishes of tiny strawberries and cream.

"Excuse me for just a moment," he said. "I have a phone call to make. I'll return in a moment."

While I waited, I nibbled the strawberries.

When he returned, he was wearing a dressing gown. Before I could say anything, he untied the sash and let the gown fall to his feet, revealing... everything. He must have oiled his body because it was so shiny. He made some overtures.

I countered with, "I'm not that kind of girl." The tears began to roll down my cheeks. "You see, I'm still a virgin, and I'm in love with a naval officer who is out in China." The words tumbled out, and I started to sob.

He slid back into his robe, and said in a most chivalrous manner, "Well, at least we can have our strawberries and cream. I hope you like strawberries. I have them flown in from France; they're called *fraises de bois.*"

I recovered my composure as he told me about Hollywood. "Don't ever go there, Joan," he warned. "It's a miserable place. Everything has an unreal look and feel about it. I lived there for a while with my father and stepmother, Mary Pickford, at their home, Pickfair. I much prefer living in England, and I hope one day to settle here for good."

We finished the strawberries. He called a taxi for me, and we said goodbye. As he handed me into the taxi, he said, "Perhaps we shall meet again one day."

And we did. When I was in North Africa with the USO during World War II, I was introduced to a young naval officer. "Anna Lee, this is Lieutenant Commander Douglas Fairbanks."

"How do you do, Miss Lee," he said shaking my hand. He didn't recog-

The dress I would have worn—had I been presented at Court, about 1928.

nize me, though. By then I was no longer auburn-haired Joan Winnifrith.
I was blonde Anna Lee. But it was fun meeting him again.

As consolation for not being presented at Court and since I wasn't
working, Auntie Winnie announced, "Joan, dear, I think it's time you forgot this foolishness about the theatre and settle down with a suitable husband and lead a proper life." She had obviously heard from Mummie that
I was engaged!

She had a plan, for which she had obviously already received approval
from my mother. "We'll take a holiday and travel around the world. We'll
stop in some interesting places, and we'll meet some interesting people.
We'll begin in Canada, then on to San Francisco, Tokyo, and places in the
Far East, Hong Kong...." What other exotic ports she mentioned, I didn't
hear after she said the magic words: Hong Kong. Gerald was stationed there,
and I had been receiving steamy love letters from him since his departure
months earlier. I was already mentally packing.

My godmother was well aware that Hong Kong was the base of many
eligible young men who were stationed there during their duty with the
Royal Navy. The city was affectionately called "the fishing fleet" by mothers
of young ladies in the market for husbands.

Auntie Winnie had a personal motive, as well. We would, she told me,
spend some time in India. The family story was that when she was young,
she had fallen in love with a man stationed there. I think she really wanted
to relive that place and that time. I was a good excuse.

Through Thomas Cook & Son, Ltd., the tour organizer on Berkeley
Street, Auntie Winnie booked an eight-month, first-class tour of some of
the great cities of the world. The itinerary, of which I still have the original, runs eight, single-spaced typewritten pages. It is headed: "Tour for Miss
Goldsworthy and Miss Winnifrith."

We left Southampton on August 30, 1930, aboard the S.S. *Empress of
Scotland*. Seven days later we arrived in Quebec, where we remained for two
nights at the Chateau Frontenac. Then we traveled by train, the *Chicago
Express*, to Montreal. We had sleepers on the train, but there was too much
to see, and I sat up most of the night peering out the window. Toronto, Nia-
gara Falls, Banff Springs, and by the *Trans-Canada Limited*, across the
magnificent Canadian Rockies to Vancouver—these were my first glimpses
of North America.

At each stop, our schedule called for a "drive by sightseeing auto" to
points of interest. Although I found it all interesting and educational, I
wanted everything to go faster, faster, faster, until the day we would reach
Hong Kong—and Gerald.

Finally, we crossed into the United States and arrived in San Francisco on September 19, where we were booked into the grand Fairmont Hotel atop Nob Hill. I thought San Francisco was the most beautiful city I had ever seen. How it sparkled by the Bay. I had heard so much about the city that I wanted to explore on my own, but Auntie Winnie would have none of that. In fact, she would not allow me to leave the hotel.

"America is full of gangsters and horse thieves," she told me. "No one is safe on the streets." Where *did* she get those ideas!

We had one "evening trip to Chinatown and a Chinese drugstore, Joss House, the Telephone Exchange, etc.," according to the Cook-prepared itinerary.

We also visited the Presidio and Golden Gate Park. My impression of San Francisco was a lasting one, and years later, when I had to get away from a difficult situation, I fled to the City by the Bay.

On September 20, we boarded the S.S. *Tatsuta Maru*, bound for points in the Far East.

From Yokohama, we took a train to Nikko and then to Tokyo where we stayed at the Imperial Hotel, designed by American architect Frank Lloyd Wright. As much as I was impressed with Japan in general—Kamakura, Odawara, Miyanoshita, Kyoto, and Kobe—I wondered if we were ever going to get to Hong Kong.

At last! We boarded the *Empress of Canada*, and on October 19, 1930, we steamed into Hong Kong harbor.

When we arrived, Gerald was at sea. I would have to wait several more days to see him.

We stayed at the Repulse Bay Hotel, a large modern hotel on the north end of the island near the fishing village of Aberdeen. My room faced across the Bay where I could see two British destroyers at anchor. A British Union Jack flew from the roof of the hotel. Auntie Winnie immediately felt at home.

Shortly after our arrival, we paid a formal visit to Government House, where I met a number of important but dull government officials. I also met two girls my own age: Margaret, whose father was an admiral, and a pretty girl with red hair, Mary Hayley Bell. Her nickname was Paddy, which is what I call her to this day. Her father, Colonel Hayley Bell, was Commissioner of Chinese Imperial Maritime Customs.

Paddy, Margaret, and I became a trio. We galloped around Kowloon in rickshaws, complete with pointed bamboo hats, all of which we rented from their owners. We generally behaved in a rather unladylike fashion. In fact, we behaved so badly that we received a call from one of the governor's aides-de-camp who scolded us, saying: "Young English girls do not behave in such a manner."

But, oh, did we have fun!

At last, Gerald returned, and we spent many romantic afternoons on the beaches surrounding Repulse Bay. It was on one of these afternoons that he presented me with a beautiful emerald and diamond ring. We were formally engaged. Auntie Winnie was delighted.

To celebrate the occasion, we were given a round of parties at Government House and on board some Royal Navy ships in the harbor. It was exciting to be the center of attention, surrounded by government officials and Navy personnel all in full regalia and Gerald by my side.

With just a few more days before we were due to leave Hong Kong for India, Auntie Winnie was eager to visit Macao.

One morning, we boarded the Hong Kong–Macao ferry and set off for the Portuguese colony. We left Bias Bay and were out on the open sea when I became aware of a commotion. One of the passengers, an American, screamed, "Good God! Chinese pirates! They're going to board us!" At this announcement, I thought Auntie Winnie was going to faint. She didn't.

"Don't worry," soothed one of the crewmembers, obviously having been through such an event before. "They only rob wealthy Chinese. They seldom bother foreigners." Auntie Winnie didn't receive much consolation from this pronouncement.

I held my breath. I could hardly wait to see the pirates. Just as they were climbing up the side of the ferry, a British gunboat suddenly appeared and fired a warning shot over their junk. I could see the pirates scrambling down the side of our ferry. They re-boarded their boat and disappeared around the corner of the Bay. The gunboat then escorted us into Macao harbor.

That was as close to real pirates as I ever came.

We spent Christmas at a Government House party where we sang carols around a Christmas tree. Gerald and I danced. Even though I received a beautiful gold lacquered box from Gerald and an embroidered Spanish shawl from my godmother, I was homesick for a real English Christmas with a log fire and snowflakes and Christmas pudding.

The following week was my eighteenth birthday. Auntie Winnie hosted a party for me at the hotel. Gerald was again at sea, but Paddy Hayley Bell, her father and mother, and two young men from Government House joined us for the celebration.

As we finished our meal and were chatting, I looked up and into the dining room walked two officers wearing full-dress uniforms of the Argyll and Sutherland Highlanders.

One of them was the most gorgeous man I had ever seen.

"That is the man I want to marry!" I announced in a loud whisper as I pointed in his direction.

All heads at our table turned to see this Adonis.

"Don't be silly, Joan!" huffed my godmother. "You're already engaged to Gerald."

I turned to Paddy. "Who are those beautiful men?" I asked.

"They're from the 42nd Battalion that was stationed in Shanghai when we were there," she explained. "Now they've been sent down here to replace the Welsh Guards who left yesterday." She certainly knew the movement of the troops.

"How can I meet them?" I asked, looking at them again out of the corner of my eye.

"Oh, that's easy," she said, rising from her chair. "Come with me."

I followed her as we zigzagged our way around the tables.

"Hello, boys," she said. Paddy was no shrinking flower. "Remember me? Paddy Hayley Bell. I met you in Shanghai. But I'm sorry to say, I've forgotten your names." She smiled in a most engaging way.

"I'm Freddy Graham," said the older of the two, "and this is Lieutenant Terence Roper-Caldbeck." He cocked his head toward the gorgeous one, who smiled at me and asked, "Would you like to dance?"

"I'm afraid I don't dance very well," I said.

"Good, neither do I," he said as he led me to the dance floor.

The orchestra was playing a waltz. We glided around the floor, our hands clasped tightly together, my arm resting on his shoulder. I could feel his right hand at the small of my back, pulling me close to him.

"This is the loveliest birthday I've ever had," I thought.

When the waltz came to an end, I ushered Terence to our table to introduce him to Auntie Winnie and the others.

He said, "I'd like to see you again. Where are you staying?"

"Right here. But we're moving to the Peninsula Hotel."

"I have a few days' leave coming up. May I call on you? Perhaps we could have lunch?"

I thought I saw Auntie Winnie's mouth tighten as I answered "yes" a bit too quickly.

We left Repulse Bay a few days later and moved into the Peninsula, the newest, most luxurious hotel in Kowloon. It is still one of the great hotels of the world.

Gerald was still on pirate patrol. Terry came over from his barracks several times a week. We would sit and talk for hours in the second floor lounge, and before long, we found ourselves hopelessly, desperately in love.

The day was approaching when we were due to leave the Crown Colony. I didn't want to leave. Terry didn't want me to leave. What to do about Gerald? I prayed for a miracle.

The miracle came on wings.

A mosquito somehow managed to creep through the netting that hung over Auntie Winnie's bed and bit her on the arm. The next morning she awoke with a high fever, and her skin began to turn yellow. The hotel doctor was summoned. "She has malaria," he told me. He wanted to put her in the hospital immediately. She would have none of it, saying that germs there would kill her. We sent for a round-the-clock nurse, and I moved into another room.

Poor Auntie Winnie. She was miserably ill until the fever broke. The doctor informed us that she would be unable to travel for at least three weeks. Thomas Cook was notified, and our passage on a ship of the Cunard Line was cancelled.

How guilty I felt when I left her with the nurse and spent the days with Terry!

A really serious problem loomed ahead of me, though: Gerald had returned to Hong Kong. I would have to tell him that I had fallen in love with someone else. I dreaded the thought.

Gerald and I met in the same second floor lounge where Terry and I had had our daily rendezvous. After several minutes of small talk, I told him as gently as I could what had happened while he was away. Not unexpectedly, he was hurt and angry.

"You have humiliated me," he said, with a catch in his voice. "You cheated me. All those days we spent on the beach together, I had a difficult time controlling my passion for you. You see, I always thought of you as being pure and untouched. That is how I wanted you to stay until we were married." He was on the verge of tears. "Now this other fellow will have all the pleasure that should have been mine!" The tears ran down his cheeks, and I cried as well. I offered to return the engagement ring. He insisted I keep it. "Perhaps it will remind you in years to come what wonderful times we had together. I know I will always remember."

I never saw Gerald after our last meeting. I hope he found a lovely girl, married her, and had a happy life.

Terry and I became engaged and vowed eternal devotion to each other.

As soon as Auntie Winnie recuperated, we rescheduled our departure from Hong Kong.

Finally, the day arrived that I had been dreading, the day for our departure from Hong Kong. I had said my goodbyes to Terry at the hotel because I could not bear the thought of watching him standing on the dock, waving farewell. I left behind a broken heart, a new love, friends, and many memories.

Because of Auntie Winnie's illness, we had to eliminate several of the stops on our original itinerary. Among those that we did visit were Bangkok where we had an excursion to the Floating Market and a visit to the Christian College for Boys; Penang; and Singapore, where we stayed at the venerable Raffles Hotel and where I had my first Singapore Sling.

Finally we reached Calcutta via a British India Line steamer. Auntie Winnie and I remained in India for several weeks. Our itinerary had been revised and would now take us as far north as Rawalpindi on the Northwest Frontier. We continued on to Darjeeling where my itinerary indicates, "Leave hotel at 2 a.m. by rickshaw, dandy, or pony, arriving Tiger Hill Resthouse at about 4 a.m. when coffee will be served; return to Darjeeling, arriving hotel about 9:30 a.m." All this was to view Mt. Everest at sunrise, and I can't even remember it. I do remember our visit to Agra to see the exquisite Taj Mahal. We visited Madras, Kandy, Colombo, and then moved on to Port Said and Naples, where we boarded a ship for our return home.

Auntie Winnie may have been eccentric and had ideas that to me, even then, seemed old-fashioned. But she gave me an opportunity to visit places and see sights of which people only dream. I shall always be grateful to my godmother for that wonderful journey. It enabled me to see the glories of the British Empire before they sadly disappeared and were replaced with new nations, many of them with new names.

Auntie Winnie was sometimes difficult to get along with, and she never gave me the freedom that I would have liked. But she was kind and generous, and I wish I could have been more loving toward her. I shall always remember her with gratitude.

So, at the age of 18, I had already fallen in love, become engaged, fallen out of love, fallen in love a second time, and had become engaged again. I had been around the world, appeared on the stage, and had a variety of adventures.

What else was there in store for me?

7

After Adventures Abroad

Life in London seemed dull and dismal after my adventures abroad. Terry and I wrote to each other every week. His letters were comforting and gave me great joy, but I missed him terribly. He was no longer with the Argylls in China. He had been posted to Ankpa, Nigeria, where he was serving with the Royal West African Frontier Force.

Of all the letters I've kept, the 17-page handwritten one from Terry dated July 3, 1933, from Ankpa, Nigeria, is the most poignant. This is just a portion:

My dearest Joan,

Oh, God, how I wish you were here with me now, instead of miles away, because I love you more than you can ever realise. Honestly, darling, my love for you still continues to increase every day, and you mean just everything in the world to me. Oh, God, how I love you, my precious.

Darling, darling, darling, to-day I have completed 8 whole months of my tour and by the time you receive this letter, the half-way mark will very nearly have passed!! Isn't that a truly magnificent thought?! ...

Darling, would love to see you playing your part in 'Mayfair Girl.' I cannot imagine you playing the part of a permanently blasé young woman!...

Dearest, you say in your last letter that I am probably bored stiff with hearing all your very stale news about who you lunched or dined with each day during the last fortnight. Well, I can assure you that it isn't stale news to me and I simply love hearing every little bit of news about what you have been doing.... I only wish to God I could write really interesting letters to you in return. But that is impossible from Ankpa. Damn these far flung outposts!!

...Well, darling, it is now 10 o'clock ... so I think it is about time I had a bottle of beer as I am feeling grand and thirsty!! So here's to you, my very own darling Joan! You are my very own, aren't you, darling?

On Monday night, Sgt. Young, the Doctor, and I all dined with Brown, as the C.O. was dining there and on Tuesday night Major Stronge and Brown came over here and dined with me. It was the first time that anybody had dined with me in Ankpa, and I was a wee bit anxious about the dinner! But I needn't have been, as the cook produced an excellent dinner and Sam did his job as a waiter very well indeed! I had to borrow a bottle of sherry and a bottle of port from Brown for the evening, as I don't allow myself such luxuries in the wilds of Ankpa!! Too much of a temptation, my love! I am rather too partial to a nice drop of sherry, now and then! ...

The climate here at present is well-nigh perfect.... It really is amazingly cool and the nights are grand on the whole. Quite honestly if you were here, I believe you would say that it wasn't warm enough for your liking!! You must have been reveling in the hot spell at home, when the temperature was over 90 degrees!!! We seldom get it over 85 degrees in the shade!! This is not what one imagines 'darkest Africa' to be like....

Well, good-night darling Joan and God bless you, my sweet. I love you desperately.

> Your very own,
> Terry

I read the letter two, three, even four times. Of all the love letters I received over my life, this one was the most heartfelt, tender, and moving.

I began the daily routine of visiting the Bramlin Agency. Eric Goodhead told me, "Theatre work is practically non-existent. The best we can hope for will be crowd work in small films." He told me that there were still a great many "quota films" being made.

"They are not too particular about experience—or even talent, for that matter," said Mr. Goodhead matter of factly. "All they need is someone who will be there on time and work cheaply."

He shuffled through a pile of papers on his desk and pulled a sheet out of the jumble. "Here's one going on now, and they need a few people for a crowd. The picture is called *Ebb Tide*, and it's being directed by," he checked the paper, "Arthur Rosson. They want girls for a barroom scene and are looking for a couple of prostitute-types." He gave me a quick glance to see my reaction. "So wear something, you know, revealing."

He gave me instructions: "Be at British and Dominion Studios at Elstree tomorrow morning at 7 a.m. sharp. Tell the man at the door that I sent you."

The next morning, I drove to the studio in my Morris-Oxford—a gift from Auntie Winnie—parked it in the yard, and joined about 20 other actors waiting by the door. The assistant director, a fatherly-looking man, herded us onto a dimly lit stage.

"Stand here, and look as if you're enjoying yourselves," he instructed us.

"You," he said, pointing to me. "What's your name?"

"Joan Winnifrith. I'm from the Bramlin Agency. Eric Goodhead sent me."

"Yes, Joan. Well, I want you to sit on the piano with Queenie and swing your legs. You're supposed to be 'ladies of easy virtue.'" He grinned. Then he called out, "Queenie? Queenie Thompson? Where are you?"

A beautiful young girl emerged from the gloom and came forward. She had a perfect profile and dark, smoldering eyes that slanted at the corners.

"Hello, Queenie. My name is Joan," I introduced myself. "We're supposed to sit on the piano and pretend to sing. I'm rather nervous. Are you?"

"Yes," she replied. "I always am."

"At least we're together, and we don't have to worry about standing in the right place," I said. "Do you know who is in the film?"

"Chili Bouchier is playing the lead, and the blonde girl over there is Joan Barry."

We both jumped up onto the piano and sat, swinging our legs, until the director came in. He walked over to us and explained that he wanted Queenie to do a "bit."

"I want you to run up that staircase," he said as he pointed across the set. "Then open the door, look in, and run down again."

Queenie was so nervous that she was shaking.

Everything was ready for a "take."

"Action," called the director. Queenie slid down from the piano, ran up the stairs... but she was unable to open the door. It was stuck.

She burst into tears. I was called upon to do the "bit."

Queenie was still sobbing when I climbed back onto the piano, and when the scene was over, she had disappeared. I wanted to console her but couldn't find her anywhere.

At the end of the day's work, I collected the princely sum of three guineas, about $5. By the time I returned to my car, it was pouring rain. As I turned out of the yard, I saw Queenie waiting for the bus. She was wearing a thin, cloth coat and was soaking wet.

I pulled up to the bus stop. "Queenie," I called, "jump in. I'll take you back to London."

"Oh, thank you! The bus is always late, and I'm so cold," she said with a shiver as she opened the door and climbed in.

I handed her the lap rug that I kept in the car.

"I live with my godmother," I told her. "She has a flat in Knightsbridge. Why don't we stop there and dry you off? You could have supper with us, if you like."

"Yes, I'd like that, if it's not too much trouble."

We drove on for a while in silence, the rain splashing all around. Then, my passenger asked in a small voice with a curious undulating cadence that I had not noticed before, "Joan, is there a bath in your flat?"

"Of course," I replied. "And plenty of hot water."

"We only have a shower where I live," she explained. "More than anything in the world, I would love to lie in a bath with warm water up to my neck."

When we arrived at Auntie Winnie's flat, I introduced my new friend, "This is Queenie Thompson, and she's having supper with us."

"Why, that's splendid," said my godmother. Looking at Queenie, she added, "I hope you like roast beef and Yorkshire pudding. It's Joan's favorite. But let's get you out of those wet clothes. Joan," she said to me, "find a warm dressing gown."

I hurried off as Auntie Winnie said to Queenie, "We'll hang your clothes in front of the fire to dry."

At supper, Queenie had two helpings of everything. She was ravenous. I wondered when she had last had a proper meal.

"Where are you from, dear?" asked Auntie Winnie, passing the Yorkshire pudding.

"I was born in Calcutta," said Queenie, "but I've lived in England for some time."

"Is your mother with you?"

Queenie lowered her eyes. "I have no mother," she said. We didn't pursue the topic any further.

After supper, I showed her the bathroom and filled the tub with hot water, tossing in a handful of lavender bath salts.

"This is heaven," she said as she tied up her dark hair. "One of these days, when I'm a big star, I'll have a bathroom of my own."

Years later, I remembered those words. When I visited her home in Beverly Hills, she was true to her word: she had multiple bathrooms. We didn't see much of each other, then. I don't think she wanted to see anyone who reminded her of her past.

Queenie and I did not work together again, but we continued to see each other. We went on long walks in Kensington Gardens. I asked her why she wanted to be an actress.

"Oh, I don't want to be just an ordinary actress. I'm going to be a *star*," she said with emphasis on the last word. "The greatest star in the world. I don't care what I do or who I have to sleep with to get there. But *I will get there*." The last words she said with such vehemence, it was frightening. I don't think I'd heard anyone say anything with such determination and purpose.

"But, Queenie," I said pragmatically, "how are you going to start? You have no experience. You don't even have an agent."

"*I* don't need any help," was her response. "It's not what you've done. It's who you know. Tonight I'm going to a party at the Dorchester. There will be a lot important people there, and I may get lucky. Why don't you come, too?" she said, as an afterthought.

I had done some serious thinking about the very subject that she was talking about. After some moments, I said, "I'm not a prude, Queenie, but I'm going to be famous without having to sleep with someone I'm not in love with to further my career."

She just smiled.

I did not attend the party.

Some weeks later, I was walking past Harrods, the department store, when I saw Queenie again.

She was gazing in one of the windows. We greeted each other warmly, and she introduced me to her companion, an Indian woman dressed in a *sari*, as her *amah*, or nurse. "She doesn't speak English," Queenie added, a little too quickly. We chatted for a few minutes and agreed to meet the following week.

I learned much later that the woman to whom she had introduced me as her nurse was, in fact, her mother!

Queenie's climb up the ladder toward stardom did not take long. One evening, I was having dinner with a friend at the Café de Paris in Piccadilly when I saw a beautiful woman coming down the staircase. She was wearing a gorgeous gown, and as she reached the bottom stair, the maitre d' and Charles, the club manager, greeted her. Every head—male and female— turned to look at this dazzling creature.

"Who *is* that?" I asked my friend.

"She's the new hostess. Her name is Estelle O'Brien, and the boys say she's a pushover."

As she came nearer, I recognized Queenie. She came to our table, and I complimented her on how lovely she looked.

I turned in my chair and asked her quietly, "Why did you change your name?"

She bent forward and replied, "I think it suits me better. 'Estelle' means 'star,' and that's what I'm going to be. Remember?"

Not long afterwards, I saw a photograph of her in the paper. The caption read: "Merle Oberon to star as Anne Boleyn in Alexander Korda's production of *The Private Life of Henry VIII*." It was 1933, just a year after our uncredited roles in *Ebb Tide*. She was 22.

After she married Alexander Korda in 1939—she was 28; he was 46—

I continued to see her. But eventually, they both left for Hollywood and further triumphs. When Alex was knighted in 1942, she became Lady Korda, a far cry from her beginnings in Calcutta. They divorced in 1945.

My career didn't move quite so swiftly.

I continued working in quota pictures, and I did one regular feature. It was called *Yes, Mr. Brown* and starred musical comedy star, Jack Buchanan. I actually had a scene with him and a line or two of dialogue.

When the film opened in London, my mother invited several of her friends to a screening. We all sat in the front row of the dress circle, anticipating my feature debut. The picture began. Scene after scene went by. I realized that my part had been completely cut from the film. I was desperately embarrassed for my mother who had wanted to show me off to her friends.

"Never mind, dear," she said. "Worse things happen at sea! [This was one of those *non-sequiturs* she often used.] We all enjoyed the film, and I thought Mr. Buchanan was very funny."

Some of the less-than-notable quota films in which I appeared in 1933 were *The Bermondsey Kid*; *The King's Cup*, again with Chili Bouchier; and *Chelsea Life*, with handsome Louis Hayward. I remember nothing about these films except the titles.

Then, in the autumn of 1933, I received the glorious news that Terry was coming home on leave. On his return, we became officially engaged, and he gave me an exquisite diamond ring, which had been in his family more than a hundred years.

We drove down to his home, near Haywards Heath, Surrey. Terry's father, Colonel Roper-Caldbeck, had served in the First World War with the Irish Fusiliers. His mother, a gentle, charming lady, obviously adored her son as much as I did. His older brother James was in the Black Watch. He also had a sister.

We decided to celebrate our engagement by driving up to Scotland for the Regimental Ball at Stirling Castle where the Argylls were stationed.

I will never forget the Ball. The men were resplendent in full-dress uniforms and the women wore ball gowns with tartan shoulder sashes. I was not able to dance the Scottish reels as the steps were too intricate for me. As it was, Terry and I managed to skip through "The Gay Gordons" without falling over each other.

On the way back, we stopped at a hotel somewhere on the east coast. This was my idea. I wanted to spend at least one night alone with him before he returned to Africa. The room at the inn was ugly, but there was a double bed, and that was all I was interested in.

Terry was very gentle with me, and I thought it was all wonderful, especially when it was over, and I lay in his arms, listening to his heart beating.

"I hope I didn't hurt you, darling," he whispered. "It will be much better after we are married, and I don't have to worry about making you pregnant."

When we returned, we spent several days visiting my mother in Rochester—in separate rooms. We also had separate rooms when we visited Auntie Winnie, who was now living in Sevenoaks.

A week before he was to leave for Africa, Terry told me he had to return to Scotland for a day to visit his commanding officer. "I have to ask his permission to marry," he explained. "It's just a formality, but it's a regimental regulation, and I have to have his consent."

When he returned, he was beaming. Evidently all was well.

"Apparently someone had told him that you were an actress, but I said this would not be a problem as you were going to give up your career as soon as we were married. I assured him you would become a proper regimental wife."

A *regimental wife*! My heart sank. It never occurred to me that once we were married, my entire life would change. Wherever his regiment was posted, I would be expected to follow. I realized that I could never be happy with him, when all I would do is traipse around after him. His career would flourish, and I would have none. I knew I would never make a good officer's wife.

I broke off my engagement, the second one in two years. Terry was inconsolable.

"I can't believe this is happening," he cried. "I love you more than you will ever know. You mean everything in the world to me." Tears were streaming down his handsome face. He kissed me and said, "Let me know if you ever change your mind, Joan, and I will come to you from the ends of the earth."

This time I returned the ring.

Oh, my poor Terry. How could I have done this to you? What was wrong with me? First Gerald and then Terry. I was stupid and thoughtless and inconsiderate, and I brought unhappiness to you both.

Although I do not know what happened to Gerald, I do know that Terry distinguished himself in World War II as the first commanding officer of Camp X, which was organized just outside Toronto, Canada, to train Allied agents in espionage for assignments behind enemy lines.

I continued with my career. The only picture of any importance in 1933 was Noël Coward's *Bitter Sweet*, starring Anna Neagle. I played one of her bridesmaids. It was my first costume picture. Each morning, the wardrobe lady came in carrying a beautiful pale blue Victorian dress. Each morning she laced me into a corset—very tightly. I stood with my hands on the back of a chair while she tugged and pulled until I thought I would faint. In the

With Anna Neagle *(center)*; I'm on the far left. Noël Coward described my décolletage as "The Great Divide," and the scene was cut.

end, I had to admit the result was well worth the pain. My waist shrank to 23 inches, while my bosoms rose to where they almost popped out of the dress.

The resulting cleavage did not escape the discerning eye of Noël Coward, who was on the set during production. At one point he said to director Herbert Wilcox, just loudly enough for me to hear, "You'd better change the angle of the camera. It's pointing right down the chest of that girl in blue who is leaning over the banister." He was pointing at me. "All you can see is 'the Great Divide.'"

So I was moved to the back of the group of bridesmaids. Not that it mattered. That scene, too, was cut from the finished film. My career so far was on the cutting room floor.

While I was working on *Bitter Sweet*, I became friends with a young actress who was also playing a bridesmaid. She was Russian, and I called her Natasha. I don't think I ever new her real name. One evening after work, she invited me to accompany her to the Berkeley Hotel, where she wanted me to meet some of her friends.

"Don't worry about taking off your makeup," she told me as I reached for the cold cream. "Everyone is used to seeing me like this." So off we went.

At the hotel, the doorman the waiters, everyone, seemed to know Natasha. We were escorted into the Berkeley Grill and to a corner booth where two young men were already seated. She introduced me. "Joan, this is Dickie Norton, and this is Jack Dunfee." They both stood up "They are known as 'the Bentley Boys,' and we have a lot of fun together." Did I see Dickie wink at her?

Dickie (who later became Lord Grantley and headed Pinewood Studios) and Jack were called that nickname because they raced their Bentleys at Brooklands track. Several of these wealthy young men died tragically from racing injuries.

From that first evening, I became part of the Berkeley circle.

I fell in love with Jack Dunfee and he with me.

Knowing my love of horses, Jack introduced me to polo, and I learned to play. I became a member of the Ham Common Women's Polo Club. Jack and I had wonderful times riding together, and when we finally went our separate ways, he gave me a beautiful pair of silver spurs. My daughter Caroline has them now.

Another man who came into my life in the early '30s was Bernard Rubin. By the time I knew him, he'd been out to Australia and had won some sort of flying record, but he was living at the Berkeley and had become part of the Bentley circle. He fell in love with me. Although I liked him very much, I was never in love with him. I did feel a strong physical attraction to him, however. He used to give me wonderful presents, including a black-and-gold Cartier cigarette lighter. I kept it for years, even when I gave up smoking.

"Look outside your front door," he instructed me when he phoned one day. I ran downstairs, and there, parked on the street, was an Alfa Romeo, all tied up in ribbons. It was a gift for my 21st birthday.

Auntie Winnie made me give it back.

"The only things you may accept from a young man," she told me, "are flowers and chocolates." Obviously, I never told her or Mummie about the other gifts I received from Bernard.

I did have one wonderful drive in the Alfa Romeo. The same evening I received it—and before I returned it to Bernard—I drove down to Portsmouth where I had been invited to a party on board the HMS *Ark Royal*. I remember that drive. I was wearing a black and scarlet chiffon evening dress and a white racing helmet, which was on the seat of the car when I first saw it. The top of the car was down, and it was a glorious sensation hearing the wind whistling in my ears and the engine throbbing as the car sped down the Great West Road.

Quota films were my bread and butter for the next two years. Sometimes I did as many as two or three a month, so many, in fact, that my friends called me "Queen of the Quotas."

The money was not good; I had to provide my own wardrobe; and there was also the expense of driving back and forth to the studios, often as far away as Islington and Twickenham.

To help with the finances, I began modeling for commercial photographers. I posed for magazine and newspaper advertisements, including several for Reslaw Hats. One of them was printed on a large placard.

My mother saw a man walking down the street carrying the placard. "That's my daughter!" she exclaimed and persuaded him to give her the placard. It now hangs on the wall in my home.

I also posed for several coffee, face cream, and jewelry advertisements. I even posed in a highly acrobatic pose for the logo for one of the photography firms, Tunbridge.

The owner of one photographic studio for which I worked told me that one of his clients was introducing a new line of cosmetics called Venus. They wanted a girl to pose in a seashell, reminiscent of the famous Botticelli painting, *The Birth of Venus*.

"There is only one thing," the photographer pointed out. "They want the model to be nude... or almost nude." He knew I would balk at anything like that so he offered a compromise. "I thought we could drape you in seaweed. It will be a beautiful and tasteful photograph." Then he added, "They are willing to pay a lot of money."

A few days later, there I was draped in seaweed, with nothing between the cold, clammy leaves and me. But the picture was beautiful. I kept it for years, until my jealous second husband destroyed it.

Mayfair Girl, also in 1933, in which I had a small role, starred Sally Blane. She and I became friends, and years later, I worked with her sister, Loretta Young.

Between quota pictures and modeling, I thought it might be helpful to work on my singing. Along with several other aspiring actors, I took lessons from Madame Clara Novello-Davis, the mother of the matinee idol Ivor Novello.

During our lessons, we were required to stand barefoot on our toes, all in a row. She'd say, "You're birds in a tree," and we would sing, "Ning. Ning. Ning."

Although I was busy in 1934, I couldn't break out of the quota pictures. *Mannequin*, however, brought me into contact with my old friend Charles Bennett, who wrote the screenplay.

On *The Bermondsey Kid*, I met a young actor, Peter Sutton. Both of us were frustrated with the way our careers were stagnating. "We need to get out and meet people and be seen," I said. "Otherwise we are never going to get anywhere."

Our respective agents were not helpful. When we complained, their reply was, "You're lucky to be working at all."

I had an idea. From what I had heard, the Savoy Grill (the same place I'd had my dinner with Howard Hughes) was where producers and directors gathered after they finished work. This was the place to be seen.

One evening, Peter booked a table at the Grill, and we sat sipping wine, hoping that someone important would notice us.

I noticed a man staring at me. He was seated at a table across the room. He sent a waiter over with his card. It read:

Albert Parker
Fox Studios, Hollywood

"The gentleman would like you to join him for coffee," said the waiter.

"Peter," I said as we walked across the room, "I believe we have been discovered."

Al Parker was middle-aged with dark hair and a strong American accent.

"I'll come directly to the point," he said, looking directly at me. "I'm over here to direct a film called *Rolling in Money*. Isabel Jeans and John Loder are playing the leads. We're looking for someone to play the ingénue, and when I saw you just now, I thought you might be right for the part." My heart was pounding as he continued. "I'd like to give you a test. Be at my office at 10 o'clock tomorrow morning. Sixth floor of the Grosvenor House. We'll talk then."

I smiled, nodded, and said something like, "Thank you, Mr. Parker."

He never even looked at Peter. Not long after Peter left acting and went home to tend to the family estate.

On the stroke of 10 the next morning, I was at the Grosvenor House. Al Parker's suite was large and luxurious. He sent for a photographer who took several head shots of me.

"Good cheekbones," he said. "And your eyes are excellent. He handed me the script of *Rolling in Money*, and I read the part of Lady Kathleen Eggelby, the daughter of the Duke of Braceborough, who would be played by Lawrence Grossmith.

Mr. Parker seemed pleased with my reading.

"Come again tomorrow evening, and we'll discuss the details," he commanded.

When I arrived the following evening, my worst suspicions were confirmed. After room service brought in dinner, it became obvious he had more on his mind than discussing the role. He chased me around the table and tried to kiss me. I pulled myself away.

"Mr. Parker," I said as firmly as I could, "when I started as an actress, I promised myself that I would never make love to anyone in order to get a job."

"But, my dear girl," he replied, "this is not to *get* the job. You already have it. This is to say thank you for it!"

I allowed him to kiss me. It was like kissing a piece of wood, but he was a nice man, and in the long run, I grew quite fond of him. He never again made a pass at me.

"I'm going to make you a star," he told me. I looked at him in astonishment. "I've done it for others, and I can do it for you."

The result was that I signed a contract with Fox-British, with the hope that Mr. Parker would take me to Hollywood after *Rolling in Money*.

He had some advice for me: "There are two things you must do. First, auburn and brunette hair photograph too dark. You must become a blonde. But," he cautioned, "not a Jean Harlow blonde, something softer and warmer." The other change: "Joan Winnifrith is too difficult to say and is too long for a marquee. Choose something short and glamorous."

I decided to change the color of my hair first. I went to Antoine's in New Bond Street and told the stylist what I wanted. My hair was covered with a strong solution of peroxide and ammonia, which smelled dreadful and remained on for about an hour. The pain on my scalp was intense. When they were finished, however, I was a blonde. I looked in the mirror and liked what I saw.

Finding a new name was not easy. "Something short and glamorous," Mr. Parker advised. I made a list of all my favorite names: Cordelia, Miranda, Perdita, Tamara. All too long.

At the time I was reading Tolstoy's *Anna Karenina*. "Anna," I thought is a beautiful name, short and romantic." For my surname, I took the name of the American Civil War general whom I admired: Robert E. Lee.

So Joan Winnifrith became Anna Lee.

When my friend, Charles Bennett, heard about this, he phoned me. "Joan," he said in a reproachful tone, "if you had to change your name, why did you choose one that sounds like a Chinese laundry."

A few days after my dual transformation, my picture appeared in one of the trade papers: "Al Parker Discovers Anna Lee." The article said that I had signed a seven-year contract with Fox and would be leaving shortly for Hollywood.

Work began on *Rolling in Money*, the first picture in which I had a proper part. I remember little about the picture, but I do remember John Loder, who was extremely handsome and had a profile that surpassed even that of John Barrymore. John had served in World War I with the 15th Hussars at Gallipoli. He was taken prisoner in 1918. After the war, he married a French woman, the first of his five wives.

A few days after *Rolling in Money* was completed, I received a call from a theatrical agency called Connie's. Connie had started the agency some years previously with a partner, and was known as "The Captain." Since they were only interested in big name actors, I was surprised when she called me.

"Michael Balcon of Gaumont-British wants to see you," she told me. "They are making a picture starring Jack Hulbert and want to find a new face to play opposite him."

I pinched myself to make sure I wasn't dreaming. Jack Hulbert, along with Jack Buchanan, was one of the biggest musical comedy stars in London.

And *I* might be given the chance to work with him.

Michael Balcon was a delightful man. He told me about the part I was to be tested for: Anita Rodgers, who piloted a plane all over the Sahara Desert looking for smugglers.

"We are going to make this picture in Egypt, near the Suez Canal. You'll be there for at least six weeks. Do you suppose your parents will mind?" he asked.

I assured him that my mother would have no objections. Then he introduced me to his brother, Shan, and they arranged for a screen test.

A few days latter, Connie called, "Congratulations, Anna, you've got the part. Gaumont-British liked you so much they want to sign you to a five-year contract."

"Connie," I said, "that may be a problem." I told her about the previously signed contract with Al Parker and Fox.

"Don't worry," she counseled. "Gaumont-British has an excellent team of lawyers. They will find some way to work this out."

Their lawyers were able to get me released from my legal entanglement. It was easier than I expected. They found out that I was under age when I signed the first contract so it was not valid.

I became the property of Gaumont-British and its sister studio, Gainsborough, when I signed the new contract... with my mother's signature alongside mine.

Al Parker was upset and angry. "You are a stupid girl," he said. "I could make you a star in Hollywood. Gaumont-British will do nothing for you. In three years' time, you'll come to me, begging for a job. Just you wait and see."

I never saw him again. I will always remember the three things he left me with: a new name, a different hair color, and confidence that I could become a really good actress.

So thank you, Mr. Parker, wherever you are.

8

Yet Another Love,
and My First Feature

There was another romantic interlude, this one with Lord Simon (an Anglicization of the Gaelic name "Shimie") Lovat, the seventeenth Lord Lovat.

When I first met him in 1930, he had not yet succeeded to the title, but was known as Simon Fraser, Master of Lovat. He was proud of his Highland heritage and preferred being called Shimie rather than Simon.

I had been invited to Oxford for the Magdalen College Ball in June. I was sitting with some friends when Shimie appeared, wearing his kilt, playing his bagpipes, and slightly drunk. He was tall and wonderfully handsome, and my heart started to beat faster. Someone took the pipes away from him and sat him down next to me. I still have the menu from that evening, with its title, "*Souper de Bal.*" In the corner, faint but still legible, is the inscription: "Joan, dearest, from Shimie Fraser, drunk piper."

I can't remember what we talked about that evening; I think he tried to teach me how to speak Gaelic. The following day we had lunch together. He invited me to Oxford again. We saw a great deal of each other during that summer, and I think we fell in love.

One day I arranged to have a picnic lunch near Holmby Woods. I remember we spread a blanket on the grass and before I knew what was happening, I was in his arms, and he was kissing me passionately. Suddenly, he broke away.

His voice was harsh. "Joan, darling, we must stop this. I'm a wild Highlander, and I'm afraid of what might happen, and I don't want to hurt you. You see, my dearest Joan, I can't marry you. I'm Catholic, and you're Church of England, and as the Chief of the Fraser Clan, it is my duty to marry into one of the old Highland Catholic families."

We continued to write to one another, and I saw him once in London, but when I left for America, we lost touch.

Shimie became one of the great heroes of World War II; he led his commandos across the beaches of Normandy, accompanied by his piper, Bill Millin, who played "Scotland the Brave" all the while they were storming Sword Beach. He later was so seriously wounded that he was given the Last Rites, but after weeks in the hospital, he recovered.

It was wonderful to have known that brave and gallant Highland warrior. It was only for a very short time, but I shall always remember him with love.

Now that I was under contract to a film studio, there were tests to be made. Michael and Shan Balcon supervised my makeup tests. As Shan watched the makeup artists, I could see he became concerned about some aspect of my face.

He said, "We have to do something about your mouth. You have an aristocratic upper lip."

"What is an 'aristocratic upper lip'?" I asked.

"It's thin," he explained. "We must fill it out and make it look sexier."

The makeup people dabbed and daubed until they got the lip Shan liked.

I also spent a few rather painful days being vaccinated against smallpox, cholera, and black water fever prior to leaving for Egypt.

Finally, cast and crew of *The Camels Are Coming* sailed from Southampton in the fall of 1934. Fall and winter months are considered "the season" in Egypt; otherwise it would be unbearably hot.

On board were the principals: Jack Hulbert, Hartley Power, Harold Huth, Allan Jeayes, and Peter Gawthorne. Peggy Simpson and Norma Whalley, who had small roles as tourists, were the only other women in the cast, but they left as soon as they completed their scenes, leaving me the lone female.

The sea voyage was choppy, and I was seasick in the Bay of Biscay. We spent a few days in Cairo at the venerable Shepheard's Hotel, where anybody and everybody congregated. I immediately fell in love with the city. Sitting on the terrace, I inhaled the exotic smells and watched the traffic and the people.

The first sequence of *The Camels Are Coming* was shot in the hotel gardens. I particularly remember the scene because I hated my costume: a long white flowing dress. Black stripes criss-crossed my midriff; topping off this ensemble was the most ridiculous little hat.

After we completed shooting for the day, I was sitting on the terrace having tea with Harold when the hotel manager came up to me with a man close upon his heels. "Miss Lee," he said gesturing toward the stranger, "this gentleman would like to meet you." I looked up to see a handsome Arab who took my hand and lifted it to his lips, more like a Frenchman than an Arab!

"Allow me to introduce myself," he said in a voice that bore no hint of a Middle Eastern accent. "I am Sheik El Barrak, and I would like to welcome you to Egypt."

"Thank you," I smiled. "Are you really a sheik? You don't look like one." He was wearing a smart suit and tie, gloves—one of which he took off to kiss my hand—and carried a soft hat.

He laughed. "You mean you expected someone who looked like Rudolph Valentino? I dress that way when I am with my tribe, but here in Cairo, I think my secretary would die of fright if I walked into my office looking like that. I am a Bedouin," he continued. "My camp is a few miles from Luxor. I would like to take you there one day." That sounded like an intertitle from Son of the Sheik. I was intrigued.

"My hobby is breeding Arabian horses. I understand you are going to do a lot of riding in this film, and I wondered if you would allow me to lend you one of my horses. They are accustomed to galloping across the desert. It would be much easier for you than trying to cope with one of the studio horses." That was an offer I couldn't refuse.

"Yes," I said, thinking, "What a tremendously kind gentleman." I was secretly rather pleased that I had caught the attention of a real sheik, even if he didn't look like one. He asked if he could join Harold and me for tea. Harold said something about going over the scenes for the next day and left us to continue our conversation.

The sheik told me he had been educated in England at Eton and Oxford and that he owned two banks in Cairo. When we had finished our tea, he rose, took my hand once again, and promised to bring one of his prize horses to the location.

A few days later, we packed up our belongings and moved to out to the desert location where the rest of the film would be shot. The camp, complete with tents and other desert-safari paraphernalia, had been set up a few miles from the Suez Canal—about 40 miles south of Cairo—by an Egyptian firm that organized such things for tourists and film people. They were also responsible for catering; food was sent in three times a week by lorry. Giant crates of bottled water also arrived. We were warned never, ever to drink anything but the bottled variety and not to eat lettuce or fruit that might have been rinsed in contaminated water.

The largest tent was used as the mess hall. It also occasionally became our rehearsal hall. My tent, furnished with a camp bed, a chest of drawers, a candle, and an oil lamp, was hot and stuffy during the day. At night, it was moderately comfortable.

Norma and Peggy were in the tent next to mine, and nearby were Jack and the other actors in private tents. Tim Whelan, the American director, was in a tent at the end of the line, near the crew's quarters.

I was glad that he was not too close by, as he had already made a pass at me, and had been firmly rejected. I was not anxious for a repeat performance. But following the first day's shooting in the desert, he asked me to come into his tent to discuss a new scene that had been written into the script. After a few minutes, it became obvious that his mind was not on the dialogue.

"Tim," I said, in a none-too-polite tone, "can't we just avoid any trouble and remain friends while we shoot the picture."

Surprisingly, we did.

My Bedouin sheik arrived at the camp as promised, bringing with him Sheba, a gray mare, with a coat that shone like silver in the sunlight. On her back was an exquisite Moroccan saddle, encrusted with silver medallions and a large, high pommel in the Arab fashion. I was delighted with her, and with the first ride knew that we would become fast friends.

Since films are often shot out of continuity, it's not unusual that the first scene shot is often the climax of a film. So it was with *The Camels Are Coming*. It took place in the "ruins" of a stone fortress that had been built out in the middle of the desert for the film.

Jack and I spent the first few days filming the climactic fight scenes with the smugglers. In those days, there were no "stunt doubles," and the work was hard and, at times, quite painful.

During the second week, we filmed the scenes where Jack and I are impersonating the villains—the sheik and his wife, the head of a band of smugglers. We were each leading a string of camels. I never liked camels; they sneer at anyone who comes near, and they snort and grunt. And they slobber.

All went well until the return journey to the fort. I had to ride ahead of Jack, pulling my camels behind me. I galloped across the desert on my lovely Sheba and through the entrance to the fort.

Into the fort we rode, Sheba, the camels, and me. Sheba and I were suddenly surrounded by the throng of ugly, snorting camels. Sheba shied in terror and reared, causing me to crash to the desert floor with a thud. As I lay there on my back, all I could see was a flurry of furry camel legs and hooves shuffling around me and stirring up sand. They were grunting and, worst of all, they were slobbering all over me. The thick drool dripped onto my face and arms. The smell was vile and made me so nauseous that I almost passed out.

Jack Hulbert and I smile for the cameras in *The Camels Are Coming*.

The camera crew saw what happening, and two or three of them ran in and pushed their way through the camels. They picked me up and carried me to the car that had transported us to the location.

I was not hurt, except for a bump on the back of my head. I wanted desperately to wash off the camel goo. The first-aid man cleaned me up as best he could. Then I was driven into Cairo to the Hospital for Tropical Diseases. I had broken out in a rash over my face and arms. It burned and itched and was very painful. The doctors told me that camels can carry several diseases, some of which are serious, but I was fortunate to have nothing but a moderate rash.

Two days in the hospital, and then I returned to Shepheard's to recuperate further. While I was *hors de combat*, there were several scenes in the film in which I was not involved, so production did not stop. As soon as all signs of the rash disappeared, I rejoined the company.

"My" sheik came to visit me. He assured me that Sheba was no worse for her encounter with the camels.

Back at the location, after we finished with the smugglers inside the fort, the crew boarded a paddle steamer and sailed down the Nile to Luxor for a sequence in the Valley of the Kings. The site was fascinating, filled with temples and tombs and carved stone monuments. Several members of the company were eager to see the tomb of Tutankhamun and planned an excursion to the site.

I would love to have joined them on the adventure, but I had heard and read too much about the "Curse of King Tut" to risk entering the tomb. I had read about the people who had become involved with Tut's tomb and had died mysterious deaths, including our neighbor from Ightham.

Of course, none of our crew who entered the tomb complained of any ill effects.

However, after we left Luxor and returned to our camp near the Canal, a cloud of misfortune descended on the company.

Glen McWilliams, the cinematographer, began to complain of stomach pains. He was also running a high fever. A doctor from Cairo arrived and told us Glen was suffering from dysentery.

"There's a lot of it in Egypt," he said, "and there's nothing much to do for it. Keep him as cool and comfortable as possible. Don't be surprised if more of you get sick as it's highly infectious."

Tim Whelan was the next to come down with the ailment and was taken to the hospital in Cairo. Jack Hulbert, rather sensibly, saw no point in continuing to endure the heat of a tent in the desert when he could enjoy a few days' comfort back at Shepheard's Hotel.

The rest of us stayed where we were. Allan, Harold, and Hartley played cards most of the day. The remainder of the crew who had not succumbed to the disease amused themselves by playing football on the desert sand until overcome by the heat.

As the only woman on location, I played Florence Nightingale. I did my best to take care of my sick crew. With the help of our first aid man, Joseph, I ministered to the ill men, helping to change the sheets and put cold compresses on fever-ridden brows.

We suspected that the Arabs who were in charge of the camp and were supposed to bring in bottled water had become neglectful and filled up the empty bottles with tainted water. Hence, the illness.

Every evening, as soon as the sun set, I'd saddle up Sheba and gallop through the desert twilight, hoping to find a new adventure.

With no director, no star, and no cinematographer, *The Camels Are Coming* became *The Camels Aren't Going Anywhere*. No footage was shot for about ten days.

Back in London, the executives at Gaumont-British were becoming

Between takes outside my tent in the desert, from *The Camels Are Coming.*

frantic because no rushes were coming in for them to screen. They tried to call the camp, but the connection was so bad it was impossible to carry on any conversation. Finally, a cable arrived that someone was coming out to see what was going on, but they didn't say who it would be.

As I returned from my ride into the desert one evening, I saw a man walking out of the camp toward me. He was dressed in a cream-colored safari suit, like someone out of a Noël Coward play. He looked so clean. For weeks, I had been surrounded by ill-shaven, rumpled men, and when I saw this vision in white, I was immediately smitten. As I reined in Sheba directly in front of him with a slight spray of sand, I saw that he was of medium height with a slim physique, high forehead, and a long, interesting nose.

"Hello," he said, as I dismounted. "I'm Bob Stevenson. Gaumont-British sent me here to find out what the hell is going on. I stopped off in Cairo and talked with Tim, Jack, and production manager George Rogers who seem to think we are in a bit of a mess."

"That's putting it mildly," I said. "But let me get you a cup of tea or something stronger. You must be tired after your journey. First you must meet the other lost souls," and I called Harold, who was playing solitaire in his tent.

"Come meet Bob Stevenson, and give the poor man a drink while I put Sheba away."

Robert Stevenson had written a number of screenplays and had directed two films. The studio heads had sent him out as a trouble-shooter because they knew if there were problems, he could take over.

The following evening, Bob drove me into Cairo and took me to dinner at a French restaurant. The food tasted delicious after the over-spiced, exotic Arab cooking we'd had at camp. Bob insisted on ordering a bottle of wine. I told him I really didn't drink. He laughed and said, "Nonsense! A little red wine will be good for you. You know what the Bible says: 'A little wine is good for the stomach'!"

He went on to tell me that collecting wine was one of his hobbies. He showed me the correct way to savor it. "First," he instructed," swirl it in the glass. Then look at the color." He demonstrated, and then continued. "Inhale the aroma until it permeates your palate. Take a sip, then swish it around your mouth. Lastly, swallow it."

Bob was so different from the other men I knew. He was so knowledgeable, not just about wine, but about life and movies.

He was in the process of a divorce; he told me it had been a short marriage and was ending amicably.

In very matter-of-fact tones, he said, "I found her in bed with another man, and that was that!"

His house in London was on the South Bank of the River Thames in a district called Bankside. "The unfashionable side," he laughed. In the 16th Century, this area was the site of several theatres, including The Globe, The Swan, and The Rose. The name of Bob's house was Cardinal's Wharf; it had been built in 1710 on the foundations a 14th century tavern, The Cardinal's Hat, noted for its fine food and excellent wine. Some say that William Shakespeare often dined there on his way to The Globe. Cardinal's Wharf had been the home of Sir Christopher Wren while he was building St. Paul's Cathedral, and, as I was to find out, the house has the finest view of the great church across the river from all the front windows.

As Bob described it, the house was on a small, cobblestone street, with the river flowing past the door, carrying an ever-changing procession of barges, tugs, and pleasure steamers. I longed to see it for myself.

I found myself falling in love with Bob, and, sight unseen, the house. I didn't know it then, but Cardinal's Wharf would become an important part of my life.

"Incidentally," Bob said, changing the subject, "you're very good. I've watched the rushes, and Micky Balcon thinks you're good, too."

"Well, that's a load off my mind," I admitted. "After all the problems we've had here, I was afraid they would never want me in another picture."

"There will be many more Gaumont-British pictures for you, and I am looking forward to seeing a great deal of you," he told me. "How many of the crew are still sick?"

"Only two," I told him, "and they will be well enough to travel in a day or two."

Bob, Jack, and Tim had a couple of meetings and decided to send the company back to England as soon as possible. We boarded a liner in Alexandria, with plans to finish shooting the picture at the studio at Shepherd's Bush.

"Nothing like a sea voyage to calm the nerves," Bob said. The liner was not as luxurious as the one we had traveled out on, but it was comfortable, and it was lovely to be able to relax on the deck after weeks working in the desert heat.

Bob and I spent a great deal of time together during the voyage. Our conversations lasted all day and well into the evening. I learned all about him. He was born in Buxton, Derbyshire, in the northwest of England, in 1905. His father, who died when Bob was sixteen, was the head of a paper box factory. As a student at Cambridge, he told me, he attended St. John's College, and in 1928 was elected president of the Cambridge Union Society. After leaving Cambridge he worked for Gaumont-British as a reader. His first two directing assignments were *Falling for You* and

Happy Ever After with the husband and wife team of Jack Hulbert and Cicely Courtneidge.

His mother remarried and, until recently, had worked as a midwife. One of the babies whom she had brought into the world, I learned later, was actor Reginald Gardiner, with whom I would work in my first Hollywood film, *My Life with Caroline.*

Bob Stevenson was brilliant, and I used to tell him he was a walking encyclopedia. He seemed to know everything.

The love I felt for Bob was not the sudden, passionate infatuation I had felt for Gerald or Terry. This love was slow and comfortable and gave me a feeling of belonging to someone.

The first time he kissed me we were walking around the deck, watching the ocean slide away behind us when the ship gave a lurch, and I fell against him. He wrapped his arms around me, tilted my head up toward him, and kissed me gently, but firmly, on the mouth. Two passengers who witnessed the event applauded.

"I think we had better continue this where we have a little more privacy," he said and led me into his cabin.

By the time we sailed through the Straits of Gibraltar, we were lovers.

The subject of marriage came up.

"I'd like us to get married soon," he said, "but, unfortunately, my divorce won't be final until sometime in December. This will give you plenty of time to make sure you really want to marry me."

I spent a long time thinking about marrying Bob. I was not *madly* in love with him, but it was comfortable being with him. I wanted desperately to be married and have a home of my own and to be away from Auntie Winnie and even from my own family. I was very fond of him, and we had a lot in common; the most important was our profession. By the time we reached England, I had accepted his proposal, and we decided to marry when his divorce was final.

When we docked at Tilbury, my godmother was there to meet me. Mummie was home with a cold. I introduced Bob to Auntie Winnie. She asked him, "What part do you play in the picture, young man?"

As Bob excused himself to phone Micky Balcon, I explained to my godmother that he was *not* an actor but an important writer and director.

"A nice young man, but obviously not quite out of the top drawer," was her response.

I tried to hide my anger. "I don't care what drawer he's out of. I love him, and I'm going to marry him."

"Of course, you can't marry him, Joan," objected my godmother. "He's divorced."

Robert Stevenson and I pose outside the Kensington Register Office on our wedding day in 1936. Just after this photo was taken, Robert dashed off to the studio for a story conference with Micky Balcon. (Collection of Venetia Stevenson)

When I told my mother, she was upset. "But he's divorced! It's a good thing your father is not alive. It would have broken his heart." Then, ever the pragmatist, she added, "Darling, if you really love this man as much as you say you do, then of course you must marry him. But I beg of you to think long and hard before you commit yourself."

Bob and my mother became good friends. She admired his intellectual qualities and his quiet good manners.

Because of his divorce, we were unable to be married in the Church of England. In the spring of 1936, we had to settle for a dull, unromantic ceremony in the Kensington Register Office in a room covered with a thin layer of dust. I was disappointed that neither my mother nor Auntie Winnie attended the ceremony.

My dress, designed by Molyneux, was a pale grayish blue, called "sea foam." The belt and the collar were covered in pale blue crystal. I did not want a conventional gold wedding ring. Instead I had Asprey in Bond Street make a clear crystal one for me. I carried a bouquet of gardenias, jasmine, and stephanotis.

For one fleeting moment during the short ceremony, I closed my eyes and saw myself in Rochester Cathedral, dressed in a white satin gown with a long train, with the Bishop performing the service. The vision faded, and a voice said, "I pronounce you man and wife." We signed a few documents, and it was over.

Bob and I stepped outside into a crush of press photographers.

We had decided to hold our wedding reception at the Berkeley Hotel. As we stood outside the Register Office, Bob looked at his watch.

"Darling," he said, "I'm terribly sorry, but I have to get back to the studio. I have to look over some scripts with Micky and help him iron out some problems. I promised I'd be there by noon, and it's a quarter past now."

I protested. "Bob, it's our wedding day. I can't appear at our reception alone."

"I'll join you there just as soon as the meeting is over. Run along and enjoy yourself." He turned to Jack Hulbert. "Jack, please do the honors, and take Anna to the reception at the hotel. I have some work at the studio. I'll be along as soon as I can."

"Of course, old boy," said Jack obligingly, flashing one of his toothy smiles. "What's a best man for but to escort the bride to her reception?"

Bob hailed a cab and was gone.

But Jack too had to leave me as soon as we arrived at the Berkeley. Cecily was not well, and he wanted to be at home with her. My friends, Dickie Norton and Jack Dunfee, were there waiting for me and greeted me warmly.

"Where is Bernie Rubin?" I inquired.

"Oh, he's upstairs in his room, sulking," said Jack. "He's hardly been down here at all ever since he heard you were going to be married. No more funny stories, no laughs, just a long, unhappy face."

"Oh, poor Bernie," I laughed. "I'll just ring up his room and see if I can persuade him to come down and join us.

After a few rings, Bernie answered. His voice sounded hoarse and blurry; he had obviously been drinking.

"Go away," he mumbled. "You have broken my heart, and I never want to see you again." But he eventually joined us for a glass of champagne and wished me well.

True to his promise, Bob finally joined us. By that time, the guests were enjoying the effects of an afternoon of champagne, and the party had become noisy and rambunctious. As soon as we cut the cake, we slipped away to Cardinal's Wharf.

The best wedding present I received were the positive reviews of *The Camels Are Coming*. The picture was a great success.

9

Life at Cardinal's Wharf

Bob and I agreed to postpone our honeymoon until he could get a few weeks off from Gaumont-British. He had recently completed a film starring Charles Boyer and was doing research for a picture about Lady Jane Grey, entitled *Tudor Rose*. It would become one of the most successful of his films. Our honeymoon for the moment would be 49 Bankside, Cardinal's Wharf.

Of all the homes I've lived in, 49 Cardinal's Wharf is my favorite.

Bankside itself has a fascinating history. In *A History of London*, written in 1886, the area is described as once with "public bawdy-houses, licensed by the Bishop of Winchester...."

Bankside was the entertainment center of London during the reign of Elizabeth I. More than two decades ago, the foundations of the Globe Theatre were discovered beneath the cellars of a nearby warehouse. Today, thanks to the decades-long efforts of actor Sam Wanamaker, the new Globe Theatre stands close to the site where many of Shakespeare's plays were first performed.

Four stories high in the Queen Anne style, Cardinal's Wharf overlooks one of the most beautiful views in all of London. I never tired over looking out over the Thames at St. Paul's.

Somewhat to my surprise, Robert had furnished the house with ultra-modern furniture. The divans, long benches, and window seats were all upholstered in creamy white linen, matching the walls and woodwork. The only piece I disliked was the dining room table, which was a highly polished black slab of heat-resistant stone on bent chromium steel legs. It was hideous. Bob refused to get rid of it; so when we gave dinner parties, I covered it with a white damask cloth.

We entertained very often. The house was always filled with people, among them John Houseman, Angus McPhail, John Betjman, and, of course, Micky Balcon and his wife, Aileen.

Robert and I had a cook named Marta, whose only problem was that she drank too much. One evening, when we had guests, she came stumbling into the drawing room where we were serving drinks. She was shouting obscenities; then she fell to the floor and passed out. That night we took our guests to a restaurant in Piccadilly. The next morning we dismissed Marta.

I am not a very good cook, but I enjoy making desserts, "sweets," as they are called in England. My specialty was fruit trifle. I still serve to my friends in California. I make it with pieces of sponge cake and almond macaroons soaked in rum and brandy and then layered mixed with raspberries and egg custard and topped with whipped cream; then I decorate it with candied violets.

I set about adding my own touches to Cardinal's Wharf. At the back of the house was a paved garden, at the end of which were a pond and fountain. The pond was on the site of the Royal Pike Pond, which in medieval times supplied the Royal table. I was unable to find a pike to place in the pond, so I filled it with goldfish.

My favorite spot was high up on the roof. Here, with the help of our gardener, Seymour Kusumoto, we created a Japanese garden. It had a miniature stone bridge and a pagoda. After dinner, Bob and I had coffee there, listening to the hoot of tugs on the river and watching the soft glow of the lights of London around us.

I had always loved prints and paintings, and together, Bob and I scrounged all the second-hand print stores in London and found innumerable prints of Old London, which we hung in the various rooms and on the walls of the narrow stairway.

Then came the books. I had always loved books, especially those illustrated by famous artists. I found a shop at the far end of Old Bond Street that sold first editions and rare books. Although I cannot remember the name of the shop, I remember Mr. Godden, the proprietor. He and I became good friends, and he always seemed to find exactly what I was looking for.

The first book I bought from him was illustrated by Arthur Rackham. The one I really yearned for, however, was Le Morte d'Arthur, a four-volume edition bound in white vellum with exquisite illustrations by William Russell Flint. The set was enormously expensive. I thought about it and dreamt about it for several weeks. I knew that I had to have it. Meanwhile, encouraged by Mr. Godden, I bought several other books illustrated by Flint: The Heroes by Charles Kingsley; The Odyssey by Homer; and Iolanthe, from the Gilbert and Sullivan opera of the same name.

I told Bob of my longing to buy *Le Morte d'Arthur.* "I know it's terribly expensive, but perhaps it would be a good investment."

"If you want it that much, darling, then buy it. At least it's a lot better than wanting a mink coat," he said.

I rang up Mr. Godden and told him the good news.

In the meantime, Russell Flint happened into the shop. Mr. Godden told him that a young lady was very interested in the books that featured his work, especially his *Le Morte d'Arthur.* "And," he told Russell Flint, "she's an actress," implying, I thought, that it was incredible to him that an *actress* would be interested in buying expensive books.

Mr. Godden arranged for Russell Flint to meet Robert and me at Cardinal's Wharf. He asked if he could paint my portrait. He writes of the meeting and the subsequent painting in *More Than Shadows:*

> ...I was indulging myself in a bookshop when the proprietor showed me a copy of one of the books I had illustrated ... years ago. He told me that a very beautiful lady, a film star, was collecting them. Quite flattered, I asked her name. Alas, not being a filmgoer, I had never heard of her. However, one [*The Camels Are Coming*] was showing; I went to see it. There she was, young, pretty, fresh and delightfully English, having all sorts of adventures. Correspondence followed. She and her husband had an old house ... and I visited them there. She was so paintable that a picture just had to be produced. ... The result [was a] double portrait of Anna, the blonde star, and Joanna, the wife of Robert Stevenson....

Russell Flint had already explained to Bob and me what he had in mind for the picture: "...the Actress would be lying indolently on a couch while the Wife would be leaning over her protectively."

My mother was concerned when she heard that I was going to pose for him. "Joan, dear, the pictures I have seen of his are beautiful, but most of the models are nude. Is he expecting you to take your clothes off?" I assured her that this would not happen and that Mrs. Flint would be there to chaperone me.

Mrs. Flint bought a beautiful golden dress for me to wear as "The Actress" and for "The Wife," I was swathed in silver brocade. The completed portrait is entitled *Bronze and Silver.*

Russell Flint was anxious to include a few of my personal items in the picture. Among them are a porcelain camel which had been given to me when I was making *The Camels Are Coming, a* Staffordshire plate, a small watercolor of me wearing jodhpurs and riding shirt that Russell Flint had painted of me and gave to me as a present. Of course, the vellum-bound volumes of *Le Morte d'Arthur* were on the shelves in the background.

Russell Flint (he became Sir William in 1947) and his wife, Sybille, lived at Peel Cottage on Campden Hill in Kensington. His studio at the top of the house had two north-facing windows and a sky light. Oriental shawls and pieces of colored brocade were draped over the furniture. There was a small oil stove at one end of the room and a dressing room for the models.

The picture took about six weeks to complete. It was a happy time for me. Every morning when I wasn't working, I would drive to the Flints' cottage. Mrs. Flint would be waiting for me with a cup of Earl Grey tea and ginger biscuits. Russell Flint arranged the long, upholstered bench on which I was to lie. My feet were placed on a golden cushion. He wanted me bare footed because, he told me, "You have the most beautiful feet in London."

Bronze and Silver hung in the Royal Academy in 1936. Bob and I went to the opening of the exhibition. It was fun to eavesdrop on the flattering comments about the portrait.

On the same wall of the Academy where my portrait hung was a painting of another actress. "What an exquisite face," I thought, as I stood before it. The eyes were blue-green and stared down with an imperious—almost defiant—look, as if to say, "I shall be famous one day!" Indeed, she would be. The portrait was of Vivien Leigh.

Bronze and Silver was bought by a Scottish earl, whose name I have forgotten. He later donated it to the Edinburgh Art Gallery. After that, I lost touch with its whereabouts. I can't imagine why Bob and I didn't purchase it.

A few weeks after I married Bob, I played in a dreary film called *Heat Wave*. Playing opposite me was a young singer, Les Allen, who had just been placed under contract by Gaumont-British. I had little to do except gaze in rapture at Les while he sang some senseless lyrics. *Heat Wave* is *not* one of my favorite pictures.

My next picture in 1935, *The Passing of the Third Floor Back*, is one of my favorites, and I enjoyed making it. The principal player was Conrad Veidt, who would later play Colonel Strasser in *Casablanca*. I had always admired his work and was fascinated by his wonderfully dark, hypnotic eyes. When he looked at me, it was as though he saw right through into my very soul; it was not a comfortable feeling. However, I thought Veidt was dreadfully miscast as "The Stranger," who was supposed to be a Christ-like figure who takes a back room in a boarding house and changes the lives of his fellow boarders.

Dear Cathleen Nesbitt, with whom I was to play opposite in the theatre many years later, was part of the wonderful cast, as were Sara Allgood, Mary Clare, and Beatrix Lehman. One of the leading roles was played by the lovely young actress Rene Ray, who I believe would have become a great star had she not decided to quit acting and marry a count. Berthold Viertel directed. I would meet him later in Hollywood.

I finished production and was immediately assigned to *First a Girl*, playing opposite Jessie Matthews and Sonnie Hale, a real-life husband and wife team. Jessie Matthews is almost forgotten today. But in the late 1920s and '30s, she was one of the great musical comedy stars, known as "The Dancing Divinity." Just to see her float across the stage, light as thistledown, those wonderful long legs kicking far above her head, was a wonder. Beneath that lovely elfin smile, though, was a deep sense of insecurity and guilt that was to torment her through her life and affect her career. She suffered several breakdowns.

Early in her career, Jessie had fallen in love with her then-leading man, Sonnie Hale, who at the time was married to actress Evelyn Laye, one of the best-loved actresses in England. Accounts of their affair appeared in the newspapers, and the press skewered both of them. The ensuing divorce was ugly. Jessie was called a "home wrecker" and was booed as she left the stage door at the theatre where she was appearing. She and Sonnie had married in 1931.

Her rejection by audiences never completely healed. If a show in which she was due to appear had to be postponed due to her "illness," it was usually reported as a "nervous breakdown due to overwork." Finally, no one would risk backing her in a musical show. Gaumont-British director Victor Saville brought her back as a film star and signed her to a three-year contract.

The location for *First a Girl* was the South of France. We spent several weeks in Monte Carlo and Nice. What a gorgeous location! I can still remember my beautiful room in the Eden Roc Hotel, overlooking the incredibly blue-green Mediterranean.

Jessie's character in the film pretends to be a man who plays a female impersonator on stage. After one scene as a female dancer, she whips off her wig to disclose that she is a "male." The story was from a German film, entitled *Viktor, Viktoria*, made just two years earlier. The same story with a different background was made again in 1982, also entitled *Victor, Victoria*, and starred one of my favorite actresses, Julie Andrews.

I played the role of a princess. Molyneux and Chanel designed my lavish costumes. The credits indicate Marianne as the costume designer; she must have been responsible for other actress' outfits. A young Welsh actor, Griffith Jones, played my fiancé; we would work together several times. In this film, his character falls in love with Jessie; I end up with Sonnie at the fade out.

Just after *First a Girl* was released, Victor Saville left Gaumont-British, and Sonnie took over Jessie's career. He lacked Saville's behind-the-camera knowledge and ability to work with actors. The films Jessie made under Sonnie's aegis—*Head Over Heels* and *Gangway* in 1937 and *Sailing Along* in 1938—were not successful. Their marriage collapsed in 1944, leading to Jessie's further nervous breakdowns. Her third marriage, to Brian Lewis, also ended in divorce.

Astonishingly, she made a comeback two decades later in the radio soap opera, *Mrs. Dale's Diary*, a BBC production in which she starred for more than 20 years.

The last time I saw Jessie was in 1975 when she came to Hollywood for discussions about a possible film with Fred Astaire. She confided to me that her great ambition was to dance with him. It never came to anything, which caused her additional heartbreak.

That same year, she performed at a benefit at the Mayfair Music Hall in Santa Monica. She could no longer perform any of her famous dance routines with the high kicks, but she could still sing and hold an audience spellbound.

Jessie made a few more films, including *tom thumb*, the Peter Cook-Dudley Moore version of *The Hound of the Baskervilles*, and a television movie, *Edward and Mrs. Simpson*.

She died in 1981 at 74 from cancer. I was shocked to learn that she was buried in an unmarked grave. Her brother had told the press, "Jessie does not need a tombstone or a monument.... The memory of her is enough. It does not have to be words carved into stone." I thought this very unfeeling and apparently so did a number of other people in the business because before long, funds were raised, and now Jessie has a stone marker where she is buried in St. Martin's Parish Church cemetery outside London. Admirers also raised funds for a plaque on the home in Soho where she was born.

I miss her smile and her energy and, especially, her talent. Jessie Matthews was truly one of a kind.

Best known for his role as Frankenstein's monster, Boris Karloff was my next co-star in *The Man Who Changed His Mind*. The subtlety of the title was lost on American distributors who changed the name to *The Man Who Lived Again*.

The excellent cast, all of whom I had worked with before, included John Loder, Frank Cellier, Cecil Parker, and Donald Calthrop. The only two members of the cast that I didn't like were the two chimpanzees. Although they were well trained and docile, they smelled horrid. They had a dressing room next to mine, so every time I had to change costumes or see to my makeup, I had to endure the revolting odor as I passed their door. I was thankful when they completed their "roles" and left the studio.

As Dr. Clare Wyatt in *The Man Who Changed His Mind*.

In the film, Boris plays Dr. Laurence, a brain surgeon and scientist who discovers a method for transferring the contents of the brain from one chimpanzee to another. At a meeting of the leading scientists of the day, he is derided for these experiments. This humiliation causes him to become deranged, and he decides to test his theory on humans. I play his assistant, Dr. Clare Wyatt, who is engaged to Dick Haslewood (John Loder).

Although I look frightened of Boris Karloff in this still from *The Man Who Changed His Mind*, I found him to be a soft-spoken, poetry-loving gentleman.

Dr. Laurence falls in love with Clare but realizes she will never return his affection unless he assumes the mind of Dick.

The climactic scene takes place in the laboratory. Dick is strapped to the table, and the doctor has completed the brain transfer when the police burst in, having been alerted by Clare. A shot is fired; the doctor is mortally wounded. Clare immediately sees that Dick's mind has already been transferred to the doctor's and will have to be reversed before the doctor dies. So, without a moment's hesitation—wearing a lovely evening gown by Molyneux—Clare performs the operation before the doctor dies.

The reviews were excellent, one critic even calling it "powerful melodramatic fare, with obvious stellar appeal."

The comment I liked best read, "Anna Lee is both intelligent and beautiful as Clare." Never before had a reviewer referred to me in any role as "intelligent"!

Many critics had kind words to say about Boris as well, some considering it the most sophisticated of his horror films.

Boris was a joy to work with. I thought I would be intimidated working with him, but he was one of the kindest, gentlest, most considerate people I have ever known, completely the opposite of his cinema persona. He had a great sense of humor and kept the crew laughing by doing impersonations of himself as Frankenstein's monster. What I liked about him most was his love of poetry, a trait we shared. We both adored the traditional poets—Keats, Shelley, Wordsworth, Tennyson, among them—not those "modern" poets. We both felt that the modernists not only didn't scan or rhyme but they also had no feeling of beauty or wonder. Together, we swept through the pages of Francis T. Palgrave's *Golden Treasury of English Verse* and *The Oxford Book of English Verse* in a sort of poetic jam session.

I would start a poem, with, say, a line from Lord Byron: "The Assyrian came down like a wolf on the fold," and Boris would complete the line, "And his cohorts were gleaming with purple and gold." We did this without referring to the source. Only as a last resort did we use the text.

I think the only time I stumped him was with a poem by Milton: "For Lycidas is dead, dead ere his prime." Boris struggled but couldn't remember the subsequent line, "Young Lycidas, and hath not left his peer...."

As soon as *The Man Who Changed His Mind* was completed, Bob and I decided to take our long-postponed honeymoon. We went to the Austrian Tyrol and walked a great deal, an exercise we both loved. We also visited Vienna and Budapest.

On our return, I was assigned to another film, *O.H.M.S.*, which stands for "on his majesty's service." Not being familiar with the terms, American distributors retitled it: *You're in the Army Now*, which sounds appropriately robust.

It was made with the full cooperation of the British War Office, which obligingly loaned Gaumont-British 10,000 troops, as well as tanks, armored cars, and machine guns.

I play Sally Briggs, the sergeant major's daughter; Frank Cellier plays my father; and John Mills as the lance corporal is the love interest. Wallace Ford plays an American who steals a murdered man's passport and finds himself forced to join the army. Although I thought Wallace was American, I learned that he was actually born in the north of England.

Our director, Raoul Walsh, was American through and through. He had lost an eye in a freak accident in 1928 and had worn a patch ever since, giving him a roguish appearance. He had directed a number of action-oriented pictures, including *The Big Trail* with John Wayne, and went on to direct Errol Flynn in *They Died with Their Boots On* and *Objective Burma!*

I liked Walsh very much, but I was mystified how an American was able to so brilliantly portray the life of a soldier in the British Army.

Much of the film was made on the Salisbury Plain, and several famous regiments took part, including the Queens, The Royal Warwickshires, the Royal Engineers, the Argyll and Sutherland Highlanders, Scots Greys and the 4th Hussars. It was a colorful spectacle. One magnificent scene at the end of the picture is a review of cavalry, infantry, artillery, and tanks, with King George V taking the salute. I must admit that as I watched the Argyll and Sutherland Highlanders march by, with their kilts swinging and bagpipes droning, I felt a twinge of nostalgia as I remembered Terry.

During the making of O.H.M.S., I ran into an old friend. Walking down Sloane Street one afternoon, I saw a familiar figure on the other side of the road. There was no mistaking that jaunty stride and bright red hair.

"Paddy," I called.

It was my friend from Hong Kong, Paddy Hayley Bell. We found a teashop, and while we sat drinking tea and eating raisin buns, we shared everything that had happened to each of us since we last saw each other several years ago.

"I became engaged to Terry Roper-Caldbeck," I told her, "but I broke it off because he wasn't too keen on me continuing as an actress."

"Jolly good," she said. "Terry was gorgeous, but you would have been bored stiff after a while being an officer's wife."

"I'm married now to Robert Stevenson, the director."

"Yes," said Paddy. "I read it in the papers."

Paddy told me that she had been signed by Seymour Hicks to tour in a play called It's You I Want and had been working on the stage and films.

"As for you, Joan, or I suppose I must call you 'Anna' now, you have done great things. I hear you're making a film with John Mills." I nodded. "I want to ask you a big favor," she confided. "Would you be a darling and let me come down to wherever you're shooting, so that I can see him? Actually, I did meet him a few years ago in Tientsin when he was playing in Journey's End, but I'm sure he won't remember me. I would so love to see him again."

"If it means all that much to you, I think I can arrange it," I offered. "We're shooting interiors now at Shepherd's Bush. Johnnie and I will be working the day after tomorrow, so come down to the Bush then. I'll leave your name with the man at the door, and you and Johnnie can have a long chat." As an afterthought, I said, "You know he's married."

"I know," she said with just a hint of impudence, "but that makes no difference because I'm going to marry him one day."

"Not a chance," I thought.

I arranged the meeting, and she and Johnnie seemed to get on very well. "She's a jolly nice girl," he told me. "I look forward to seeing her again."

He *did* see her again. Four years later, in 1941, they were married. I have a picture of them taken after the ceremony at the Westminster Register Office. Johnnie was wearing his army uniform, and Paddy has an orchid corsage pinned to her coat.

Delighted with the news, I showed it to Robert. "It won't last," he said pessimistically. "Those wartime marriages never do."

Little did I know that *I* should have listened to those words.

But how wrong Robert was. In January 2004, they celebrated their 64th anniversary. I no longer call her Paddy. She is Mary Hayley Bell, author of the novel *Whistle Down the Wind* and other works, as well as her autobiography, *What Shall We Do Tomorrow?*. Today she is Lady Mills, as Johnnie was knighted in 1976. They have three children, actresses Juliet and Hayley, and a son, Jonathan. Although Mary has suffered with Alzheimer's disease for many years and Johnnie* has lost his sight, they still live in their lovely home.

I finished my assignment on *O.H.M.S.* in late December. It received excellent reviews and became a box-office success. The opening night was held at the Tivoli and attended by the Secretary of War Duff Cooper and Lady Diana Cooper.

My next role was ready and waiting for me.

*John Mills died at the age of 97 in April 2005.

10

A Picture, a Party,
and a Pregnancy

During the time I was making *O.H.M.S.*, Bob was busy working on the script for our next picture, *King Solomon's Mines*. We both loved the book, a wonderful adventure story by H. Rider Haggard.

There was only one problem with the original story: there was no woman except for Gagool, the old witch doctor, and I didn't think I was right for the role!

"Not a problem!" said Bob. "I'll fix it."

Fix it he did. He added the role of Kathy O'Brien. She is a young Irish girl who makes her way across Africa in a stolen wagon in order to find her father who is searching for King Solomon's mines.

Not everyone at the studio was happy about the inclusion of a girl in the classic adventure. My old friend, Charles Bennett, who also worked on the script, declared angrily, "It's an insult to the memory of Rider Haggard. How would he react to the idea of a girl being brought into the story just to add sex appeal? I want no part of it. I'll have my name taken off the credits."

He did.

Playing opposite me is Cedric Hardwicke as Alan Quartermaine. (The name "Quartermaine" would come back into my life so many years later.) John Loder is again my love interest; Roland Young is Commander Good; and the great Paul Robeson is Umbopa.

A few days before we started filming, Bob and I decided to take Paul out to dinner. We thought we should get to know him a little better.

"Let's go to the Berkeley," I suggested. "The food there is always good."

"We'll have to call first and find out if they will allow him in the dining room," said Bob.

"What do you mean? Why on earth wouldn't he be allowed in the dining room?" I asked, incredulously.

"Because he's a Negro, dear girl," answered Bob. "And we don't want to embarrass him. A few years ago when he was in London, a friend invited him to the Savoy Grill. When they arrived, the maitre d' informed him that he would not be allowed to eat in the dining room due to management policy."

"But that's monstrous!" I cried.

"I know it's monstrous," said Bob. "But that's the way the world is at the moment, and there is little we can do to change it. But I am sure we can find a restaurant that does not discriminate."

We found a charming Greek restaurant in Soho with no "management policy" and had a delightful evening.

Although I knew that Paul had spoken passionately against racial bigotry in America, the treatment of his people, the killings, the lynchings, he never spoke to me about these matters.

Looking at him, dressed in his warrior costume as Umbopa, I thought what a great leader he would make: tall, with a magnificent physique, a quiet dignity, and his sense of nobility. I began to think of him as Moses, longing to lead his people out of oppression into the Promised Land.

Paul was wonderful to work with, always on time, word perfect, always receptive to Bob's direction, popular with the other actors and the crew, and he never complained, as some of us did, about the long hours and the heat.

His wife, Eslanda, whom everyone called Essie, came to visit several times at Shepherd's Bush, accompanied by their young son, Pauli. She was attractive and intelligent. Her love for Paul was extraordinary. She overlooked his infidelities, which were numerous.

Eventually, Essie moved out of Paul's apartment, taking Pauli with her and went to live with some friends. They implored her to get a divorce, but she refused.

While we filmed at the studio, a second unit was sent to South Africa to look for suitable locations. Second unit director Geoffrey Barkas did a superb job and brought back film shot by Cyril K. Knowles at Otto's Bluff and the Umgeni Valley in South Africa.

Finally, the two largest stages at Gaumont-British were joined together, and a giant volcano, complete with a lake of seething lava, was built. On the neighboring stage, four thousand tons of fine sand had been laid down for the scene where we crawl through the desert in search of water. In this scene, I was supposed to be dying of thirst. To make me look really thirsty, the makeup man put powdered alum in my mouth.

It certainly did the trick. My lips were cracked, and the inside of my mouth was so dry that for several days I was scarcely able to speak.

The film and I received mixed reviews, but was generally well-received:

The Daily Sketch: "[Anna Lee plays the role with] ... intelligence and sincerity, she has good looks, and in this picture, she has the authentic Irish brogue. An agreeable mixture."

Sunday Pictorial: "Anna Lee is a gifted actress, who should have been before now a great star, but this film is unfair to her in decking her out as if she were an entrant for hairdressing competition...."

Screen Pictorial: "Anna Lee with her pleasant, flirtatious smile and ... charm becomes a tremendous asset for British films."

Even the formidable Graham Greene in *Night and Day* wrote:

> [There is] an introduction of an Irish blonde who somehow becomes the cause of the whole expedition. Miss Anna Lee's performance is rather like one of Miss [Madeleine] Carroll's seen through the wrong end of a telescope, with the large tortuous mouth, the intense whispers and the weighty whispers.... Yet it is a "seeable" picture....

More than six decades later, the University of California, Los Angeles, Film and Television Archive presented a retrospective of Paul Robeson's film work. On October 4, 1998, I attended a screening of *King Solomon's Mines.* I'm happy to say that the film received a warm reception, and so did I.

Bob subsequently directed me in *Non-Stop New York*, one of my favorites, a romantic thriller with a touch of science fiction. I play a chorus girl on the run from England to the U.S. to save a man from being put to death for a murder he didn't commit. The real villains, along with the hero, John Loder playing a detective, are on the double-decker plane.

To show how naïve the concept of trans–Atlantic travel was, the design for the plane included an outdoor deck, where passengers could step outside *during the flight.* I remember a scene in which John and I had the wind in our faces as we talked about the situation. The idea foreshadowed the first real trans–Atlantic flight in July 1939 by Pan Am, which didn't have a balcony.

Sadly, it was the last film to be shot at Shepherd's Bush. The studios were closed in April 1937.

Immediately following the completion of the film, Bob announced, "Let's give a party!"

"Darling, we just gave a party. Remember the ten people we had for dinner last Saturday?"

Bob shook his head. "I don't mean that kind of party. I mean a *special* party, the sort of party they used to give on Bankside two or three hundred years ago, a River Party. We'll rent a steamer and take our guests down the Thames as far as Greenwich, and then return."

So began preparations for the greatest and most memorable party given in London in the 1930s. Bob studied tidal tables and astronomical charts so we could pick the right date for the party; it had to be a night with a full moon and a tide high enough for a Thames steamer to moor at the wharf in front of our house.

With the date decided, we ordered the invitations, which were written in Old English style and printed on parchment paper:

> Mrs. Robt. Stevenson desires the pleasure of
> your company on Saturday, the nineteenth of June at
> ten o'clock for a Water Party from Bankside. At
> midnight, the Assembly will embark from
> Cardinal's Wharf in the ship *New Dagenham*
> and proceed towards Greenwich, returning to the
> bridge at Westminster towards two in the morning.
> An answer is desired to Cardinal's Wharf on the Bankside, Southwark.

There was, of course, the question of the menu for the supper onboard the steamer. Bob insisted on the kind of food that would have been served at Elizabethan banquets: roast swan, jellied eels, whelks, whitebait, and Chinese birds' nest soup. To drink, he planned to serve red wine and champagne and, in case the night turned chilly, hot rum.

A few days before the party, the provisioning company we had hired told us their swans had gone "broody," meaning they were pregnant, and we would be unable to have that delicacy. We had to make do with goose instead. But roast goose, covered with swan feathers, proved a good substitute, and nobody seemed to notice the difference.

The weather on June 19, 1937, was beautiful. The air was warm and still, and the full moon—as calculated by Bob—hung in a cloudless sky. On Bankside, everything was in readiness.

Because the newspapers had covered the pre-party preparations, a large crowd of onlookers had assembled by 9 p.m. The spectators hoped to see film celebrities who had been invited. They were not disappointed. Lili Palmer and Rex Harrison arrived, as did Jack Hulbert and Cicely Court-neidge, Francis Sullivan, Boris Karloff and his wife, and so many others. Everyone was elegantly dressed. Lili Palmer wore a black tulle dress covered with golden stars. I wore silver brocade with a wreath of stephanotis in my hair. The men all looked dashing in their tuxedos or dinner jackets.

Police held back the crowds so the cars could drive up to the front of the house. By ten o'clock, every room at Cardinal's Wharf was filled with guests.

A staff of forty had been employed for the evening: waiters, barmen, two chefs, electricians, ship's crew, a bargeman, bugler, and a river pilot. Three barges had been hired for the evening and were moored to the wharf opposite the house. A gangway was built across them that led to the steamer. At midnight, a naval bugler sounded, "ship preparing to depart," and guests began to board.

"All aboard," was sounded, followed by "Hoist the anchor."

And off we went.

We had installed a dance floor on the lower deck and Louis Levy and His Orchestra played foxtrots, waltzes, and an occasional rumba. As we sailed down the Thames, we ate and drank and danced the night away.

We sailed as far as Greenwich, then turned around, arriving back at Westminster Bridge at three o'clock in the morning.

The London newspapers wrote about the party. *The Evening Standard*'s headline was: "Whelks for Thames Midnight Party; But Roast Swan in Jeopardy." *The Daily Mirror* wrote about "Anna Lee's Water Party."

A few weeks after the Water Party, I found out I was pregnant. Bob and I were delighted, but we felt that we had to find a home in the country. London was too sooty and noisy to raise a child properly. We needed somewhere with shady lawns and green meadows.

By August 1937, we had sold our wonderful Cardinal's Wharf home to Mr. William Montagu-Pollock, who was with the foreign service.

Bob finished up his picture *Owd Bob*, and we both decided that we needed a lengthy holiday from filmmaking. He hadn't been happy doing the picture, saying, "It wasn't my story or one that I wanted to do." In a *Daily Express*, interview, he said he didn't like what he called "the committee system of directing." He was used to writing the script and directing and having a free hand. He didn't feel he could give individuality to his work without that.

Besides, Bob was eager to begin a novel about the plague in London that he had in mind for a long time. Set in 1665, it was entitled, *Darkness in the Land*. I recall that it was published, but unfortunately, I don't have a copy.

When we finally set October 1937 as the date for our departure for the country, we took out an advertisement in the trade papers:

Anna Lee and Robert Stevenson
thank all their friends in films and film
journalists for their many kindnesses to
them and hope to be back in a year's time
or earlier if their bank manager insists.

Just before the train departed, I gave a "station party" for friends at Paddington Station.

We had found a charming Elizabethan house, Priors Farm, in Mattingley, Hampshire. It had low ceilings and old beams that jutted out in unexpected places. Bob bumped his head several times until he got used to where they were.

The gardens were beautiful, with herbaceous borders, roses and honeysuckle, and a small lily pond. At one time, it had been a working farm, and there were still chickens and ducks running about. An old granary stood at the back of the house, which Bob converted into his study. Every morning after breakfast he would disappear to work on his book. It was so quiet there in the country that I could hear the peck-peck-peck of the typewriter from across the garden.

I spent the days gardening or lying on the couch listening to music.

When I was eight months pregnant, we thought it best to move back to London and to stay with my mother in her flat at 3c Morpeth Terrace, near Westminster Cathedral. I had already had several visits to the doctor in Harley Street who was going to deliver the baby. I had decided that when the time came, I should go to the London Clinic for the delivery. I was certain my first child would be a boy, and had already trimmed the cradle with blue ribbons. We were going to call him "David," after the former Prince of Wales, who had been my idol before he married Wallis Simpson.

One day early in March, my mother suggested we go to the House of Commons to hear a speech by Anthony Eden. We were given seats in the Strangers' Gallery. We hadn't listened to Mr. Eden's speech for more than a few minutes when I started having pains. I clutched my mother's hand. "Mummie," I whispered, "we'd better leave. I think David is due to arrive."

We hailed a taxi and sped to the London Clinic. We telephoned my doctor but found he was in the north of England attending to an emergency. He had left word that I would be taken care of by his colleague, a young Scotsman named Angus McKensie.

I was put in a lovely, airy room, which I heard afterwards had been occupied by Mrs. Charles Lindbergh, when her second son was born.

"False alarm!" announced Dr. McKensie. "You're not ready yet. Your water hasn't broken, and you're not dilated." Then he added ominously, "But I'm glad you came in because there's a slight problem. The baby is in a breech position. This means that the head will not come out first, which makes the birth difficult. Not to worry, though," he assured me. "I will turn it. It may take a little time and be uncomfortable, but I've done it before, and I promise you, everything will be fine. Meanwhile, just stay here and rest."

I asked my mother to telephone Bob and ask him to bring over the things we had packed in preparation for just such an event.

Meanwhile, word had been leaked to the local press that I was at the London Clinic, and several reporters were outside waiting for news. In those days, very few actresses had babies for fear of hurting their careers. But I had been boasting about my pregnancy and was happy to talk to any reporters who wanted interviews.

One headline read: "Anna Lee's Baby Almost Born in House of Commons."

The following day, March 7, 1938, the headline read: "Anna Lee Expects 'David' Today."

When the baby did arrive on March 10, it was not "David," but a beautiful baby girl.

In those days, it was routine for a new mother to stay in bed for several days after giving birth. I remained in the London Clinic for a week, surrounded by flowers and telegrams of congratulations, rather like an opening night. With the birth of my fifth child many years later, I was made to stand up and walk across the room almost immediately, and I was sent home the following day.

We engaged a private nurse, Margaret Davis. I was able to nurse the baby for the next six weeks, with the help of three glasses a day of Guinness Stout, a dark beer that was believed to produce a rich mother's milk.

When I left the hospital with Nurse Davis and the baby, I rode in an ambulance back to Mattingley. Everything looked beautiful in the March sunlight, and I was happy to be home.

Now we had to choose a name for our little daughter. She had been known as "David" for so long that it was hard to think of her as anything else. I wanted to name her after my mother, but somehow the name "Edith" or "Maude" did not sound right. Then I remembered a portrait I had seen at Sherborne Castle. It was of a beautiful young girl, the daughter of Sir Edward Stanley. Her name was Venetia, and she married Sir Kenelm Digby, who loved her so much that when she died, he was inconsolable and dressed in black for the rest of his life. The name and the story appealed to my romantic spirit.

A portrait, *Sir Kenelm and Lady Venetia Digby* by Anthony Van Dyck, hangs in the Red Drawing Room at the Castle. I gave a copy of the painting to my baby daughter, along with her first name.

Venetia's middle name, Invicta, meaning "invincible," came from a childhood memory. I used to watch the street being repaired, and I loved the smell of the thick, black tar as it was poured over the gravel and then flattened and smoothed by a giant steamroller. It was the huge, formidable steamroller that fascinated me. On the front of this piece of machinery was a brass plaque of a horse, rearing up, with the word "Invicta" beneath it. Much later the Kent County Council knew that I longed for one of the plaques and presented one to me. It hung in every house I had until it was destroyed in a fire.

Our old friend, Hewlett Johnson, the Dean of Canterbury Cathedral, baptized her at the cathedral. Her godparents were Jack Hulbert, Aileen Balcon, and Honor Earl, the portraitist.

My friend, the dress designer, Molyneux, helped me design the christening robe. It was made from the Brussels lace-trimmed heavy white satin fabric of my godmother's court train. She had worn it when she was presented to King Edward VII and Queen Alexandra. It was worn at the baptisms of all five of my children. I had hoped to pass it on to my grandchildren, but it too was destroyed in the fire that nearly destroyed the house I live in today.

Nurse Davis finally returned to London, and I had to find a nanny. I interviewed several women. The one I engaged was Alice Radcliffe, whose references were excellent. She was sturdy, had large brown eyes, and a friendly smile. From that day on, Nanny Radcliffe became part of the family. She would also become my closest companion, the one to whom I would confide all my secrets. Her favorite expression was, "A little of what you fancy does you good." Oh, dear, how I remembered that during the next few years. I was to fancy a great many things, and they certainly did me *no* good.

The owner of Priors Farm was returning from Australia and had decided to resume residence there; so we had to find another home. We located one, Fingest Manor, in Ibstone, near High Wycombe, a reasonable distance from London and the studios. The house had large, comfortable rooms and was surrounded by a daisy-studded lawn sweeping down to a burbling stream. Our furniture, which had been in storage, was shipped from London, and I spent the next months decorating the rooms. I even found charming wallpaper with small angels floating around pink clouds for Venetia's nursery.

We were very happy there. Almost every weekend, friends came down from London to visit. My sister, Ruth, and her husband, Peter, bought a small house nearby, amusingly called Sparepenny Cottage, up on Ibstone Hill. One of our neighbors was a lovely lady, Mrs. Andrews. I used to visit her every few days, and we would have tea on her lawn and talk about our gardens, what was going on in London, and how to make gooseberry jam. When my mother came to live with us after leasing her flat in London, she too visited with Mrs. Andrews

Not until I left Ibstone did I discover my friend was the novelist Rebecca West.

I also continued my singing lessons with a dear man, Mr. Sanders, who came from London every week and spent the day with us. I don't think I ever knew his first name, but he liked to be called "Dudja," Russian for uncle. I called him "Uncle Sasha." He had been born in St. Petersburg and had come to England shortly after the Revolution. At one time, he told us, he had been a music teacher to the Czar's family. Now, in England, he was earning a frugal living as a Russian interpreter and a singing teacher.

One day, he asked me if he could bring his two nephews with him, as he was also teaching them. He thought they would enjoy a day in the country. His nephews were George and Tom Sanders. George, of course, became a famous actor, and Tom, who also became an actor, changed his name to Conway.

I eventually worked with George in Hollywood and found him cold, rude, and supercilious. His rudeness, I found out later, was a kind of protective barrier that shielded him from a world he despised. During his long and happy marriage to actress Benita Hume, Ronald Colman's widow, there was no sign of unpleasant behavior or temperament. But it is still hard to forgive him for the note he left when he committed suicide in 1972, "I am committing suicide because I am bored." *Bored!* He was in good health, had plenty of money, and had scored many successes as an actor and was still in demand.

His brother Tom did not achieve the same success as an actor. He is best known for his role as The Falcon in several films. He married a great friend of mine, Queenie Leonard. He died, an alcoholic, in 1967.

Queenie was very hard up for money at the time, having spent most of her money taking care of Tom.

"I'll call George," I offered. "After all, Tom *is* his brother."

I was shocked at George's reply. "Why the hell should I pay for his funeral? I never really liked him, and we were certainly not close. Besides, we have other problems at the moment!" And he hung up.

I learned later that this was about the time that Benita had been diagnosed with cancer, which she fought with her usual gallantry until her death the same year.

The Screen Actors Guild paid for Tom's funeral.

Of course, all this happened decades after our singing lessons at Fingest.

With Nanny Radcliffe to watch over Venetia, I felt comfortable enough to return to work.

On April 5, 1938, *The London Evening News* announced, "Anna Lee Will Come Back with a Bang!" And what a bang it was!

I was to play "Miss Ada, the Human Cannonball" in *Young Man's Fancy*, which Bob wrote for me. He had seen a story in a newspaper about a 19th century music hall artist named "Zazel, the Human Cannonball," who is fired from the mouth of a cannon into a net which is hung above the audience.

Bob's take on the story was that the cannon's aim went wrong and the girl, instead of landing in the net, landed in the arms of the leading man. It would be a new and amusing twist on "boy meets girl."

I loved playing Miss Ada. My costume was a lovely black-and-silver leotard. The tights I wore were pure silk; nylon had not yet been invented. The first time I was fired from the cannon and landed in the net, my tights tore to shreds. The friction in the barrel of the cannon had been too much for the delicate fabric. I had to re-shoot the scene, this time wearing black cotton tights, which were not nearly as attractive or sexy as the silk ones.

Young Man's Fancy was photographed by Ronald Neame, an up-and-coming cinematographer, who would later join Noël Coward, David Lean, and Anthony Havelock-Alan in the famed Cineguild producing company. The film had a great cast. Griffith Jones plays opposite me as Lord Alban. Sir Seymour Hicks is his father, the Duke of Beaumont, and Martita Hunt plays his mother, the Duchess.

Martita had heard about the role and came to me with tears in her eyes, begging me to use my influence with Bob. "I just have to play that part," she cried. "I will be wonderful in it."

She was!

Many years later, when we were both in America, Martita had the leading role in a picture. I was trying desperately to get a job and wrote to her, asking if she could help me. I never heard a word from her.

Another scene I love takes place in Kensington Gardens. Ada climbs up the Albert Memorial and watches sadly as Alban, thinking she is not meeting him, walks slowly away.

It's one of my favorite films.

Four Just Men is a mystery-drama, directed by Walter Forde. It is the story of the most unusual quartet of heroes who are out to defend England. Griffith Jones was again my leading man. The best aspect of this film was again being photographed by Ronald Neame.

The last film that Bob and I made together was *Return to Yesterday*. We shot on location in Hope's Nose, near Torquay, Devon. *Return to Yesterday* stars Clive Brook who plays Robert Maine, an English actor who has become a famous movie star in Hollywood. As a person, Clive was slightly pompous, a good actor but personally rather dull. As Maine, he returns to England for a short holiday and decides to visit some of the places where he had worked as a struggling young actor. At a small seaside town, he calls on one of his former landladies who introduces him to her tenants as Robert Manning.

The boarders, a group of actors who are performing at the theatre on the pier, are in great trouble because their leading man has just left them following a quarrel with the producer. They are unaware that the newcomer is the famous Robert Maine, but they persuade him to read the part in the play so it will not close.

The young actress, Carol Sands, my role, falls in love with him, and after a romantic afternoon on a sandy beach, he admits that he is in love with her and asks her to return to Hollywood with him, although Maine's wife refuses to give him a divorce. The elderly character actress, played so beautifully by Dame May Whitty explains to him that it will ruin Carol's life and career if she goes with him. So, amidst a great many tears, Carol returns to her former boyfriend, and Robert sails away. The film was adapted from a play, *Goodness, How Sad*, by Robert Morley, which accounts for its bittersweet ending.

This was the third film in which I was photographed by Ronnie Neame. And it was on this film that I fell in love with him. He photographed me using a light he called an "inky dink." I never looked better.

One evening, after we had finished shooting scenes in a rocky cove, Ronnie asked my husband, "Bob, do you mind if I take Anna out to dinner tonight?"

"Yes, I *do* mind," retorted Bob, "because I have an idea that she is in love with you, and I have no wish to encourage it."

Although neither the question nor the response was addressed to me, I was flattered by both.

But I had an idea: the wardrobe lady and I sneaked into Ronnie's room and dressed a pillow in my costume and placed it on the bed. He and I had a laugh about it the next day. Bob never knew.

The studio congratulated Ronnie for making Clive look so good. Ronnie didn't tell anyone but he knew that Clive had a facelift while he was in America!

With production complete, we returned to Ibstone. With war clouds gathering over Europe, we were instructed to build air raid shelters. Gas masks were distributed to the villagers. Blackout curtains were fastened to the windows, and at night, Ibstone looked dark and foreboding.

Not long after our return to Ibstone, Bob's agent called to tell him that David O. Selznick, the Hollywood producer, had just seen *Nine Days a Queen* (the U.S. title of *Lady Jane* Grey), the film Bob had finished some months

Before Robert Stevenson and I left for America on the *Normandie* in
August 1939, the family came to see us off. *Left to right:* **Mummie,
me, Ruth, Robert, Nanny (Alice Radcliffe) holding Venetia, and Robert's mother.**

earlier. Selznick was so impressed that he wanted Bob to come to Hollywood
immediately to direct a picture for him. The money he offered was enormous compared to what Bob usually made, and the offer was tempting.

He turned it down. With England on the brink of war, we felt we didn't
want to desert her.

Then Neville Chamberlain returned from a conference in Munich,
announcing, as he descended from his plane, that Hitler had promised not
to invade Poland. On that September day in 1938, he waved a paper that
assured us that there would be "peace in our time." I remember hearing the
wild shouts of enthusiasm that greeted the Prime Minister's speech on the
radio. Foolish man! How could he have trusted Hitler to keep his word! But
for the moment, it was a case of relief over reality.

Life returned to normal. Blackout curtains came down, and I planted sweet peas in the garden. Venetia lay happily in her pram on the lawn while Nanny knitted.

With the political crisis seemingly defused, Selznick phoned several more times. He now wanted Bob to direct his new star, a Swedish actress named Ingrid Bergman, in her first American picture, *Intermezzo*. Again, the salary he offered was enormous, and we were told that first-class transportation would be arranged for both of us, along with Venetia and Nanny.

"Bob," I said, "it's a wonderful opportunity for you, and I think you should go. But not me. I'll stay here. I've never wanted to go to Hollywood, and, besides, Micky Balcon has another picture coming up for me. I am still under contract to him."

"Why don't you just come for a short holiday for two or three weeks," he suggested. "We'll have a restful sea voyage, and you will be able to see something of California. Then you can come home and tell your friends how beautiful it is."

He was very persuasive. On a sunny morning in August 1939, Robert and I, together with Nanny and Venetia, boarded the French Line's premiere ship, the S.S. *Normandie*, en route to New York. My mother agreed to stay on at Fingest Manor and look after it until we returned.

Ruth and Mummie came down to Southampton to see us off. My mother was wearing a red hat with feathers on it, which she called her "cheer up hat." She only wore it when things looked gloomy.

"I'll be home in three weeks' time," I told her as I choked back tears.

Ruth was holding Venetia, who was wearing a white woolen jacket with pink ribbons, her golden curls shining in the sunlight. A man came up to admire her. It was actor Monty Banks, who, with his wife, Gracie Fields, was also going to America on the same ship. Venetia stretched out her arms to him, crying, "Dada. Dada." Ruth flushed with embarrassment and tried to silence her. Monty thought it a big joke, and so did Bob.

We all boarded the ship and found our way to a magnificent stateroom. It was filled with flowers and fruit from the Selznick Company and the Balcons. Nanny and Venetia had the cabin next to ours.

Finally, Ruth and Mummie had to leave the ship as the sound of "all ashore who's going ashore" blared from the loud speaker. They stood on the dock as the *Normandie* set sail. The ship's orchestra was playing, and the crowd on the dock was shouting and waving as the ship's horn blasted a final farewell.

I stood at the stern, watching Mummie's red hat slowly disappear into the distance. Sadness swept over me. I kept saying to myself, "It's not for long. It's not for long."

It would be several years before I would see the coast of England again.

11

Hollywood and All That

The *Normandie* was a magnificent ship. The sweeping stairways. The paneled dining room with Lalique light fixtures. The luxurious lounges. The Grand Salon with a 32-glass panel, "The Chariot of Aurora," by famed Art Deco designers Jean Dupas and Jean Dunand. The golden wall coverings.

Sadly, this was almost her last voyage from England to New York. On December 7, 1941, she was taken over by the United States Navy and renamed the U.S.S. *Lafayette*. Plans were to make it a troop ship, but during its refurbishment, a spark from a welder's torch caught a bale of flammable material on fire. The ship sank. What a humiliating end for such a glorious lady. Ships like that will never be built again.

But for us, that five-day crossing was a voyage to be remembered. As we sailed into New York harbor, the purser led us to the rail on the port side to see the Statue of Liberty and the jagged skyline of New York City's skyscrapers.

As we docked, several representatives from the New York office of Selznick International met us. Among them was Kay Brown, Selznick's story editor. Kay took us to lunch at the Colony Club and then escorted us to Grand Central Station where we boarded the *Twentieth Century Limited*, which would take us to Chicago. There, the cars would be switched to the *Super Chief*, and we would move on to Los Angeles.

The *Super Chief* was almost as luxurious as the *Normandie* or any five-star hotel. The porters assigned to each stateroom were like guardian angels. They catered to every wish, bringing hot cups of tea in the early morning and ice-cold cocktails later in the day. They pressed our clothes and polished our shoes. Highlighting the journey were the fresh flowers on white linen tablecloths in the dining car. Gourmet food, including trout, grouse, or

Robert and I chat up Producer David O. Selznick at a Hollywood party.

pheasant, was accompanied by crisp vegetables. I was almost sorry when we arrived in Los Angeles.

Looking back, I realize how fortunate I was to have traveled not only on the *Normandie* but also aboard the *Super Chief.* Travelers today cannot imagine what it was like. Airplanes have taken over, and it's rush, rush, rush, nothing compared to the luxurious and leisurely ship and train travel. Like so many other beautiful things in my past, these, too, have faded away.

We disembarked in Pasadena, then a small town several miles from Los Angeles. Our first glimpse of California was orange trees, whose blossoms gave off a powerful but pleasant odor, and snow-capped mountains glistening against the azure sky.

Harry Ham, who would be Bob's Hollywood agent, met us at the station. He was from the Selznick Agency, headed by Myron Selznick, David's brother,

We were led to a limousine that took us to the Garden of Allah at 8152 Sunset Blvd., our first home in Los Angeles. This apartment hotel was then one of the most prestigious hotels in the city. It was originally the home of Alla Nazimova, the silent picture star. Later, when her career foundered, she built 25 separate villas and turned her estate into a residential hotel.

Within walking distance of many of the popular nightclubs on Sunset Boulevard—the Trocadero, Mocambo, Ciro's, and the Players Club—the Garden of Allah soon became the temporary home of Ronald Colman, Buster Keaton, Bessie Love, Clara Bow, Gary Cooper, and Charles Laughton. John Barrymore stayed there between divorces, and Laurence Olivier rented a bungalow when he first came to Hollywood. It also became a home-away-from-home for several of the members of the famous literary lions of New York's Algonquin Round Table, including George S. Kaufman, Robert Benchley, Dorothy Parker, and Alexander Wolcott. They sat around the pool arguing and writing.

Like so many places with a history, the Garden of Allah is no more. It was torn down in 1950 and standing on the property today is a strip mall and a bank. Another fading memory.

When we arrived at the hotel, I was utterly exhausted. I made sure that Nanny and Venetia were comfortably installed in their room next to ours. Nanny complained that the closet was too small.

"Where am I going to put all the baby's clothes?" she asked. Nanny was never happy unless she had something to complain about. I took no notice. I returned to my room, leaving her to sort out the problem.

I took a warm bath and sank into bed, hoping I could sleep for at least ten hours.

It was not to be. The telephone rang. It was David O. Selznick asking us to come to his house for a screening of a rough cut of a picture he had just completed. He would send a car for us at 6:30. He added that there would be coffee and dessert before the screening.

"Oh, Bob," I groaned, "*please*, not tonight. It's already 4 o'clock, and I'm so bloody tired that I'll fall asleep before we even get to his home. Call him back and ask if we can do it tomorrow. Tell him your wife is exhausted from the travel. Or," I suggested, "why not go alone?"

"Joan, dear," Bob replied gently but with authority, "there is something you will have to learn: an invitation from David Selznick is not a request; it's a *command*. We have to go, both of us. So be a good girl and make your-self pretty, and I promise you that tomorrow you can sleep all day."

After a quick cup of tea, which always revives me, and a light meal, which I shared with Nanny and Venetia, we were driven off to Beverly Hills and the most incredibly wonderful evening of my life in Hollywood.

As we drove up through the streets of Beverly Hills toward the Selznick home, the chauffeur pointed out some of the houses. "That's where Fred

Astaire lives. And there's Buster Keaton's home. Up on the hill is where Ronald Colman lives."

Selznick lived on Summit Drive in a large white colonial-style house. Two magnolia trees, heavy with white blossoms, stood on either side of the entrance.

The butler led us into the drawing room where the producer joined us.

"I'm sorry Irene isn't here to meet you," he apologized, "but she's spending a few days in New York." His wife Irene was the daughter of Louis B. Mayer, the second "M" in MGM.

"Help yourselves to drinks," he said. "We'll have coffee and something to eat as soon as the others arrive."

"The others" turned out to be Clark Gable and Carole Lombard, and the rough cut we saw that night was *Gone with the Wind*.

There were no words to adequately describe the film. With a few scenes yet to be cut and some of the musical score yet to be recorded, it was still a magnificent picture. Vivien Leigh was exquisite; no one could have been a better or more beautiful Scarlett O'Hara. I felt proud she was English.

Clark Gable was wonderful as Rhett Butler, although he did not seem to be entirely pleased with the picture, and he and Lombard left abruptly when the screening was over. I learned later that he and David had argued throughout the making of the film.

Bob wrote a note to Clark Gable about his performance in *Gone with the Wind*. On October 5, 1939, he received a typed, signed reply:

Dear Mr. Stevenson:
    Your kind letter was very generous in its praise of the characterization of Rhett Butler. As you probably know there are many times that you doubt whether you will be able to come up to what is expected of you. If I have been able to convince you for the sincerity and honesty of Rhett Butler, then I feel my efforts have not been wasted. Many thanks and kindest wishes to you.
                    Clark Gable

After a good night's rest, we went sightseeing the following day. We saw Grauman's Chinese Theater and its famous foot- and handprints of stars embedded in the cement courtyard. We had lunch at the Brown Derby, which was shaped like the hat for which it was named. It was demolished years ago, faded into the past and seen only in books about old Hollywood.

We drove to Forest Lawn. There were billboards advertising this prominent cemetery along Sunset Boulevard. One of them I particularly remember. It showed a coffin against a background of a flower-filled meadow and the words "No Seepage." To visit a cemetery sounded grim and a bit ghoulish. When we arrived, I was surprised that there were no tombstones, which are commonplace in England.

I asked, "Why are there no tombstones?"

"In America," said our guide, "we generally do not mark a grave with a headstone. Engraved bronze tablets are placed on the ground. It gives a peaceful aura to the place." And then he gave the real reason: "Also, it makes it easier for the lawn mowers to move around the graves!"

I found that Los Angeles had strange ideas about death. It seemed that there were almost as many mortuaries as there were grocery stores. A large mortuary stood at the corner of Sunset Boulevard and Holloway Drive. Its only identification was a big bronze clock with no hands.

A few days later, Bob took me out to dinner. When we returned, Nanny was waiting up for us. One look at her face and I knew we were in for trouble.

"Mr. Stevenson, sir, and Madam [for some reason, Nanny always called me Madam], we 'ave to find somewhere else to live! Some place quiet. Two nights now I've lain awake without a wink of sleep, wot with them noisy gentlemen shouting and swearing and singing at the top of their voices. The poor baby can't get any rest either."

Bob called Harry Ham, who suggested the Chateau Marmont, another celebrity haunt (it still is!), but it was fully booked. Harry then found us accommodations at the Beverly Hills Hotel. It was a bungalow, one of several set in a courtyard behind the main building. Herbert Marshall and his wife, Edna Best, occupied the bungalow opposite ours. The one immediately next to us belonged to Marlene Dietrich, who was then living with Erich Maria Remarque, author of *All Quiet on the Western Front*.

The bungalow was much like a small house. It even had its own kitchen, so we could do our own cooking. I remember one day Marlene Dietrich brought over a beautiful chocolate cake for us. She had baked it herself!

It was pleasant living there, but I was intent on going home. I had already been in America longer than I had expected. Plans were made to return to London, and I was busy packing when Bob came into the room and flung a newspaper on the chair beside me. I read the headline: "Germany Invades Poland; Britain Declares War."

It was September 3, 1939, and England, my England, had declared war on Germany.

The British colony in Los Angeles was in an uproar. Basil Rathbone organized a meeting in the Polo Lounge at the hotel, which included Ronald Colman, Boris Karloff, and Nigel Bruce, among them. British Consul General Eric Cleugh spoke. He said he hadn't received any information from Washington about British subjects wanting to return, and for the moment, he said, we would all do better to stay here and help raise funds for Britain. However, several young men, including David Niven, left for England immediately. Niven rejoined his old regiment, the Highland Light Infantry.

"I'm going too," I announced.

The following day, I went to the Consul General's office to obtain a visa, which was then required by all aliens before leaving the United States.

"I'm sorry, Mrs. Stevenson," said the Consul General, "but I cannot issue you a visa. We've just been advised that no mothers with small children will be allowed to cross the Atlantic."

"You mean I'm stuck here?" I wailed. "I want to go home. I *have* to get back to England. How can they do this? Why are they doing this?"

"German U-boats are swarming all over the Atlantic," he explained. "Yesterday, the Cunard passenger liner, the S.S. *Athenia*, was torpedoed with more than 100 drowned, including women and children." The ship was coming from the UK to Canada and was the first civilian casualty of the war.

Saddened and angry, I was still determined to get home somehow or other. We had wired my mother, telling her how worried we were about her and begging her to come to America and stay with us. I was surprised that her return wire was not censored. It read: "Do not worry. We are all keeping our peckers up."

I had already learned that the word "pecker" has a very different meaning in America than it does in England! It is strange how, in the same language, some words can have an entirely different—and surprising—meaning.

I tried to keep busy. I joined the Bundles for Britain group. A group of us spent day after day knitting dark gray woolen balaclava helmets in a room on Sunset Boulevard near the Trocadero nightclub. Together with my English friends, Edna Marshall, Pat Boyer, Queenie Leonard, Heather Angel, and Dame May Whitty, we chatted and knitted. For every helmet, I pulled out a strand of my hair and blended it into the wool for good luck. I sometimes wonder if any British soldier ever wore one of these balaclavas.

There were a number of fund-raising parties held by the British contingent.

Charlie Chaplin attended one of them. A group had gathered around him, and he was saying, "Oh, *we're* neutral" referring to the U.S. I told him, "You were born in England. You're British. How can you say you're neutral!"

I would probably have said more, but Bob grabbed my arm and led me outside.

"You can't say things like that," he said. "We're living in America now, and America *is* neutral."

"Well, I will *never* be neutral! I just want to go home and be part of what's going on."

At another party, I was standing with some friends, a glass of champagne in my hand when a man with a red face came staggering towards us. He was quite drunk. He raised his glass and in a loud voice said, "I drink a toast to the Fatherland and to more glorious German victories."

"You dirty bastard," I shouted, flinging my glass of champagne in his face. "Why don't you go back to your beastly Fatherland?"

Bob didn't stop me that time.

All of us British expatriates were terribly worried about the situation. I certainly was.

We decided to leave the Beverly Hills Hotel and rent a house on Tilden Avenue in Westwood, a beautiful area near UCLA. The home had recently been occupied by the Earl of Warwick who, as Fulke Warwick, had come to California hoping to find success as an actor. He did have a few small roles. When war broke out, he returned to England. He must have been quite the man about town. For several days after we moved in, there were telephone calls from women asking for Fulke or Mr. Warwick. We finally had to have the number changed.

Laurence Olivier came to lunch with us, bringing Vivien Leigh with him. They were now living in a house above Coldwater Canyon. Larry was making *Rebecca*, opposite Joan Fontaine. At the time, she was angry with Samuel Goldwyn for not allowing her to play Cathy opposite Larry in *Wuthering Heights*.

When our lease on the house on Tilden Drive was up for renewal, Bob decided that we should buy a house of our own.

"I'm tired of moving around from place to place," he complained. "We can send for our furniture and books and really make a home here in California." I wasn't sure how this could happen with U-boats prowling the Atlantic shipping lanes.

Bob was involved in his first American film, *Tom Brown's School Days*, at RKO, and after a long day at the studio, he wanted a place he could call his own.

Before the house hunting began, Harry Ham called and said Joe Pasternak wanted to see me about a picture he was doing.

"Who is in it?" I asked, without much enthusiasm. I still wanted to go home.

"Marlene Dietrich and John Wayne," replied Harry.

At the name "John Wayne," my heart leaped up. Ever since I had first seen one of his pictures in England, I had been madly in love with him, and I remember thinking that the only reason I would ever go to Hollywood would be to meet John Wayne. And here I was! It was an offer I couldn't refuse.

When I met Joe Pasternak for the first time to discuss my role as Dorothy Henderson in *Seven Sinners*, he looked at me with a critical eye.

"There's one problem," he said. My heart sank. "We'll have to darken your hair. In a Dietrich picture, there is only one blonde, and that blonde is Dietrich." So even though the film was going to be in black and white, he was concerned about how my hair color would photograph against Marlene's.

I was sent to the Westmore Salon in Hollywood. They immersed my hair in dye until I came out a dark, drab brown.

"Too dark," declared Perc Westmore. "Put some henna on it, and give it some highlights."

When they finished, I was a dark auburn color, and I liked it. Marlene liked it too. I was no longer an Al Parker blonde.

Along with Wayne and Dietrich, the cast included Mischa Auer, Billy Gilbert, Oscar Homolka, and Reginald Denny.

John Wayne plays a young naval officer, and I am his fiancée. But he falls in love with a cabaret singer named Bijou, the Dietrich role. I spend almost the entire film trying to win him back.

The first scene I have with him is at the Officers' Ball. While we were dancing, he asked me if I were a Republican. This, of course, was not in the script. I didn't understand him and thought he said "publican," meaning someone who owns a pub. I said, "No, I don't own a public house" or 'pub' as they're called in England." And then I added, "But I'm very fond of beer," which I thought was terribly clever. He looked at me bewildered and confused. He must have thought I was completely mad.

I asked Broderick Crawford, who was also in the film, what a Republican was. He explained that it was a political party, that America had two main parties, the other being Democrats.

That was my first briefing on American politics.

The greatest pleasure I derived from making the film was the friendship I developed with Marlene Dietrich. At first, I had been a little apprehensive about working with her even though I had known her on a personal basis when we both lived at the Beverly Hills Hotel. Even though we had met when we were neighbors at the Beverly Hills Hotel, I thought that when she was working, she might not be as friendly. I needn't have worried. She was wonderful.

The first day on the lot at Universal, Dietrich sent her dresser, Nellie Manley, to my dressing room. "Miss Dietrich would like you to come to see her."

As I walked in, she smiled and handed me a bowl. "I thought you might like this: fresh peaches in champagne."

I thanked her and said, "It's so nice to see you again."

"Yes, of course, I remember. We were neighbors at the Beverly Hills Hotel. Your little girl used to play with my daughter Maria."

"Venetia is almost three now and growing so tall. Is Maria with you?" I asked.

"Yes. We have a house in Beverly Hills. You must come and visit us ... soon."

Marlene Dietrich was very generous to me. I casually mentioned how much I loved the perfume she wore. The following day, Nellie brought me a package. It contained a bottle of that very perfume.

Nellie and I became good friends. We were such friends, in fact, that I ventured to ask her something I had wondered about. "Nellie, is it true that Miss Dietrich wears nothing under her costumes? I mean... no underwear?"

Nellie smiled and said, "Just a minute." She went to Dietrich's dressing room. When she returned, she was carrying something tucked under her arm.

"This is what she wears underneath her dresses," she said, holding out a roll of wide surgical tape. "I strap her breasts up with this until they point to the ceiling. And that's all she wears."

I marveled at the exquisite Dietrich face. She largely owed her cinematic beauty to her mentor, director Josef von Sternberg, who painted a silver line down the center of her nose and a white line beneath her lower eyelids. He also taught her exactly how she should be lit. Every cinematographer for whom she worked listened to her suggestions. I recall her saying to the cameraman, Rudolph Mate, "Move number eight just a tiny bit down, darling. It's casting a shadow across my nose."

When the scene was finally lit to her specifications, a cheval mirror was wheeled in and placed in front of the camera so that Dietrich could see how her body would look when it was photographed. She would adjust her beautiful legs and tilt her head until she was certain that the result would be perfection.

The crew adored her, and she knew most of them by name.

"Hey, Bill," she'd call to one of the gaffers high up in the rafters, "has the baby arrived yet?"

"No, Miss Dietrich," came the reply from above, "but any day now."

Even director Tay Garnett said, "She was the most generous person who ever lived!"

When *Seven Sinners* was complete, Dietrich gave gifts to everyone. I received a beautiful white lace shawl and a crystal bottle of perfume.

As far as I was concerned, *Seven Sinners* was a forgettable picture. It did moderately well at the box office, but with two great stars, how could it have failed?

Far across the Atlantic, the war raged. Those terrible days of the Battle of Britain with pictures of St. Paul's Cathedral rising above black smoke and flames of a desolate London tore at my heart. I thought of our former home, Cardinal's Wharf, and wondered if it had survived the bombing raids.

Life in Los Angeles was hard for me to bear, especially when Joseph Kennedy, the former Ambassador to the Court of St. James, began his campaign to keep America from joining the war.

On May 26, 1940, we read the news about the siege of Dunkirk. Over 500,000 British and French troops were trapped on the beaches of France with no means of escape. Then, just as in a film script, from the coast of England a gallant fleet of small boats, river steamers, and anything that could float sailed from the coast of England and rescued 330,000 British Expeditionary Force soldiers and brought them home.

While I was agonizing over Dunkirk, the American poet Robert Nathan was also moved by the thought of that armada and was writing a poem called "Dunkirk: A Ballad."

> There was no command, there was no set plan,
> But six hundred boats went out with them
> On the gray-green waters, sailing fast,
> River excursion and fisherman,
> Tug and schooner and racing M,
> And the little boats came following last.
> From every harbor and town they went
> Who had sailed their craft in sun and rain,
> From the South Downs, from Cliffs of Kent,
> From village street, from country lane...
>
> They raised Dunkirk with its harbor torn
> By the blasted stern and the sunken prow;
> They had raced for fun on an English tide,
> They were English children bred and born,
> And whether they lived, or whether they died,
> They raced for England now....

I also didn't know that one day that great poet would become an integral part of my personal life!

12

A Ford in My Future

I had ceased to worry about my career in England. Margaret Lockwood, I learned, had replaced me in the film I was supposed to do for Micky Balcon. That was not my primary concern. I just wanted to get back home to be with my family.

My younger sister, Ruth, was now in the Women's Royal Naval Service; she was assigned to a flying photographic unit in the south of England. Margaret, my older sister, was working in a military hospital. Mummie was still living at Fingest Manor, and John was in the Treasury at Admiralty House in London. Somehow or other I had to get home to be with them and do my part.

Bob had just finished directing *Tom Brown's School Days* and was busy with editing. I knew he was an ardent pacifist and would never go home to enlist. Although I did not agree with his views, I respected them.

Nanny was worried about me. "You're looking peaky, Madam," she said. "What you need is a little 'oliday. Get away from 'ere for a few days. Meet some new people." She pointed out, "Mr. Stevenson is busy on his film. I'll take good care of little Venetia. You go off to some nice place, and 'ave a good time. A little of what you fancy does you good!"

Heeding her advice and with Bob's blessing, I took a train to San Francisco and found a small hotel on a quiet street close to Union Square. The weather was cooler than in Los Angeles, and the air was fresh and stimulating. Every day I took long walks through the city and climbed up and down the steep hills the city is famous for. I felt stronger and more invigorated almost immediately. Auntie Winnie would have been shocked that I was alone there.

I even went to the Red Cross office with a request for overseas service,

With charming Ronald Colman, in My Life with Caroline.

but they were not encouraging. They told me they could not send me anywhere without a visa and asked, "Why not help us here?" I told them I would
let them know.

With really nothing to do, I soon became bored. I decided to begin
writing the novel that had been running through my head for years. I bought
a thick pad of paper and several pencils and shut myself up in my room,
leaving only for meals. Thinking about it today, I haven't the faintest idea
what the book was about, except that the heroine's name was Diana Shane,
and the hero made his first appearance carried in on a gate, having been
brought home on it following a hunting accident.

One afternoon as I was busy writing, the telephone rang. It was Bob.
My immediate thought was that something had happened to Venetia.

"No, dear, everything is fine here," he assured me. "I have some good
news. You have to come home right away. Lewis Milestone wants to see you."

"I don't know Lewis Milestone, and he doesn't know me," I said.

"That's just the point," he said. "He wants you to play in his next picture. How it all happened is a strange story, which I'll explain when you get

back here. Meanwhile, start packing, and get the first train in the morning. I'll be at the station to meet you, and if you're not there," he warned, "I'll come up to get you. Be a good girl, and do as I say!"

The explanation about how Lewis Milestone found me was a typical Hollywood story. He had been searching for an actress to play the leading role opposite Ronald Colman in *My Life with Caroline*. He had tested several young actresses—Miriam Hopkins, Paulette Goddard, Jean Arthur— but they lacked the quality he needed. He was in his projection room one morning watching tests when he saw some footage of a young girl being shot out of a cannon.

The projectionist came running in. "I'm sorry, Mr. Milestone. I brought that in by mistake. It's a film belonging to Robert Stevenson, the English director. He is storing it here. I got it mixed up with your tests."

Milestone turned to someone in the screening room. "I have to find that actress."

"Better call England," came the reply.

The answer from the U.K. came back: "Contact Robert Stevenson at RKO. He directed the film. He'll know where she is."

Milestone found that Robert's office at the studio was on the same floor as his. When he walked through the door, he came straight to the point.

"I've been watching your picture, *Young Man's Fancy*, and Anna Lee is exactly the girl I have been searching for to play opposite Ronald Colman in my new film. Where can I find her?"

"That's easy," Bob laughed. "She lives with me. She's my wife."

The story sounded so improbable. But, I thought, if Bob's story is true and there is a possibility of playing opposite Ronald Colman, it was tempting. So my novel was never finished, and the fate of Diana Shane will never be known.

Two days later, I was sitting in Lewis Milestone's office at RKO with Lewis Milestone and Ronald Colman.

My Life with Caroline is based on a French farce and adapted for the screen by John Van Druten and Arnold Belgard. Caroline is the frivolous wife of Anthony Mason, the head of a publishing company. She loves Anthony, but when he is away on business, which is often, she becomes involved in romantic, though completely innocent, relationships with any man who strikes her fancy. The first to enter the picture is Paco Del Valle, a South American gaucho, played by Gilbert Roland. He wants her to ride the pampas with him, and Caroline, in her infatuation with him, dresses in black velvet breeches and rolls her own cigarettes. Her next romance is with Paul, a sculptor, played by Reginald Gardiner, who persuades her to elope with him, but Caroline is thwarted by her loving and understanding husband. She realizes that he is her only true love.

My Life with Caroline was a happy picture. We all liked each other, which is not always the case on a film.

Ronald Colman was a joy to work with. At first, I was a little anxious. After all, he was one of the most sought-after leading men in Hollywood at the time. How would he react playing opposite an actress who was virtually unknown in America? I needn't have worried. From the moment we met, he was kind and courteous and considerate. It was hard for me to believe that I was actually playing love scenes with an actor who had played Sydney Carton in *A Tale of Two Cities* and Robert Conway in *Lost Horizon*.

Mr. Colman—I just couldn't call him Ronald or Ronnie—was wonderfully helpful to me in our scenes together, and he particularly endeared himself to me when he named a bulldog that was in one of our scenes calling it Winston, saying to the dog, "I'm glad you're on our side!" referring, of course, to Winston Churchill.

As a romantic comedy, *My Life with Caroline* should have been directed by someone with a lighter touch. Maybe Ernst Lubitsch. Milestone was a great director of films such as *All Quiet on the Western Front*, for which he won an Oscar as best director, and *Of Mice and Men*, a film that he had both directed and produced, and was nominated as best picture. But I don't think he was the right director for *Caroline*. Some of the scenes fell as flat as an over-done soufflé.

My own reviews were very flattering.

Louella Parsons in the *Los Angeles Examiner* wrote, "...I don't know when I have seen an actress who impressed me as much as Anna Lee.... Not only is she photogenic, but her timing, the way she puts over a scene, and her naivete as Caroline are all extremely effective."

From *The Hollywood Motion Picture Review*: "...Top acting honors go to Anna Lee, whose performance shows great promise of eventual stardom."

Another reviewer wrote: "...Anna Lee, who makes her American screen debut ... establishes herself at once as one of the most attractive and skillful light comedy actresses in Hollywood."

Based on this picture, I was signed to a contract to star with Charles Laughton in a film titled *Three Rogues*. It was never made, but William B. Hawks, Charles Boyer, Colman, and Milestone, the principals in United Producers, said they had big plans for me they said and had already purchased the rights to Ferenc Molnar's *The Swan* for me.

My new agent, Nat Deverich of the William Morris Agency, called with some disturbing news. "United Producers are no longer united," he told me.

I model the latest 1941 fashion. I wore this ensemble in *My Life with Caroline*. I liked it so much I bought it from the studio.

"Lewis Milestone and Bill Hawks have split up and are disposing of the company. They've sold your contract to RKO."

"They can't do that!" I protested. "I'm not a piece of meat that can be sold from one market to another. They don't own me!"

"Oh, yes, my dear, I'm afraid they do and they can. When you signed that contract with them, it gave them the right to loan you out or to sell your contract to another studio," he explained in his soothing agent voice. "Anyway, RKO is a perfectly respectable studio. It has a lot of good people—Ginger Rogers, Lili Palmer, Lucille Ball, and Orson Welles. You'll be in good company."

"Well," I said, still bristling with indignation, "I won't do any of their beastly pictures if I don't like them. I'd rather be put on suspension."

"That can be rather expensive," continued Nat. "Anyway, cheer up. I have an interview for you. They're making a film of *How Green Was My Valley* from the novel by Richard Llewellyn. Have you read it?"

Indeed, I had read it and loved every page. The story is told through the eyes of the young Huw, the youngest of the Morgan family's six boys and one girl in a Welsh coal mining village. The harsh realities of the life are told by Huw. Bronwen comes from the other side of the mountain to marry the oldest Morgan brother. When he is killed in a mining accident, Huw moves in with his sister-in-law, whom he secretly loves. The father is also killed in the mine, and the family begins to disintegrate. Huw recognizes the strength of his family, but also sees that there is no future for him in the valley and leaves, remembering "How green was my valley then, and the valley of them that have gone."

"I want you to be at 20th Century–Fox tomorrow afternoon and meet with William Wyler, who's going to direct," Nat instructed.

The next day, I drove to the Fox studios and was directed to Mr. Wyler's office. He was not only one of the best directors in Hollywood, he was also a nice man, and I could see why women liked to work with him. We talked for a minute or so. Then he said, "I understand that you would like to play Bronwen."

"Yes, I would," I replied.

"Your timing is unfortunate," he told me. "Just this morning, I gave the role to Greer Garson."

He must have seen the disappointment on my face because he said gently, "But now that you are here, perhaps you would like to know about the preparations we're making. Originally," he continued, "we were going to make the picture on location in Wales, but now, with the war going on, this is impossible. We will have to find somewhere in the hills of Northern California or Utah." Then he added, "You might be interested to know that we've found our Huw. He is the young English actor, Roddy McDowall."

He opened a drawer and handed me a photograph of Roddy McDowall, who had huge soulful eyes and an impudent little grin. It was the face of someone who would be a dear and loving friend for years.

My heart, however, was heavy as I left the studio and drove home that afternoon. I had wanted so much to play Bronwen.

Some weeks later, I heard that the production of *How Green Was My Valley* had been cancelled. The money men at Fox in New York didn't like the script and were worried about the pro-labor scenes which might prove to be a political problem and were also concerned by Wyler's reputation for extravagance. They were convinced that the film would be a disaster and refused to finance it.

I decided to keep my mind off my disappointment by busying myself decorating the house that we had bought while I was making *My Life with Caroline.*

715 North Palm Drive, Beverly Hills, was to be my home for the next few years; it was a beautiful two-story Georgian-style house, designed by architect Paul Williams in the early '30s. Williams was the first black member of the A.I.A. and became the "architect to the stars" in the '40s and '50s.

The house had a massive front lawn, a brick walkway leading to the front door, and columns supporting a balcony over the front door. Featuring a huge living room, beautiful dining room, and a library, the house was beautifully laid out. There was a large fir tree in the front, which we decorated with colored lights at Christmas.

My mother had somehow managed to ship out more of our furniture from Fingest Manor, but I needed additional pieces. So I searched for an interior decorator who would help me find what was necessary. I found the talented Beatrice Lenane; we remained friends for years after the project was complete.

Our bedroom had an enormous bed with a headboard upholstered in blue satin. A door led to the bathroom where the walls were covered in mirrors. There was a little room for Venetia just down the hall with the same bed in miniature.

Upstairs in the attic, Bob had built an elaborate train set that went all around the upstairs. He was always building things; he was great with his hands.

Nanny had a suite to herself, including a small kitchen. We had a cook and a parlor maid. Bob hired a chauffeur to teach me to drive my new blue Cadillac on "the wrong side of the road."

Venetia attended elaborate birthday parties, accompanied by Nanny.

VENETIA STEVENSON: The nannies were known by the last name of their employer—Nanny Stevenson, or Herbert Marshall's daughter's was Nanny Marshall—would stand behind the chairs in the dining room. Parents just weren't there. I didn't know my nanny's real name until much later. I was completely devoted to her. She raised me from the time I was born until I was about 12. She was actually my surrogate mother. This situation was not uncommon in the Beverly Hills community in those days.

In April 1941, I discovered I was pregnant again. I was rather pleased. Now Venetia could have a baby brother. The new nursery would be ready just in time.

Then, very unexpectedly, Nat phoned to say that Fox wanted to see me again. Darryl F. Zanuck had decided to make *How Green Was My Valley* in spite of protests from New York. He felt that Philip Dunne's script was the finest that he had ever read, and he was determined to make the picture. William Wyler had returned to MGM and would not be available, so the film was going to be directed by John Ford.

Ford had directed *Stagecoach*, one of my favorite pictures and the film that brought John Wayne stardom. I knew Ford was a great director, but someone told me that he would never cast an English actress in the role of Bronwen. "He only likes to work with Irish actors," I was informed.

"Is that so?" I thought. "Well, we'll see about that." So I invented a fictitious grandfather whom I called Thomas Michael O'Connell, or maybe it was O'Toole.

John Ford's office at the studio was smaller than Wyler's and was filled with pictures and models of sailing ships. Ford was tall and wore dark glasses, even though we were in a rather dark room, and he was chewing on what seemed to be the end of a very old cigar.

"So you're the Limey, huh?" was his greeting to me.

"My father was English, Mr. Ford," I said defensively, "but my mother is Irish, and my grandfather's name was Thomas Michael O'Connell."

"I understand that some time ago you talked with Willy Wyler about playing the part of Bronwen. What happened?"

"He had already given the part to Greer Garson," I said.

"Greer Garson, huh? She's a good actress, but I don't see her as Bronwen. She always sounds to me as though she's opening a charity bazaar. We'll, I'm not going to test you. I just want to see how you match another cast member." He called to his secretary, Meta Sterne. "Bring in the boy."

I recognized Roddy McDowall from the photograph Wyler had shown me.

Ford looked at us both.

"Sit there," he directed, pointing to a wooden rocking chair. "Roddy, you kneel beside her, and both of you, talk about something. I doesn't matter what. Just talk."

I don't remember what we said. My arm was around Roddy, and the chair was gently rocking. Ford seemed to be pleased with us because he smiled and said, "Yes, that's good. We start shooting two weeks from tomorrow. Check with wardrobe, and start learning your lines. Meta will give you the script."

I could hardly believe it: I was to be Bronwen after all. I did not tell anyone at Fox that I was pregnant for fear that it might cause a problem with the insurance people. After all, I thought, Bronwen herself becomes pregnant and has a baby half way through the picture. As long as they shoot the wedding scene first, all will be well. In fact, the schedule called for the wedding scene to be shot first, and I was able to wear that beautiful white satin wedding dress. For the rest of the time, Bronwen wears a skirt and blouse with an apron tied around her waist, and that apron would conceal any signs of pregnancy... I hoped.

Production began on *How Green Was My Valley* on June 11, 1941. We worked on location at the Fox Ranch off Las Virgenes Road in the Malibu Hills. Originally scheduled to be shot on location in Wales, the location had to be changed because of the war.

A superb replica of the coal mining town of Cwm Rhondda, with the tall mine shafts rising behind it and the black slag heap covering the green of the hillside was constructed. A row of small cottages lined the street, and at the bottom of the hill was the chapel.

The first scene we shot was where Bronwen comes down the steps by the chapel and meets Huw, and he immediately falls in love with her. Dear little Roddy. Those eyes. That smile. Who could have imagined that in a few years, he would be one of the best character actors in Hollywood!

Roddy's father, Tom McDowall, was a captain in the Merchant Marine. He had brought his family to America at the outbreak of the war and then returned to England to take part in the conflict. Mrs. McDowall, or Win, as every one called her, accompanied Roddy to the location every day. His sister, Virginia, also played a small role in the film.

Donald Crisp plays Gwylim Morgan, the patriarch of the family. Sara Allgood, from Dublin's Abbey Theatre, plays his wife, Beth. My old friend John Loder, along with Patric Knowles, Richard Fraser, James Monk, Evan Evans, and Roddy were the brothers. Maureen O'Hara played the sister. There are also several great character actors: Barry Fitzgerald, Rhys Williams, and Arthur Shields. Walter Pidgeon plays the village preacher, Mr. Gruffydd.

Rhys Williams taught us all how to speak with a Welsh accent. We were coached to lift our voice at the end of a line, but with the Llewellyn and Dunne dialogue, that was easy.

Maureen, who plays Angharad, and I are still friends. She named her daughter Bronwyn after my character, except that she changed the spelling, using a "y" instead of an "e."

Every morning we would meet in the makeup department to have our

With my favorite film actress, Maureen O'Hara, in *How Green Was My Valley*. Maureen and I have remained friends for more than 60 years.

hair and makeup done. "No makeup for Maureen or Anna!" was John Ford's instruction. Maureen was one of the only actresses I ever knew who looked gorgeous without makeup.

Each day before we started to shoot a scene, he would take his thumb and run it down our cheeks to make sure that we were not wearing any. One day, I think it was during the wedding sequence, I thought I looked too pale, so I brushed a little rouge on my cheeks. Down came the thumb. Ford's voice thundered, "Take off that stuff. You're playing a Welsh virgin, not a Hollywood hooker!"

At 6 a.m., we all climbed into the studio limousines and started the long drive to the San Fernando Valley, more than an hour away. No freeways then. After Tarzana, the road became little more than a dirt track, winding between sun-scorched fields and dairy farms. I remember Patric Knowles pointing to a spot way up in the hills and telling me that was where he was building his home.

"But, Patric," I protested, "it's so isolated. Not another house in sight. Won't you and your family be very lonely there?'

He shook his head. "That's what I like. No crowded streets. No bothersome neighbors. Just my house all by itself."

Today the area that Patric chose for isolation is home to a beautiful and expensive area known as Westlake.

I was now a little over three months pregnant, but I felt very well indeed. The aprons that I wore every day concealed any sign of the small bulge. I had no morning sickness in spite of the bumpy ride to the location every day.

It was bound to happen: trouble. We were shooting the scene where Bronwen's husband, Ivor, has been killed in the mine and the men are bringing his body down the hill to the cottage. Bronwen runs to meet them but is turned back by the brothers. She staggers down the hill and through her cottage gate. She is supposed to go through the door and up the stairs. But I must have tripped on the threshold of the doorway and fell face down on the stony floor. The first aid man was summoned, and besides my injuries, he immediately noticed my "condition."

"Take her home. She's pregnant," he announced.

John Ford was devastated. He closed down production for the day and drove to my home to explain to Bob what had happened. He insisted on calling his own doctor, a Dr. Rooney, who had delivered both the Ford children, Patrick and Barbara.

Apparently, I had been carrying twins, and just like my mother who fell down the steps of St. Paul's Cathedral years earlier, I miscarried one. John Ford came to visit me in the hospital that first evening. "Why the hell didn't you tell me you were pregnant?" he asked.

"Because I was afraid that you would replace me," I replied truthfully.

"Well, don't ever do that to me again! In the future, when you work for me, just be sure that you let me know ahead of time whether or not you are pregnant."

That was the beginning of a very long personal and professional association.

True to his word, before shooting started on each of the subsequent seven films on which I worked with him, he would gather the cast and crew together and in front of everybody ask me, "Anna Lee, are you pregnant?"

"No, sir," I would say.

"Good! Then we can start production."

This little ritual would continue long after my childbearing days were over.

I was in the hospital for only one day after my miscarriage, and a week later, I was back working.

My daughter, Caroline, who was born on January 24, 1942, didn't seem to be the worse for the incident, and we named her after the character I played in my first American picture.

Every June for many years after production had finished, John Ford held a party at the Motion Picture Country Home in Woodland Hills for what he called "the ladies of the Green Valley." Maureen, Ethel Griffies, who had played Mrs. Nicholas, and I would get together. Although she wasn't in the picture, Jane Darwell, who was a great favorite of Mr. Ford's, joined us. Had she been available at the time, he would certainly have cast her as Beth.

It was a wonderfully happy picture. All of us felt a strong sense of "family," which seemed to blend into our personal lives as well. For years, every June 11, Roddy would bring me flowers or send me a postcard to remind me of the day that we started filming.

The only discordant member of the entire cast was Sara Allgood. When we first met on the set, I said, "We played together years ago in *The Passing of the Third Floor Back*. I think you played my mother." She gave me a cold look. "I don't remember," she said and walked away.

In the introduction to his book, *How Green Was My Valley: The Screenplay for the John Ford Film*, Philip Dunne writes:

> My biggest disappointment [in the film] was Sara Allgood [as Beth]....
> When I heard that the great Sara Allgood of the Abbey Theatre was to play it, I thought she would steal the picture. She had it in her hands; she blew it.... Ford didn't like Sara Allgood and didn't hesitate to tell me so in language that would blister this page.

How Green Was My Valley won five Academy Awards in 1942. In 1990, the National Film Registry chose the film as one of the 25 films to be preserved as a national treasure that year.

I have often been asked what it was like to be directed by John Ford. The answer to that is not easy because I can never remember actually being directed by him. He was unlike any other director for whom I had worked. He never gave me line readings or told me where to place my hands or how

Dressed for my wedding to Ivor Morgan (handsome Patric Knowles) in *How Green Was My Valley*.

to walk. When the camera was set in place, the lights adjusted, and the scene was ready to begin, he would draw me aside and start talking... not about the scene in the picture but about something entirely different—some place he had visited in England or a book he had just read. Then he would take the corner of the grubby handkerchief which he chewed on incessantly when he was working and tuck it in my apron or attach it to whatever I was wearing. Then he would say, "Start working!" And I would walk to my marks and start the scene.

On a Ford picture, I never played a scene the way I had originally intended. It was as if some strange force guided me, and I found myself doing things I had never thought of. Perhaps it was some kind of thought transference. I shall never understand it or be able to explain it.

Nobody was a star in a Ford picture except Ford. But he was a wonderful character himself. He could be absolutely hideous to people, very nasty and unpleasant. On the other hand, he had a very loving heart. He was always kind to me.

I found that the way to keep working in John Ford films was never to refuse one. We rarely got to see a script. We were told that we had a part but never knew if it was going to be the leading role or just a line or two, which often happened to me. You didn't say "no" to John Ford. Arthur Shields, I was told, turned Ford down once and never worked for him again.

The film was a John Ford film from start to finish. Even though he produced it, Zanuck had little to do with the creative aspect of it. I never saw him during the production of the film; in fact, there was a rumor that Ford would not allow him on the set.

I am very proud to have been associated with *How Green Was My Valley*.

Today, Maureen O'Hara and I are the last surviving members of the principal cast. Roddy died in 1998 at 70.

On September 11, 1941, John Ford was inducted in the U.S. Navy as a lieutenant commander. He had already begun the formation of his Naval Field Photo Unit, which consisted of cameramen and writers from Hollywood. This became the Eleventh Naval District Motion Picture and Still Photographic Unit and worked closely with the Office of Strategic Services.

The day after we finished shooting *How Green Was My Valley*, John Ford left for Washington, D.C.

Decades later, I wrote a strongly worded letter to the editor of *The Los Angeles Times*, which appeared on January 27, 1980, complaining about the brutal butchering of *How Green Was My Valley* for television.

> I feel [editing the film] is a crime akin to slashing a landscape by Constable or Turner and the stations that are responsible should be prosecuted for vandalism!
>
> ...it was Ford who created the masterpiece from the book by Richard Llewellyn and the magnificent screenplay by Philip Dunne, and it is...appalling to think that their masterpiece can be desecrated at the whim of an ignorant station manager.

I think John Ford would have been pleased.

Movies and I Go to War

On Sunday, December 7, 1941, I was lying in my bathtub, listening to music on the radio. The music abruptly stopped, and an ominous voice said, "We interrupt this program to bring you an announcement from Washington, D.C. Pearl Harbor has been attacked by the Japanese."

The next day, President Franklin D. Roosevelt, his voice strong and forceful, came over the air: "Yesterday, December 7, 1941, a date that will live in infamy, the United States of America was suddenly and deliberately attacked by naval and air forces of the Empire of Japan."

Los Angeles was in a state of panic. War with Japan, and we were the closest to the enemy. There had been rumors of a Japanese submarine lying off the coast near Santa Barbara. There were thousands of Japanese living in and around the city, and rabid Japanese racism reared its ugly head. This led to one of the most shameful acts committed by the U.S. government. Thousands of Japanese, including a great number who were American citizens, were rounded up and sent to camps where they were held during the whole of the war. These places were euphemistically called "relocation camps," but they were, in fact, concentration camps.

Our Japanese gardener was picked up one morning by two MPs.

As he said goodbye to us, his eyes filled with tears, as did mine. "Why are they taking me?" he cried. "I am an American citizen. My wife is an American citizen. We do no harm to anyone."

They took him and his wife away to Manzanar in the Owens Valley, which was where most of the Japanese in California were sent. It was a long, long war for these people.

War or not, we still had to select a godfather and a godmother for Caroline. John Ford was my choice for godfather, but since he was now in the

John Wayne gives me orders in *Flying Tigers*, one of several films I appeared in with this American icon.

navy and was at sea, he sent Henry Fonda to stand in for him. Caroline's godmother was actress Geraldine Fitzgerald.

When Caroline was a few months old, I started another picture with John Wayne. *Flying Tigers* is the story of a group of American flyers helping the Chinese in Burma who were being relentlessly bombed by the Japanese. Since the story takes place in 1939 and America was not yet in the war, the flyers were unable to be part of any company. They formed their own squadron, calling themselves the AVG, the American Volunteer Group, and were under the command of Generalissimo Chiang Kai-Chek. The aircraft were P-41s, single engine fighters. The nose of each plane was painted with shark's teeth, giving them an intimidating look.

Most of the scenes were shot on what was supposed to be an airfield in Burma, not far from Rangoon. The location the studio found was a bare expanse of land miles away from civilization on what was then called the Ventura Highway.

John Wayne plays the hero, of course, and John Carroll, on loan from MGM, plays the villain who, at the end of the picture, turns out to be a hero. I am John Wayne's love interest.

I liked Wayne, and I think he liked me, but there was never a romantic involvement between us. John, or "Duke," as everyone called him, was not really attracted to blondes. All three of his wives were dark-haired Latinas. His much-publicized affair with Marlene Dietrich was, I think, wishful thinking on her part. From what I saw of them in *Seven Sinners*, it seemed as though she was only concerned with adding him to her string of lovers.

I had several love scenes with Duke in the picture. It was strange to be in the arms of this man on whom I had a wild schoolgirl crush. Now there was only a warm affection.

Duke and I worked together on other Ford-directed pictures, including *Fort Apache* and *The Horse Soldiers*, as well as an episode of the television series *Wagon Train* directed by Ford in 1960, entitled "The Colter Craven Story."

With America now in the war, many of the films that were made had a propaganda element, including my next picture, *Commandos Strike at Dawn*, produced in 1942.

The story is about the Norwegian resistance and takes place in a fishing village on a fjord leading to the Atlantic Ocean. Columbia Pictures, the producing studio, found several locations in and around Vancouver, British Columbia, that stood in for the Norwegian landscape. Paul Muni would be my co-star.

Before we left for Canada, I was summoned to the studio office of Lester Cowan, the producer. With him was John Farrow, the director. Lester began the conversation.

"We have something to tell you," Lester began. "You will find Paul Muni very easy to work with. He's a fine, dedicated actor, but with one idiosyncrasy we feel you should know about."

Lester paused and shot a glance at Farrow, then continued, "Paul does not like any unnecessary physical contact with his leading ladies. Obviously, when you're playing a love scene with him, there will have to be some physical contact between you, but just don't fling your arms around him and hold him in a passionate embrace."

Farrow laughed and said, "The trouble is that wife of his, Bella. She's an extremely jealous woman, and unfortunately, we all have to put up with her because Paul has it in his contract that she must be on the set with him at all times. If she doesn't like the way he plays a scene, we have to shoot it again. So you see, we have our problems. But don't worry. It will be a good picture. You'll love Canada."

I did love Canada, just as I had years before. Paul, Cedric Hardwicke, from *King Solomon's Mines*, who plays my father, and I, stayed at the beautiful Empress Hotel in Victoria. Paul's room was at one end of the building. Mine was at the opposite end, making it a long walk every evening when he wanted to run lines with me. While we worked, Bella would sit in an armchair, knitting. She was quite friendly to me during the production. Apparently, she had decided that I didn't constitute a threat to her.

My biggest problem was John Farrow. He had a notorious reputation for his sexual activities. Maureen O'Hara had warned me about him when she heard I was going to be on location with him.

"Lock your door, Anna," she instructed.

My encounter with him began early, our first night in Vancouver. After dinner, John, in a most charming and courteous manner, offered to escort me to my room. As I unlocked and opened the door, I said goodnight to him, but he followed me into the room... with obvious intentions.

"John," I said as calmly as possible, "I was told all about you by a friend, and I don't want to go to bed with you. I'm a married woman with two small children, and you have a lovely wife [Maureen O'Sullivan]. So why don't we leave it that way and just be friends?"

His face reddened with anger. "Why, you pious little Puritan," he hissed. "You're probably no good in bed anyway, but I'm not going to waste my time tonight to find out. But just remember, if I want something badly, I always get my way, no matter how long it takes!" He stormed out of the room, and I locked the door.

"Mission accomplished," I congratulated myself. But I wasn't taking any chances. I asked my hairdresser, Helen Lehirly, to move in with me.

John Farrow's secretary was Frances Howard. She had a beautiful face and a voluptuous body, which was obviously why he had chosen her. She and I used to go shopping together in Vancouver. Her mother, she told me, was severely handicapped, and she had to support her, which was why she never married. One day I found her in a flood of tears. She told me that Farrow had fired her.

"Why?" I asked. "Because you wouldn't go to bed with him?"

"Don't be silly," she said. "I've been to bed with him many times. No, it was because we had a fight, and I slapped his face. He sacked me. The worst part is he refuses to give me a reference. Now it will be difficult for me to get another job, and I have to work." She started to cry again.

"I may be able to help you," I said. "When I spoke to my husband a few days ago, he told me that his secretary was moving to New York to be married. He's looking for someone to replace her. I'll call and ask if he still needs someone."

When I phoned Bob, I told him, "She's very pretty, and I think she's just your cup of tea."

Those words have never faded from my memory. I remember them all too well.

We began production on *Commandos Strike at Dawn,* and I found Paul Muni to be a dedicated actor. He plays a Norwegian and had an authentic accent. To maintain his fluency with the accent, he used it not only when he was performing, but also when we were in the hotel or eating.

There was no need to worry about the physical contact problem. The first scenes were dancing scenes that were played in the village park. In Norwegian folk dancing, couples evidently hold each other at arms' length, and there is never any embracing. Bella looked on approvingly.

Back in Hollywood, Paul and I were called into the studio to shoot publicity stills needed for publicity.

"We're going to shoot on the roof," the photographer told me. "It's a beautiful day, and I think we can get a more natural look in the sunlight rather than being cooped up in a small, stuffy studio."

"Where is Bella?" I asked, noticing that Paul was alone.

"Oh, she's in bed with influenza," he replied. "I think she caught it up in Canada. Since we have finished production, she can take it easy for a few days."

We found the photographer already setting up his equipment when we arrived. He placed us in position, and we did one or two of the usual poses, hand in hand, gazing at each other with soulful expressions. Suddenly Paul broke away from me and shouted to the photographer, "For God's sake, can't we do something a little sexier than just holding hands? I mean like that picture of Rudolph Valentino and Vilma Banky." He then instructed me, "Anna, arch your back, and I will bend over and kiss you."

What a kiss! It was on the mouth and as passionate as any I had ever had. The photographer snapped the picture.

"There, that's better. But don't look so scared, Anna. Look as if you're enjoying it. That's the trouble with you English girls. You are so cold!" laughed Paul.

I was too surprised to respond.

With Bella away, Paul Muni played.

With so many factory and shipyard employees working 'round the clock to aid the war effort, workers were offered midnight and early morning screenings throughout the country, the first, if I recall, was at the Criterion Theatre in New York.

When I returned from Vancouver, Nanny was waiting for me on the front step of the house.

"Oh, Madam," she cried in an anguished voice, "I'm so thankful you're home. I couldn't stand it for another day. She's been sleeping in your bed and wearing your clothes, and there was nothing I could do. And with two little girls in the house."

"I don't understand," I said. "Who is 'she'?"

"That woman who says she's Mr. Stevenson's secretary. More like a live-in floozy, if you ask me. Just come and look at this, Madam." She led me to the kitchen door. Outside, in the alleyway, were the garbage cans, and sticking out of them were three or four bottles of gin.

"It looks like someone's been having a party," I thought.

That evening when Bob came home from the studio, I sensed that there was something a little different in his behavior. He greeted me affectionately, but not with his usual tenderness.

"I'm going to bed early," he said. "I've got a beastly headache. I think perhaps I'm catching the flu. It might be better if I sleep in the guest room tonight."

"Before you go, Bob," I said, "there's something I want to ask you. Has Frances Howard been staying here while I was gone?"

"Whatever makes you think that?" was his response, and I noticed a little twitch at the corner of his mouth.

"Nanny told me that Frances has been sleeping here and wearing my clothes. I can't believe it's true. I want to hear it from you."

His face reddened, and the twitch at the corner of his mouth was now more evident.

"You know how Nanny loves to gossip and make things up," he pointed out. "It's true that Frances did spend one night here in the guest room when it was pouring rain. She was soaking wet, and I loaned her one of your dressing gowns. But that was all there was to it." As he turned toward the guest room, his final words were, "Now I'm going to bed. We'll talk some more in the morning." He gave me a peck on the cheek and left the room.

By the time I awoke the next day, he had already left for the studio. I still had questions but no answers.

One of the war movies in which almost every actor in Hollywood participated was *Forever and a Day*. Victor McLaglen, Ruth Warrick (who had played a key role in *Citizen Kane*, and, many years later, would play a major role in the daytime drama *All My Children*), Edward Everett Horton, Robert Cummings, even Buster Keaton, were among the American contingent. The British contingent included old friends Jessie Matthews, Queenie Leonard, Dame May Whitty, Merle Oberon, and Donald Crisp, as well as Herbert Marshall, C. Aubrey Smith, Edmund Gwenn, Claude Rains, Cedric Hardwicke, Nigel Bruce, and Gladys Cooper. More than 80 actors donated their salaries to the British war effort.

The writers for the production read like a who's who of literary lions: my old friend Charles Bennett, C.S. Forester, James Hilton, Frederick Lonsdale, John Van Druten, Christopher Isherwood, and Norman Corwin, among them. Robert was one of several directors.

I don't know of another film of any time that had such a prestigious cast and production crew. I was delighted to be a part of this morale-building effort.

Not long after this film, Paul Kohner, who was now my agent, called one day to say that Arnold Pressburger wanted to see me about playing a leading part in *Hangmen Also Die*, to be directed by Fritz Lang. Lang and Bertolt Brecht had written the story, a propaganda piece.

It is based on a real incident. On May 27, 1942, Nazi SS *Obergruppenfuhrer* Reinhard Heydrich, known as "The Hangman," was assassinated. In retaliation, the Nazis razed the town of Lidice, near Prague, Czechoslovakia. All males over 16 were shot and the men, women, children were sent to concentration camps. A massive search was mounted by the Gestapo for his killers. The real assassins were executed.

The film takes place after the event and during the hunt for the assassin, played by Brian Donlevy. I play Mascha, the daughter of a university professor, played by Walter Brennan, who discovers his identity. Dennis O'Keefe plays my fiancé. An old friend of mine, Hans von Twardowski, who I had met through Marlene Dietrich, plays Heydrich, the hangman, with chilling authenticity. Gene Lockhart, as the quisling, gives a magnificent performance.

It was a good part, no big love interest, but some interesting scenes.

I heard that Fritz Lang wanted his current girl friend, Virginia Gilmore, to play Mascha. Pressburger refused, saying she did not have enough experience and no box office appeal. Lang was furious because he was used to getting his own way. Very reluctantly, Lang agreed to see me. He stared at me through his signature accoutrement: a monocle. He looked me up and down.

"She's too tall. She must wear flat shoes," he said and left the room.

Fritz Lang had it in for me from the start.

On my first day on the set, Lang appeared wearing Prussian riding boots, a black leather swagger stick, and, of course, that monocle.

"You walk like a duck!" he shouted at me. "Take off your shoes."

I had to play the scene in my stocking feet while from time to time he would tread on them, crunching down on my toes with his boots.

A friend of mine worked with me on a slight Czech accent, which I thought Mascha would have. Lang had a different point of view.

"Why do you speak with that silly accent? I want everyone to talk American, American from the Middle West."

I could not understand why a Czech girl would talk like someone from Chicago, but I thought it best not to argue. The studio hired an accent coach for me, a charming woman named Ruth Roberts, who had worked with Ingrid Bergman when she had to lose her Swedish accent for her role in *For Whom the Bell Tolls*.

Ruth and I became great friends, a friendship which lasted for the rest of her life. She agreed with me that the idea of a Midwestern accent was absurd, and she thought Fritz Lang was crazy. However, we both decided to do our best to please him.

When Brecht first wrote the story, he called it *No Surrender*, and he was unhappy when the title was changed. The only part of his title that is included in *Hangmen Also Die* is the song that the hostages sing as they are driven off in trucks to be executed: "Die if you must/ For a cause that is just./ No surrender."

The film was made at General Services Studio in Hollywood. James Wong Howe, one of the finest cinematographers in the industry, was the cameraman.

Fritz Lang continued to harass me, trying to bring me to the breaking point. He had not bargained for my British obstinacy and determination. There is a scene in which Mascha is in a horse-drawn carriage being taken to Gestapo headquarters. The property man had inserted a sheet of cellophane in place of glass in the carriage window.

"No! No! NO!" bellowed Lang. "It must be *real* glass. I vant *real* glass."

"But Miss Lee might cut herself when she puts her hand through it," countered the property man.

"Then ve shoot it again," cried Lang.

The cellophane was replaced with glass. We shot the scene, and it all went perfectly. My arm went through the glass without a scratch. Everyone sighed with relief.

"Ve do vun more," ordered Lang.

This time I was not so lucky. A jagged piece of glass cut my right arm, and it bled profusely. To my horror, Lang came toward me saying, "Oh, my poor darling!" and grabbed my arm. He tried to suck the blood like a demented old vampire! Everyone on the set was stunned.

Ruth was appalled. "He should be reported to the Screen Directors Guild. He has no right to treat an actor that way."

The following day, I received a large bouquet of flowers with a card that read: "Well done, Miss Lee. We are all with you. With love from 'The Crew.'"

One day, we were shooting a crowd scene, and one of the extras said something. Lang yelled at him, "Why do you not speak good American?"

The man, a tall, burly fellow from Texas thought he was referring to his Southern accent. He hit Lang on the jaw and knocked him to the ground.

The director lay there, looking up at the crew, and not one of them helped him to his feet.

Lang fired the actor, but word got around, and one of the other directors on the lot immediately hired him and gave him a small part in the film he was making.

In one scene, I get to wear the cami-knickers like the ones I'd seen Tallulah Bankhead wear so long ago.

Hangmen Also Die opened in April 1943 to good reviews. Brian Donlevy and I were invited to Washington, D.C., to attend a premiere and dinner with the Czechoslovakian ambassador in exile.

14

The Troupes Entertain the Troops

Shortly after Pearl Harbor, thousands of servicemen and women arrived in California. They were stationed in camps in and around Los Angeles. To keep their morale up while they were waiting to be shipped out, Abe Lastvogel of the William Morris Agency organized the USO and recruited Hollywood celebrities—including me—to donate time and talent to entertain them.

Anyone who could sing or dance, play the guitar or do magic tricks was encouraged to take part in the camp shows which he organized. I was only too eager to help out.

Many of the camps were situated in the Mojave Desert where the troops were training for desert warfare.

One of the camps where I performed was a few miles from Victorville. Clouds of sand were blowing everywhere, and it was hard to keep my makeup looking good. Bob Hope was hosting the show, and with him was another "Lee," a pretty blonde singer, Peggy Lee. I sang—or tried to—"Deep in the Heart of Texas." I was more than off key, but as there was a large contingent of men from Texas in the audience, my rendition was greeted with a great round of applause.

Along with the USO, there was another group organized for the welfare of the troops. Co-founded by Bette Davis and John Garfield, the Hollywood Canteen, located in the heart of Hollywood, was a haven for military men and women on their way overseas. Anyone wearing a uniform could eat and drink and dance with movie stars like Rita Hayworth, Betty Grable, and so many others who came to the Canteen. I went two or three times a week after work and stood behind the bar handing out hot dogs or hamburgers or helping with the dishwashing or dancing with the men.

Washington notified the USO that performers would be needed to entertain troops overseas. The first group to go overseas included Merle Oberon, Al Jolson, Frank McHugh, and Patricia Morison; they were in England. Martha Raye, Kay Francis, and Carol Landis followed them. I went to the USO office in Beverly Hills and spoke with Abe Lastvogel.

"Abe," I begged, "please send me overseas, if possible to England. I want to be where the action is."

"Anna," he assured me, "we have your name on the list, and I promise you, as soon as we get another troupe together, you'll be with it. Meantime, please do some more camp shows for us."

Weeks went by. More camp shows. Finally, Abe called.

"We have an overseas troupe that's going to be headed by Jack Benny. Larry Adler and singer Wini Shaw are already scheduled. Interested?" he asked.

"Where will we be going?" I asked.

"That I can't tell you," he replied. "The War Department in Washington won't give that information to the USO until the very last moment. I'm afraid it will be 'destination unknown' for all of you until you have actually left the U.S."

I had never met Jack Benny so a meeting was arranged, and I went to his home on North Roxbury Drive. Mary Livingstone, his wife, was there.

"You're a brave girl!" she told me. "I'm terrified of flying. You couldn't get me up in one of those machines for all the tea in China. Jack insists on going, and I'm proud of him for it. I'm afraid you'll have to be his 'straight man' while I stay home and water the plants."

Jack told me that we would leave for New York the second week in July. We would meet Larry Adler and Wini Shaw there. "And once we're all together," he told me, "we'll get further instructions from Washington about baggage and the sort of clothing we should take."

To prepare for the trip, we had to get shots: inoculations against smallpox, malaria, and tetanus. Tetanus was the most painful. I ached all over for the next few days.

Jack had heard a rumor that we might be going to England. I could only hope it was true. Just in case, I bought woolen underwear and packed all the sweaters I had.

In early July, when I was planting a row of carrots in my Victory Garden, I received the news. An army transport car would pick me up at 8 a.m. in two days and take me to the airport. From there, Jack and I would fly to New York.

By now, Bob and I were living under an uneasy truce. He wanted to do something for the war effort. Soon after he completed *Joan of Paris* at RKO, he joined Frank Capra's Signal Corps Unit as a civilian and later was inducted and served as a captain. He filmed the liberation of Rome in 1944.

Not long before I left, there was a blurb in one of the local papers about Venetia titled "Good Business." According to the article by Harry Crocker, "Anna Lee noticed a large increase in 4-year-old daughter's war stamp fund, and questioned the tot about it. 'Oh, I've been selling radishes from your Victory Garden to neighbors and people that walk by,' explained Venetia. 'I told them the radishes were raised by Anna Lee, the actress, and they were glad to buy them for 5 cents apiece.'"

My wartime entrepreneur!

Leaving Venetia and Caroline was the most difficult for me. But they were in good hands with Nanny. They came to the airport say goodbye.

When the plane finally took off, I had a strange feeling as I watched California slip away and wondered what lay ahead of me. A flight of fighters flew ahead as if to bid us Godspeed. Jack and I had a glass of champagne and decided it was all going to be rather exciting.

When we arrived in New York, we were met by two officials from the USO who told us that we would meet Larry and Wini later that day at the Plaza Hotel. I would be staying at the Sherry-Netherland. Jack was at the St. Regis.

Winifred Shaw was a beautiful girl and a wonderful singer. Her career had started on Broadway in the early '30s. She made several motion pictures and was best known for songs from Warner Bros. musicals, especially "Lullaby of Broadway" from *Gold Diggers of 1935*, and "The Lady in Red" from *In Caliente* also in 1935. I heard both many times during our tour together. She left show business after the war when she married Bill O'Malley, who was involved in New York theatre. She died in 1982 at 72, almost forgotten.

Larry Adler was a virtuoso on the harmonica, which he called "a mouth organ." Born in Baltimore to Russian parents, he was slight in size and had an aggressive personality. Several years after our tour, in 1947, he was called to testify in front of the House Un-American Activities Committee (HUAC) during the McCarthy era and was asked, "Are you now or have you ever been a member of the Communist Party?" He acknowledged belonging to many left-wing organizations but denied being a Communist. He was blacklisted and lived in England beginning in the 1950s, where he continued his music. He died in 2001.

At Brooks Brothers, Wini and I were outfitted for our USO uniforms: a dark blue woolen skirt and jacket and a cape with the USO logo on it. This ensemble would prove absolutely wrong for our posting.

Despite the fact that we were posted to North Africa, the USO outfitted us in wool clothing appropriate for the Arctic.

"Wini," I gasped, "they must be sending us to Iceland or the North Pole. This uniform is too hot even for England."

"Well, don't worry, dear. We only have to wear it when we're traveling."

The next day we were sent to Washington, D.C., and escorted to the Pentagon. It was the largest building I had ever seen; it had rows and rows of offices. In one of these offices, we met a general who didn't seem pleased to see Wini and me.

"I'll be frank with you," he told us. "I don't approve of women going anywhere near combat zones. This is not going to be a tea party, and if either of you decides to change your mind, we will be happy to send you home."

Wini and I looked at each other and grinned. "Thank you, sir, but we'd like to go," I said for both of us. "We've been looking forward to this for a long time."

We were then escorted into another office and issued dog tags that would hang on a chain around our necks for our entire tour.

"Just in case we get killed, they can identify us," laughed Larry, as he looped his over his head.

We were introduced to a new member of our troupe: Major James Harrison would be our Special Services Officer and accompany us everywhere and decide where and when we would entertain. For the next few weeks, he was our guardian angel and solved any problem that came up.

When we returned to the hotel in Washington, I was sitting in the lobby when someone came up behind me and tapped me on the shoulder.

"I thought I'd find you here," he said as I turned around. "The last time I saw you, you were wearing an apron." It was John Ford, and he was referring to my costume in *How Green Was My Valley*. "Now look at you. I hear you're going overseas to sing to the boys."

He too was dressed differently; he was in his naval uniform and looked quite dashing.

"Not *sing*, Pappy," I said. By now I had learned to call him by his nickname. "You know I can't sing. But I'm going to help Jack Benny tell some jokes."

"Do you know when you're leaving?"

"We're supposed to be shoving off tonight, but nothing is certain, except that I'm beginning to get nervous. I've never flown the Atlantic before, and I have butterflies in my stomach just thinking about it."

"The best cure for butterflies is good British beer," he said, leading me to the bar.

After three glasses of the brew, my head began to spin, but the butterflies had flown away.

"Pappy, I think you've made me drunk!" I said with a slight slur.

"Good! Now, as soon as the aircraft has taken off, close your eyes and go to sleep. By the time you've crossed the Atlantic, you'll feel wonderful." He looked at his watch. "Have to go," he said. He put his arms around me. "You're a good soldier, Boniface. I'm proud of you." He kissed me and left.

Our luggage was packed and ready to go. I had cut my belongings down to a minimum: two short cotton frocks; one evening dress, a rather nice one of green and silver lame; three or four pairs of nylon stockings; underwear; and two pairs of shoes. With my uniform, I wore a pair of red cowboy boots, which had been given to me by a friend in Texas. I took a lot of cosmetics, as anything like that would be hard to find where we were going. I also packed a hairbrush, shampoo, soap, and perfume.

Early that evening, Major Harrison summoned us. "Let's go," he said, and we were off. We drove to the airport and boarded an army transport plane. Remembering Pappy's advice, I closed my eyes and fell asleep. I awoke to the sound of the plane's wheels bouncing on the runway.

"Miami," said the major. "Our last stop on American soil."

"What the hell are we doing in Miami?" I thought.

There, waiting in the dusk, was a B-17.

"In a few minutes I'll be able to tell you where we are going," he told us, "but not until after we've left the ground. Army regulations."

We joined the dozen or more soldiers already on board in uncomfortable bucket seats. In a few minutes, we were airborne. The major stood up and opened a yellow envelope. "We're going to the Persian Gulf," he announced.

I had never heard of the Persian Gulf, but apparently there were thousands of American soldiers in Iran and Iraq who had been there for almost two years, and their morale was low.

Jack, Larry, and Jack Schneider, our accompanist, had taken seats up front near the cockpit. Wini and I went to the rear of the plane where the soldiers were sitting. It was cooler there. Next to me was a soldier from Nebraska: PFC Joseph Obelensky.

I asked, "Are you scared?"

"No," he replied. "I always think if your number's up and it's time for you to go, you just go. But I'm already homesick for my mother and my girl." He pulled out his wallet and showed me pictures. "They worry about me," he said, "and Africa is such a long way from Nebraska. God only knows when—or if—I'll be home again."

He tucked the wallet away and looked at me. "Miss Lee," he said, "you will be back in America long before me. Would you please call or write to my mother, tell her you saw me and that I was safe and looking well and will be home soon?" He took out a piece of paper and wrote down a name, address, and telephone number.

I carefully transferred the information to my diary. I later transferred it into one of many notebooks I filled with names, addresses, and telephone numbers which I took from our boys with promises to contact loved ones. Following up on so many promises would keep me busy for several weeks after I returned home.

I fell asleep but awoke when the plane landed with a thud on a rough runway. "Are we in Africa?" I asked.

"Not quite," said the major. "This is Ascension Island. We have to stop here and refuel. We'll take off again in the morning."

I'll never forget the bleakness and desolate appearance of this tiny volcanic Atlantic island. Not a vestige of vegetation except a tiny bush struggling to survive in a crack in a rock.

The men who were stationed there had been on the island for almost a year. It was no wonder our arrival was greeted with cries of excitement. Wini and I were the first women they had seen in all that time. There wasn't even a nurse there, unusual for army bases at the time.

The afternoon we arrived, a group of soldiers came up to me. One of them said, "Please, Miss Lee, would you mind just standing there so we can look at you?"

That night Wini and I slept in a tent guarded by two MPs. Not that this was needed. The boys treated us like precious china.

As we boarded the B-17 the next morning, Major Harrison announced, "Our next stop will be on the west coast of North Africa. It's a large military encampment in Accra, Ghana. We'll spend a couple of days there and do as many shows as possible."

General James Macmillan gave us a warm welcome upon our arrival. He invited us to his quarters for dinner before the show and expressed particular concern about Wini and me. He told us, "I think it's wonderful that you girls are willing to endure all this discomfort to help the morale of our men. I just wish there was something we could do to make this more comfortable for you."

For the next couple of days, we put on shows. Each group gave us a warm reception. They were obviously hungry to see anybody from home.

I played straight man to Jack's jokes, Wini sang, and Larry played his mouth organ. I must admit that Wini and I received more applause—and whistles—than Jack or Larry. I was glad I came.

One morning, the major appeared with a broad grin on his face. "I don't know what we've done to deserve this, but General Macmillan has

Our troupe poses under the propeller of our trusty *Five Jerks to Cairo* DC-3 transport. *Left to right:* Jack Benny, Wini Shaw, unidentified colonel, me, our accompanist, and Larry Adler.

loaned us an aircraft which will be our very own until the end of the tour. It comes complete with our own crew. How lucky can we be!"

Our new transport was a C-47 (the military version of the DC-3, a Dakota). The bucket seats had been taken out and replaced by soft plush ones just like in a commercial airliner, and we had a full Army Air Corps crew.

Jack was delighted. "Imagine, our very own plane," he said, "and with all the comforts of home. Now we have to find a name for her and have it painted on the fuselage."

A popular film at the time was *Five Graves to Cairo*, directed by Billy Wilder and starring Erich von Stroheim as Rommel. Larry suggested a play on the title, *Five Jerks to Cairo*, as an excellent name for our plane.

Once we were airborne, our pilot introduced me to our co-pilot, Lieutenant George Stafford.

I gazed into a pair of wonderful gray green eyes. The rest of the face was unimportant. The eyes were wonderful. It was love at first sight!

"I don't really care very much for the name George," I told him. "Do you have another one?"

Well, my middle name is Hoyt," he said. "Will that do?"

"Hoyt? Oh, no. That's worse. It sounds like someone clearing his throat. George will have to do."

He sat down in the seat next to me. "Where are you from?" I asked.

"My home is in Texas, ma'm. A small town called Palestine. But it's pronounced 'Palesteen,' so as not to mistake it for the one near Bethlehem."

"What did you do before you went into the army?"

"Nothing more than a cowhand. You see, ma'm, my family owns a cattle ranch...."

I interrupted him. "For God's sake, stop calling me 'ma'm.' It makes be sound like your grandmother."

"Well, you certainly don't look like any grandmother I've ever seen." He smiled, and the smile was like his eyes: wonderful.

"We're headed for Khartoum," he told me. "In a little while we will be flying over Lake Chad. There's usually a lot to see there. Would you like to come up front and see what's going on? I promised Bob I'd take over for a while so that he could talk to Miss Shaw."

Seated in the co-pilot's seat, I could see Lake Chad glistening in the sun. A herd of rhinoceros splashed in the water.

"I wish we could get a little closer," I said. "I'd love to see what they look like when they're not completely submerged in water."

"No problem!" said George. "We'll buzz 'em. The Wild Life Protection League strictly forbids buzzing rhinoceros or elephants or water buffalo, but

I think we can get away with it. Make sure you've got your seat belt tight. Here we go!"

The aircraft took a sudden dive so fast and so steeply I thought we would hit the ground any minute. Then, all at once, it leveled out, and we were flying a few feet over the water. The rhinoceros herd scrambled to the shore in panic, their enormous black bodies heaving against each other as they galumphed across the desert in a thick cloud of dust.

The door to the cockpit swung open, and Bob Harris snapped, "What the hell do you think you're doing? You scared Jack Benny out of his wits. You know how scared he is of flying ever since his friend, Carole Lombard, was killed in that crash. And now you do a fool thing like this!"

There was more to come. When we arrived in Khartoum, the colonel who commanded the base met us. The first thing he said was, "What do you people mean by buzzing a herd of rhinoceros? They stampeded through two native villages, causing no end of trouble."

George admitted that it was his doing and apologized profusely. What puzzled me was how on earth the colonel had received the news of the stampede so quickly. Lake Chad was miles away from Khartoum, and there were no telephones in those villages.

Bob explained, "The natives don't need telephones. They have drums, and they beat out the message from village to village on them all the way to Khartoum."

That was the last time George and I did any buzzing in a plane. But it *was* fun.

There would, however, be more "buzzing" on a personal level between George and me.

15

My Tour of Duty

We did several shows in the Khartoum area, then boarded the *Five Jerks*, and took off for Cairo. We touched down at Heliopolis Airport where we were met by the brass and driven in a staff car to Shepheard's Hotel, where I had stayed a decade ago when we did *The Camels Are Coming*.

The 9th Bomber Command was stationed at Heliopolis, and that was where we played our first show. The audience was enormous. Jack endeared himself to the GIs by insisting that they sit in the front rows with the officers *behind* them.

Dear Jack! He had a wonderful humility, both on and off stage.

We did a skit together in which he tells me he is Hollywood's greatest lover and can kiss better than Clark Gable, Errol Flynn, or any other actor.

"Come here. I'll show you," he says and takes me in his arms. But I start kissing him until he faints. I then call two GIs in the audience to carry *him* off the stage.

Wini sang "The Lady in Red" or "Smoke Gets in Your Eyes." Larry performed his magic on the harmonica. Then it was my turn.

When I first volunteered to go with the USO, I told Abe, "I'm an actress, not an entertainer. What can I do?"

He told me not to worry as the USO had a team of wonderful writers who would give me great material. I have forgotten most of it. But I still remember this bit between Jack and me:

JACK: Anna, I hear you're going to dinner with one of the officers.
ANNA: Yes, Jack. That's right.
JACK: And you've been seeing a great deal of Lieutenant Cox?
ANNA: Yes, Jack. Is something wrong?
JACK: No, that's fine. But I have to caution you. You are allowed to go out

with officers, but you must *never* date anyone lower than a second lieutenant.

ANNA (*smiling innocently*): But, Jack, I was told there *is* nothing lower than
a second lieutenant!

This got an enormous laugh and did so in every show we played. Even
second lieutenants enjoyed it.

Our next stop was Benghazi, Libya. As we flew over the area, we saw
below us grim evidence of the desert war which had been recently waged
there. Destroyed tanks, half buried in sand, jeeps and trucks with their
wheels in the air. Everywhere a sense of abandonment and despair.

When we landed, it was dusk. We could see the silhouettes of aircraft
against the darkening sky. They looked like giant insects.

Every day, we watched and counted the bombers as they took off on
missions. Then we waited anxiously for their return, counting them again
to see what the casualties were. I remembered a scene in *Flying Tigers* like
this. But this was real!

We were assigned to another Special Services Officer as Major Harrison had left us in Cairo to go home on leave. Captain Budd Bankson had
been stationed in North Africa for some time and knew his way around.
Some years later, he sent me a copy of a book he had written about his
exploits with our troupe. It was titled *I Should Live So Long* and was very amusing and brought back many memories.

From Benghazi, we flew over the Red Sea to Saudi Arabia and the Persian Gulf. When I stepped off the plane in Tehran, we were met by a blast
of stifling hot air so intense that we were unable to do the show during the
day on the improvised stages. The nights were much cooler, but the bright
lights attracted huge flying insects. In the middle of one of my songs, one
of them flew right into my open mouth, causing me to cough and spit it
out—to the amusement of the audience—but not to the insect or me.

British and American troops were stationed all around the area. They
had been there for some time and were bored and wanted to go where the
action was.

We played Baghdad and Kuwait and Tel Aviv.

Russian soldiers were stationed in Baghdad. After the show, one of
them came up to me, and in heavily accented English asked, "You are American woman. What you doing with soldiers?"

I explained that we were entertainers and not part of the regular army.
That did not satisfy him.

"You are woman," he said again. "You should be home driving plough!"

Little did I know that was in my future!

We returned to Benghazi to complete our tour of North Africa: Tunis,

Our pilot, Lieutenant George Stafford, and me in the co-pilot seat somewhere over North Africa.

Algiers, Rabat, and Casablanca. In Casablanca we met newsmen Walter Cronkite and Quentin Reynolds.

During this period, George and I fell more and more in love. And we became more and more frustrated as the days wore on. We were unable to do anything except hold hands and kiss and embrace whenever there was a chance, which was not often.

As soon as we landed anywhere, Wini and I were delivered into the charge of the officers who met us, and we were taken away to headquarters until was time for the show. Wini and I slept in the nurses' quarters or in the Red Cross tent. Since George was under Army orders, he had to report to his quarters by 10 o'clock every night.

Wini strongly disapproved of my relationship with George.

"The USO wouldn't like it at all," she said. "We've been sent here to entertain, not fall in love.

As we traveled from place to place, I spent every moment I could in the cockpit with George, while Bob Harris sat in the back flirting with Wini.

"Why did you want to be pilot?" I asked George.

"Because I love to be in the air, far above the earth with all its ugliness and cruelty," he told me. "When I enlisted in the Army and joined the Air Corps, I hoped to be in a squadron that would take part in some of the bombing raids over Germany or Japan." And then through clenched teeth, he said, "So what happens? I'm sent to a lousy little station in West Africa where all I do is ferry aircraft from one place to another."

He went on: "The squadron leader is Elliott Roosevelt, the President's son. He isn't even a pilot! He's a navigator, and a bad one at that. I remember one time when we were headed for some place in England, and we ended up in Portugal because of him! Nobody likes him. He was awarded some kind of decoration, and his mother came over to pin it on him. We all had to stand at attention. It was as much as we could do not to burst out laughing. Elliott finally left us," he said with relief. "And we continued the dreary routine far away from the war zone where I longed to be."

George finished his tirade, saying, "And if that wasn't enough, I am now ordered to fly a bunch of entertainers across Africa. What a damn way to fight a war!"

"But, George," I said timidly, "what's wrong with show business people? Some of us are really nice." I tried to coax a smile out of him.

"Oh, I don't mean you! You're different. In any case, after we're married, you won't have to work any more. We'll have a home and cattle ranch in Texas and lots of children. That will keep you so busy that you won't miss being an actress."

"George," I asked, "are you proposing to me?"

"Yes, I suppose I am. I took it for granted from the day we met that we would marry as soon as I was discharged."

"But, George," I protested, "I'm a married woman. Bob and I have agreed to separate, and when I get home, we'll start divorce proceedings, but that takes a long time in California. Most important of all, I have two young daughters."

George assured me that he loved children and would make a good father, saying, "Think what fun it will be to start off married life with a ready-made family.

But," he sighed, "there's no point in making plans when it's all so far ahead. I will probably be stationed in Accra for at least another eight months. Then, when I get back to the States, it will take a long time before I can be demobilized. So that will give you at least a year to decide if you want to marry me."

Just a few more stops and our tour would end. As we were flying to Oran, I felt an excruciating pain on the left side of my face. It swelled rapidly and turned a nasty shade of pink. I was immediately placed in a military hospital just outside the city. The doctor, Captain Wilcox, told me I had an ear infection, probably caused by flying with the bad cold I had suffered from a few days previously. It was out of the question, he explained, for me to continue to do the shows until my temperature returned to normal.

"But we're leaving North Africa in a few days' time to fly back to America," I told him. "I'm anxious to get home and see my daughters."

Captain Wilcox was adamant. "Unless the infection is entirely gone and your temperature is normal, I cannot allow you to leave the hospital."

Two days later, I was still in the hospital. Jack Benny came to visit, carrying a large bouquet. The card read: "Get well soon and hurry home. With love from the remaining Four Jerks."

"I'm afraid this is goodbye, Anna," he said. "We're leaving for Benghazi, and tomorrow we fly to Accra, then across the Atlantic to home sweet home. The next time I see you, we'll be in Beverly Hills."

George came to say goodbye too. "Hurry up and get well, darling. As soon as you can fly, hitch a ride to Accra. I'll be waiting for you."

I was so sad at the thought of all of them leaving, but I had already made up my mind to stay in North Africa and join another USO troupe. I had heard that the actor Adolphe Menjou was on his way to Cairo. As soon as I could, I would get in touch with him and make arrangements to join his group.

Captain Wilcox was determined to keep me in hospital as long as possible, explaining, "You're the first woman patient we've had in this hospital. It does us all good just to look at you."

He even offered to take out my appendix to pass the time. I wasn't sure whether the "time" he was referring to was mine or his.

"But there's nothing wrong with my appendix," I protested.

"Not at the moment, but you never know when it will flare up. Just think how comfortable you will feel for the rest of your life knowing that you have no appendix to bother you. Besides," he added, "it won't cost you anything."

I thanked him for the offer but said I would keep it for just a while longer. I did ask, however, that he discharge me.

He did.

I contacted the USO and arranged for a meeting with Adolphe Menjou in Cairo. He was pleasant enough, but I never got to know him well. He was known in Hollywood as "Filmdom's Best-Dressed Man." Even in North Africa, he lived up to that reputation. He wore an immaculately tailored safari suit and brightly polished shoes. His moustache was trimmed to the last whisker.

His show consisted of a dancer who whirled around the stage to the accompaniment of her tambourine. A man who played the guitar was also on the bill. Adolphe's contribution was a question-and-answer game about Hollywood. Someone would call out from the audience, "Who is married to Betty Grable?" Adolphe would answer, "Harry James."

I recited the 23rd Psalm, "The Lord is my shepherd; I shall not want..." while the guitarist played *Ave Maria*. At the end of the show, I sang what had become my signature tune, "Deep in the Heart of Texas." My rendition never failed to bring on riotous applause and wolf calls.

Adolphe told me we were going to play shows in Tripoli and Tunis; we would then cross the Mediterranean to Sicily where we would stay in Palermo. On the way, he fell ill with acute stomach pains and was flown to Tunis, where he was hospitalized. The USO decided that, in view of his age—54—and the state of his health, it would be advisable for him to cancel the remainder of the tour and return home. I was instructed to remain in Palermo, visit the military hospital there, then fly back to Los Angeles.

The Excelsior Hotel was my home in Palermo. It had once been a luxury hotel but was now showing the scars of frequent bombing attacks. The main structure was still standing, but the glass in every window had been blown out. My bedroom, still somewhat intact, had a magnificent carved bed with a real mattress that was sheer heaven after the iron army beds I had been sleeping on.

That night, I took a shower and tied up my hair in cotton hair curlers that I carried with me throughout the tour. They were one-inch-long cotton strips that I had used since childhood, much lighter and easier to pack than the metal ones.

I was lying comfortably in the beautiful bed when I heard the sound of air raid sirens, and then the ack-ack guns firing and the occasional thud of a bomb hitting its target far away.

There was a loud and insistent knocking at my door and a man's voice shouting, "Miss Lee, come down to the bomb shelter at once!"

I wasn't about to go downstairs with my hair in curlers. I told him, "If I'm going to be killed, I'd rather die in this beautiful bed than in a stuffy bomb shelter."

He continued to thump on the door. Finally, I relented. Wrapping a towel around my head, I descended to the bomb shelter. Just as I had thought: hot and stuffy. That night, no bombs were dropped on the Excelsior Hotel.

The next morning, I was driven to the nearby military hospital. The moment I walked into the main ward, I smelled the ghastly odor of burned flesh, a smell that has remained in my memory to this day.

A few days earlier, a large contingent of badly burned soldiers was sent from Italy. They lay in the hospital, some too ill to open their eyes. They thanked me for coming, not because I was an actress, for most of them had never seen any of my films but because someone cared enough to come all the way from America to visit them and thank them for fighting in the war. I felt I was the one to do the thanking, just to have the opportunity to be with these young men who were making such a sacrifice for their country— and my adopted one.

I realized I could do so much more by visiting the hospitals and talking to the men than I could as an entertainer. But how was I going to persuade the USO to allow me to stay in Sicily and North Africa?

The answer came quickly and unexpectedly.

As I returned from another hospital a few miles from Palermo, a sergeant met me at the hotel entrance. "Miss Lee, ma'm, an officer here is very anxious to see you. He says he knew you in California. His name is Captain Hastings."

James Hastings owned a restaurant on the Sunset Strip in Beverly Hills. Bob and I used to eat there often.

"Jim," I cried, "how lovely to see you. What are you doing in Palermo, of all places?"

"Well, I've actually got a splendid job. I'm on General Patton's staff. He's the big cheese around here. At the moment, though, he's under a cloud. You might have read that he was visiting a hospital and foolishly slapped one of the patients, accusing him of pretending to be sick in order

Jack Benny and me on our way to one of our many performances in the Persian Gulf during our World War II USO tour. (Photofest)

to avoid being sent back to the front. Eisenhower heard the story, and there is hell to pay. Patton was ordered to make a public apology to the troops, and then he was sent here in disgrace."

We had all heard about it.

After my final visit to the Palermo hospital, I found Jim waiting for me at the hotel. "I was telling General Patton about your hospital visits," he said. "The General would like to meet you. He has some suggestions."

General George S. Patton looked as if he had stepped out of a fashion magazine. He was the epitome of a general. His uniform was perfectly tailored and resplendent with rows of multi-colored campaign ribbons. And there were the famous ivory-handled pistols on his hips. His blue eyes were set off by his ruddy complexion.

"I hear you're doing a great job with the wounded," he said in a voice that was not as deep and gruff as I expected but rather high-pitched. "I'm glad because I feel it's much more important to care for the wounded than to entertain them. Now," he continued, "there is something I want you to do for me."

What could I do for a general?

"All over Sicily and North Africa, there are many field hospitals where the men are taken directly for medical attention. Depending on how severely they are wounded, they might stay there for treatment until they are well enough to return to their units, or they might be sent to one of the larger army hospitals in the area. In some cases, they return to the States." He paused, obviously affected by what he was saying. "These wounded men desperately need someone from home to talk with. I want you to visit the hospitals, spend several minutes with each man, and find out where he is from, the names of his parents and sweetheart. Ask each man for his address, and, if possible, his home phone number. When you return home, contact as many of those loved ones as possible, and tell them you've seen and talked with their loved one. Will you do this for me and for them?"

"General Patton, sir," I said with a lump in my throat, "I will be more than happy to do whatever I can. It's what I've wanted to do ever since I came here with the USO. But I have a favor to ask of you."

He nodded.

"After I have visited these hospitals, will you please cut me orders to return to America by way of England? I want so much to see my family. If I don't have those orders, I will be sent home by way of Dakar or Accra." (I don't know what George's response would have been if he heard me ask for this re-routing.)

"I will certainly do that," said the general as he sat down behind his desk. "Now there are a few details I need. First, what is your serial number?"

"I was never given one, sir," I explained. "The dog tag I was issued in Washington gives only my name and address."

"I'm giving you the rank of Morale Builder. You are now officially MB384–751. Since you are working with us, you should wear a 7th Army shoulder patch." He turned to Jim. "Captain, find one for her, will you? Now, goodbye, Miss Lee, and thank you for what you're doing for our boys."

As I turned to leave, he asked, "Do you know how you can tell if a man is badly wounded?"

I shook my head and blinked back tears.

"Look at his mouth. A seriously wounded man moves his mouth in an odd way." I believe "Old Blood and Guts," as he was called, was actually crying as he spoke about the wounded.

The door closed behind me, and I went to meet Jim, who was waiting for me in a jeep. I asked him if the general was always so emotional.

"I think the aftermath of the slapping incident has caused him great anguish. He's is a sensitive man, and the notoriety of his act has made it hard for him." He obviously held the general in high regard.

"Thank you for taking me to see him," I said. "I'm so proud of my 7th Army shoulder patch. I'll stitch it to my uniform immediately. How soon can I get started?"

In Palermo, I met Lieutenant General Garrison (Gar) Holt Davidson, one of the nicest, kindest, most considerate men I have ever known. From 1932 to 1937 he had been head football coach at West Point and was so highly regarded by the Point that, after the war, he became Superintendent there from 1956 to 1960. At the time I met him, he was in command of a company of engineers.

"I see you're wearing a 7th Army shoulder patch," he said as we shook hands. "But you have no insignia. Would you wear one of ours?" He handed me an engineer insignia pin, which I wore on my collar for the remaining time I was overseas.

Gar gave a wonderful party for me on October 4, 1943, at the Excelsior. I still have a copy of the invitation with bright red lettering:

INITIATION BANQUET:
THE ENGINEERS ACCEPT ANNA LEE

Considering it was the middle of the war, we dined in style. The menu included fruit cocktail, special breast of chicken, Virginia ham julienne, mushroom buttons, Waldorf salad, and for dessert "1943 frozen surprise." I have no idea what the "surprise" was. It was a splendid evening.

I spent the weeks in Sicily and North Africa. That time will live in my memory and in my heart for as long as I live. I came into contact with hundreds of brave wounded men and with the doctors, nurses, and Red Cross helpers who looked after them. The nurses performed incredible tasks during their multiple shifts.

I remember one of the hospitals. Truckloads of wounded arrived, one after another, and the nurses worked from morning until late at night. They were told they could rest after the last truck pulled in and the wounded were taken care of. They would collapse, exhausted, onto their cots, only to hear the sound of yet another truck pulling in. Dazed from overwork and lack of sleep, the head nurse would say, "OK, girls. Dab on the lipstick, and let's go."

So many memories of those hospitals! Especially the smell of disinfectant. I remember a blind soldier, groping uncertainly on his bed for a letter he was unable to see, much less read. A sergeant in the Marine Corps asking me to sit by his bed and hold his hand while the nurse changed the dressing "so that I won't cry out, Miss Lee." And the wonderful light in their eyes when they showed me pictures of the homes and families they had left behind.

All this time, the notebooks in which I wrote down the names and addresses were filling up. I had my work cut out for me when I returned home.

There was one young man, a sailor named Bill Matthews, who I saw several times. I first met him when he was in a field hospital north of Palermo. He had been badly wounded and was in a plaster cast from head to toe. He was from Miami, Florida, and I wrote his mother's address in my notebook. A few weeks later, I was in a hospital in Algiers when I saw him again. This time, much of his cast had been removed. Then, in a hospital in Oran, as I was about to leave, a nurse told me someone was asking for me. There was Bill, on a stretcher, waiting to go to an embarkation center where he would be shipped home.

"We must stop meeting each other like this, or people will talk!" he laughed. "In a few days, I'll be home. If you are ever in Miami, come and visit me."

By now, I had visited all the field hospitals in the area, and I was running out of lipstick, my hair needed cutting, and I felt it was time for a quick visit to England. Armed with General Patton's orders, I headed for Tangier. Every army transport plane or bomber headed north was filled to capacity. As I was listed as an "entertainer," I had the lowest priority.

I finally claimed a seat on a transport plane heading for Birmingham, but just as we were about to take off, an army sergeant bumped me.

"Don't worry, miss," he said. "There'll be another transport coming along in a few minutes."

It was not to be. There was no room on anything flying north. So I would have to return to the States via Accra without seeing my family. At least George will be happy to see me, I thought. Although I sent word that I was coming, he was not there to meet me. When he did arrive, his face was flushed with anger.

"Where the hell have you been all this time?" he shouted. "You were supposed to come here as soon as you left the hospital in Oran."

"Didn't you get my letters?" I told him about my meeting with General Patton and his request to visit the hospitals. George wasn't the least impressed.

"I suppose all that meant more to you than seeing me again?" he argued. "And just how many of those officers did you go to bed with?"

I was appalled at his display of temper. I had never seen him like this before.

"How dare you talk to me like that," I shouted. "Yes, there were several young men who I liked very much and who would have made love to me if

I had encouraged them. I only wanted you though. Now you behave like this."
I was enraged and flung the words at him, "Maybe we had better forget the
idea of marriage because if you can't trust me when I'm away from you, then
obviously it will never work." I turned my back on him and walked away.

He ran after me and flung his arms around my neck.

"Oh, darling, I'm so sorry! Please forgive me," he pleaded. "It's only
because I love you so much I can't bear to think of you with anyone else. I
just want this damned war to be over. Then we can be married, and you'll
really belong to me."

I believed him. It was an emotional reunion for us. The stress of separation had taken its toll on us both.

Finally, there was a B-24 leaving for Miami one evening. Along with
me were twelve soldiers going home on leave. Halfway across the Atlantic,
we lost one of the engines. The engineer did his best to reassure me.

"Don't worry, Miss Lee," he encouraged. "This old bird can fly just as
well on two engines as on four. It'll slow us down, I'm afraid. But as soon
as we're over land, we'll touch down somewhere and do some repairs. Right
now, we're going to have to blow number two engine on the starboard side
so we won't make a bumpy landing."

I wasn't completely convinced, despite his words.

But we landed... in a jungle. It was Natal, Brazil. We stayed there for
about 24 hours while they patched up the engine. As one of the men
described the repair: "Scotch tape and string."

In 1995, I received a letter reminding me about the day:

Dear Ms. Lee,
    ...During the 2nd WW you passed through Natal, Brazil, on your way
back to the States. You landed at Parnamirim Air Base. This particular
night you came into the Officers' Club. I, a lowly Warrant Officer, happened to be standing at the door next to the dance floor. When you asked
if somebody would hold your Musette bag while you danced, I jumped at
the chance. When you were ... ready to leave you asked me to return your
bag. Of course I did but asked you for a dance since I had been holding
your bag.
    You said "yes" and we danced to "Ol' Rocking Chair Got Me." We
weren't on the floor very long when a Colonel tapped me on the shoulder.
I've never forgotten that short time I had dancing with you.
            Sincerely,
            Donald Hamilton

What an inspiration after all these years to be remembered so fondly.
I would never have passed up the tour.

Finally, Miami! I contacted the USO and told them I had promised to visit a soldier's mother while I was there. A Special Services officer drove me to her home. When I told her I had seen her son and he would be coming home very soon, her eyes filled with tears of happiness. It was moments like these that made all the problems and discomforts worthwhile.

Washington, D.C., where I was to be debriefed, was my next stop. I had no idea what this meant, but I soon found out when I reached the Pentagon. I was interviewed by three army colonels who asked me so many questions about every place I had been and the names of people I had met. I felt like Mata Hari. They told me that I could not tell anyone exactly where I had been or who I had met. I could only say I had been in North Africa and the Middle East.

Just behind me in the interrogation room was a poster that read: "Loose Lips Sink Ships."

I got the message.

I had one night in New York before I returned to California. I called my old friend, Kay Chaqueneux, and we went to the Stork Club together. Sherman Billingsley, the proprietor, was an acquaintance, and I was delighted to see him. The evening was a strange one after all those weeks in the war zones. Here I was in this beautiful restaurant; people were in evening dress; women were wearing silly little hats. Nobody seemed concerned with the war. I found myself wishing that I were back in the Excelsior Hotel with my engineer friends.

The following day I flew to Los Angeles. Bob was at RKO, still working on *Forever and a Day*. He didn't come to meet me, but Nanny and the girls came to the airport. It was so wonderful to hug them and see how much they had grown.

There is a clipping from a local newspaper with a picture of Venetia and me. I'm in my army uniform; the 7th Army patch and the engineer pin are clearly visible. I had been gone for more than four months, traveled 56,000 miles, entertained troops, visited the wounded, and met the man who would become my husband.

Three sacks of mail filled with letters from mothers and wives and sweethearts of those men overseas were waiting for me. It was a rewarding experience to read and reply to them.

One letter appeared in a national fan magazine. Under the headline "Letter from a Boy in the Service" it read:

> Seems funny writing to a fan magazine (I used to write for pictures), but the aftermath of a tough invasion and battle for an island, the fact that pomegranates within reach and grapes a few feet away are inviting, all tend to mellow my mood. So strictly as a fan, I am writing ... of a show that came to us doggies of the infantry in Sicily not too far from Mt. Etna.

...Adolphe Menjou and Anna Lee made two appearances for the 16th Inf. Regiment—that's my outfit.... Anna caused a riot and brought forth a salvo of hurrahs when she got a coy doggie on the improvised stage and invited him to kiss her. He did—on the cheek—the same doggie that knocked out a sniper when we were entering Treina. That's what Hollywood does to a combat line infantryman....

> Cpl. Samuel Fuller
> Reg. Hdg., 16th Infantry
> A.P.O. 1, c/o Postmaster
> New York City

War brings together a strange mix of people. In 1959, this same Samuel Fuller would be my director on *The Crimson Kimono*.

In December 1943, I spoke to the Hollywood Women's Press Club. The message I delivered was one of assurance: our boys were getting the best medical attention; their morale is high; they would like the folks at home to send more magazines.

As far as I know, I am the only civilian to have been given the designation "morale builder." No award can compare to it.

My wartime experiences, the people I met, those 56,000 air miles I traveled—those memories will never fade.

16

Home Again

I returned home in November 1943. How good it was to have a real bath, a cup of tea, and more hugs for Venetia and Caroline. Then I awaited Bob's return. He was quite affectionate. I asked about Frances, and he said she was fine and had taken a house in the Hollywood Hills. He added, "We are still in love."

Not to be outdone, I said, "Well, I am too." I told him about George.

Bob smiled. "You always did fancy a man in uniform. Do you want to marry him?"

"Yes, but you and I have to get a divorce first. George won't be home for at least another eight or nine months so we don't have to make any final decisions just yet."

We agreed that the most important thing was not to upset the girls. Divorce is especially hard on children, and we didn't want any of the gossip columnists getting hold of our plans until we were ready to divulge them. We would pretend everything was normal. "I'll continue to live here but sleep in the guest room," he suggested. "We'll go to parties together and be seen as a devoted couple until dear old George comes marching home."

I did not appreciate Bob's sarcasm, but at least he was being friendly.

Bob and I continued to be seen everywhere together. We successfully outfoxed the gossip columnists Louella Parsons and Hedda Hopper, who continued to write about us as "the ideal couple."

One evening Bob and I went to a party given by Salka and Berthtold Viertel at their Santa Monica home. Berthold had directed me in *The Passing of the Third Floor Back*. A woman wearing a wide-brimmed hat was seated on a sofa next to Salka. They stood and came toward me.

Berthold introduced us. "Anna Lee, this is Greta Garbo."

She took my hand, and in that low, strangely modulated voice said very slowly, "How... do... you... do?" I had just a glimpse of that beautiful face, and then she was gone, leaving the room with Salka.

After being home for several weeks, I became restless. After my adventures with the USO and in the field hospitals, life in Beverly Hills was suffocating. I was anxious to begin working again, but the future did not appear promising. I was offered a film, *Abroad With Two Yanks*. I misunderstood the title, which seemed to be a *double entendre*. I turned it down.

I phoned my agent, Paul Kohner, and complained, "Why can't you get me any work?"

"Anna," he replied, "a year ago your career was at a boiling point. I had calls for you every few weeks. Then, all of a sudden, you disappeared for several months. That's a long time to be away in Hollywood. People here have very short memories."

"Don't they know there's a war on?" I countered. "Aren't they concerned with those who are fighting in it?"

Not long after that conversation, he called to say I was up for a picture called *Flesh and Fantasy*.

It turned out to be one of the worst motion pictures I have ever seen... much less appeared in. The story consists of three episodes. I am in the middle one, together with Edward G. Robinson and Dame May Whitty. I play the fiancée of a man who is told by a clairvoyant that he will commit a murder. Then, for some senseless reason known only to the writers, he tries to find someone to kill in order to fulfill the prophecy.

I spoke ridiculous lines of dialogue. But I did look elegant in gowns by Vera West.

I complained bitterly to Paul and told him if I couldn't get better parts, I would go to New York and see about work in the theatre.

Just as I was about to give up hope, I was sent *Summer Storm*; the screenplay is adapted from a story by Anton Chekhov. Although my role would not be a starring one, I would have some good scenes.

One scene especially appealed to me: the leading man, George Sanders, is dying in my arms and with my eyes filled with tears, I whisper, "Goodbye, my love." In fact, the original script that I read was entitled *Goodbye, My Love*, but the title was changed prior to the beginning of production.

I did not like George when I met him years ago in England with his singing coach uncle, and I didn't like him now. But he was a fine actor. Since he was playing a Russian, his ancestry was an asset to his performance. A scene at the end of the picture takes place in a restaurant where he bursts into a song in Russian, accompanied by a balalaika. His voice was beautiful.

Although Douglas Sirk was the director, George had his own way with

I don't look particularly interested in what George Sanders has said in this scene from *Summer Storm*. George was a fine actor, but not a happy person.

everything, including the last scene, which he wanted rewritten. His excuse? "If I'm going to die, I want to die alone, not with someone holding my hand." So there went my "Goodbye, my love" scene. George died alone. Did he know that's the way he would die in real life?

The female star, Linda Darnell, was a charming, beautiful girl. She was not a great actress, but her beauty outshone everything else on screen. I remember when I first saw her in the makeup room; I was astounded by how lovely she looked without makeup. She was one of only a few actresses who looked good in the early morning.

I remember a scene we were playing: she had to hold a burning candle. She kept saying, "Please, take it away. The flame is too close to me. I'm terrified of fire!"

Poor Linda! It is dreadful to think of her terrible death in a fire on April 10, 1945, at the home of her secretary in Chicago. Did she, too, have a premonition about her own death?

Because the final credits read: George Sanders and Linda Darnell *with* Anna Lee, I felt this was the beginning of the end. Never had my name been preceded by *with*.

On a brighter note, during the making of the film, I received a letter from my George saying that he would be coming home in the next few weeks. He was going to be stationed in California at Ferry Command Air Base near Palm Springs, not far from Los Angeles.

It was time for me to get a divorce. I talked to Bob, and since it was going to be an "amicable" divorce, we decided to use the same attorney to save money.

We would sell the house on North Palm Drive and split the proceeds. We agreed to joint custody of the children, with Bob having weekly visitation rights. For their upkeep and medical expenses, I would receive $500 a month. I did not ask for any alimony as I was still making good money.

Obtaining a divorce in California was a long process. Many people went to Las Vegas, Nevada, where they could obtain a "quickie" in a matter of a few weeks. However, residence in Nevada had to be established. In order to speed the process, I moved to Nevada and rented a cabin on the shores of Lake Mead, where I lived in miserable, lonely isolation for the required time.

Before leaving California, I had received a number of disturbing telephone calls. They usually came late at night after I was in bed. A woman's voice would scream obscenities into the phone. "You're a bitch. You're nothing but a whore! Bob Stevenson is not the father of Caroline, or whatever her name is. John Wayne is probably the father or John Ford or one of the other men you've been sleeping with. You only say Bob is the father because you want him to support her."

I knew it was Frances. I appealed to Bob to make her stop.

When I confronted him about the calls, he said rather sadly, "Frances is a wonderful girl, and I love her. I know she has a problem with alcohol, and she can become abusive. I believe alcoholism is a disease, and I'm going to have her treated for it," he continued in her defense. "The trouble is that she is terribly jealous of you because we were married. I'm sorry she is behaving like this, but I'm afraid that if I say anything to her, it will only make things worse. If she calls again," he advised, "hang up. Or don't answer the phone. Once George comes home and you are married, all of this will stop."

Of course, I had written to my mother telling her about George. She was disappointed that my marriage to Bob was ending. She had always been fond of him. She said, "Darling, you haven't known this man, George, for very long. Have you met his people?"

I told her I wasn't marrying "his people," but years later I wondered if she had not been right. Perhaps I *should* have met his family before I married him.

On June 22, 1945, I had the white wedding I had always wanted. I wore a long white dress given to me by RKO after I played the bride in *Forever and a Day*. With it I wore a white veil with a garland of stephanotis and orange blossoms. I carried a bouquet of white roses and lilies of the valley. George was in his Army uniform.

My church in Beverly Hills, All Saints Episcopalian, would not marry us because I was divorced, so we were married in the nearby Beverly Hills Presbyterian Church. Alfred Hitchcock gave me away. He irritated the guests by standing behind me, concealing me with his bulk. My matron of honor was producer Joan Harrison, Hitchcock's long-time associate. She had written his first American film, *Rebecca*, and much later she became the producer on *Alfred Hitchcock Presents*.

The church was full of friends. I cannot remember them all, but I do remember Ingrid Bergman was there, as were Joan Fontaine, Gladys Cooper, C. Aubrey Smith, and many of my other British friends.

The Hitchcocks hosted a party for us after the ceremony. Later in the day, we left on our honeymoon, which was a complete disaster. A friend of George's, who was called "The Guv'nor," invited us to spend several days at his ranch in Montana.

To get there, we boarded the train, which was crowded to capacity with servicemen. We spent our first night in an upper berth. Hardly the start of a romantic honeymoon. The ranch turned out to be nothing more than a broken down wooden building surrounded by a few acres of dried-up mesquite. There was no indoor plumbing, and the food was horrible. I begged George to move us to a hotel, but he said he didn't want to hurt "The Guv'nor's" feelings by leaving too soon. We stayed for a few miserable days.

When we returned to Los Angeles, George, who had been promoted to captain, had to report to the base. He was, however, able to spend any leave he could get with me at North Palm Drive. One weekend, he brought a friend of his to spend a few days with us, a pilot named Daniel Frost. I only remember his red hair. Since he had never been to Los Angeles, we took him to all the tourist spots.

One evening, the three of us went to the famous Mocambo nightclub for dinner and dancing. George and I returned to our table after a fox trot, and Dan asked me to dance. We were waltzing around the room, and I was pointing out various actors to him. We caught sight of Buster Keaton dancing with a lady several inches taller than he was. They looked so funny that we started to laugh. I clung to Dan as we tried to control ourselves.

When Dan and I returned to the table, George's face was grim. "I think we'd better leave," he said. "I do not like watching my wife flirting on a crowded dance floor."

"But we weren't flirting, darling," I told him. "We were just laughing at something that was funny." I tried to explain. George wouldn't listen.

Dan left the next morning. That was the only time George invited one of his friends to visit. He told me he was sorry about the incident; he just couldn't help being jealous of me. Would I please forgive him? Of course, I did, as I would do many times over the years.

Ingrid Bergman and I were great friends. Our mutual friend, Ruth Roberts, had introduced us. At the time, Ingrid was Mrs. Petter Lindstrom. Petter was a doctor with a practice in Rochester, New York. Ingrid was living in Benedict Canyon near Beverly Hills with her six-year-old daughter Pia, a nursemaid, and a housekeeper. During the time she was in love with Gary Cooper, I would invite them both over to the house on Palm Drive and then discreetly leave them alone.

Ingrid invited George and me to a party at her home. There was an enormous number of people there, and I saw many of my friends. David O. Selznick came over, and I introduced him to George.

"Anna, you sure know how to choose the handsome ones," he said, looking at George.

He turned to George. "Captain Stafford, have you ever done any acting?"

"No, sir," replied George, surprised by the question.

"Well, when you get out of the army uniform, come and see me. I think I can make you into another John Wayne or Gary Cooper!"

David strolled away to another group of partygoers.

"What the hell makes him think I want to be a damn actor?" growled George.

Sometime later, he did try to call Selznick. He couldn't get him on the phone. A typical Hollywood promise!

Finally, the house on Palm Drive sold, and Bob and I split the proceeds from the $75,000 sale. It was a fair price at the time. In 1980, the house sold for two million dollars. What would it be worth on today's real estate market?

I was delighted that Louis Edelman and his wife, Rita, bought the house. Lou was an independent producer and writer, who had already produced *A Yank in the R.A.F.*, *White Heat*, *You Were Never Lovelier*, and *A Song to Remember*. He would go on to create the television series, *The Big Valley*.

The Edelmans lived there about eight years, but some time after they sold this beautiful house, it burned down and has been replaced with a modern structure that doesn't reflect the style or warmth of the original.

With George about to be discharged, I spent the next few weeks searching for another house and found one on South Hamel Drive, also in Beverly Hills, but on what was called "the wrong side of the tracks." But what did it matter? We wouldn't be there for long, and it had great possibilities for decorating.

George, however, did not share my enthusiasm for the little house. When he came in from Palm Springs, I took him to see it. "It's not very large, is it?" he complained.

"No, darling, but once you're out of the army and get a job, we can find something larger."

George was demobilized just a few months later. "Thank God I won't have to wear this damn thing again," he said as he flung his uniform jacket into the corner of the closet.

He wasn't in any hurry to find a job. But he did know how to spend money—my money. I was hesitant, but I suggested, "George, darling, I think you should get a job. You should do something."

"Look," he said, with fire in his eyes, "I commanded a squadron during the war. I went out as a captain in the Air Force. I'm not going to take any job where I can't start at the top." He was defiant. "I've given five years of my life to my country, and now they can damn well do something for me."

From then on, he used the excuse, "Something will turn up." I don't think he was the only member of the armed forces who had these sentiments.

Out of the blue one day, George announced, "I think it would be a good idea to have my mother come out here and live with us. She's a wonderful cook—pork roast with apple dumplings, real Southern fried chicken. It's not your fault that you aren't a good cook," he smiled engagingly. "You English girls are not taught to cook or clean house because you expect to have someone to it for you. But this is America, and things are different.

"Think how nice it would be after a long day at the studio to come back to a home-cooked meal. And having my mother here will give you more time with the children," he added.

It sounded like a good idea. I spent the next few days making the spare room comfortable and cozy. A new bedspread and flowered curtains and a radio on the table near her bed. George told me she loved listening to the soap operas.

Since I had never seen a photograph of George's mother, I pictured her as a plump, jolly woman who would hug the girls and me.

I was quite mistaken. When she arrived, she was gloomy, almost sullen, and hardly spoke a word.

"She's just tired after the long journey," said George. "She'll be different in the morning. You'll see."

The next day, I brought her breakfast in bed, and George and I suggested a drive to see the snow-capped mountains near Arrowhead.

"Don't care to go out this time of day," she snapped. "Don't want to miss my stories. 'Mary Noble, Backstage Wife' comes on soon."

She hardly took any notice of the children, except to complain that they made too much noise. She moved the furniture around in her room, saying, "Can't sleep with the bed facing the door. Bad luck." So the bed was pushed into a corner, and the table with the radio was jammed next to it so she would not have to get out of bed to turn it on. She never wanted to join us in the living room, and whenever George suggested going for a drive, she grumbled that she had a headache.

One afternoon, George came home from the Farmers' Market loaded with groceries of every kind, fruits, vegetables, a joint of beef, everything.

"Now, Mother," he said hoping to urge her on, "I've been telling Anna what a great cook you are. Why don't you surprise us with one of your specialties?"

"Don't care to cook in other folks' kitchens. Never seems right somehow. And I can't cook without a coal stove. This here gas thing," she pointed to the O'Keefe and Merritt stove, "scares me half to death. It might blow up."

So much for those lovely home-cooked meals.

Worse was yet to come.

We did everything possible to please her, but each day, she became more sullen.

"Mother, I thought you would love California," said George in exasperation. "The sun is always shining. The air is fresh and clean. And there is so much to see."

"It's not like Texas," she snapped. "I hate it. I want to go home." We contacted George's sister, Eunice, who lived in Northern California where she was in charge of a home for delinquent girls. She managed to get a few days' leave and come to Los Angeles.

"We'll have to get her back to Texas," she advised. "She's miserably homesick. You should never have brought her here." She berated us, saying, "You can't uproot someone of her age and expect her to settle in another place." She offered to take her mother back to Palestine... if we would pay the airfare for both of them.

That was the end of my contact with George's mother. She died a few years later so I never saw her again.

His mother's visit had a severe effect on George. He was consumed with a sense of guilt and even stronger feelings of anger and disappointment.

Perhaps my mother would have a calming effect on him. I asked her to spend some time with us. George was very unkind to her. After some minor argument, he threw a piece of cake at her. She packed up and went to stay with Robert.

I continued to encourage George to look for a job, but he decided to enroll at a local college under the GI Bill. On the first day of class, he was told he couldn't smoke. He walked out and never went back.

Perhaps out of boredom, he eventually found job as a used car salesman in Westwood Village. This certainly wasn't what he had in mind, but he seemed very good at it.

We made a lot of improvements in the house, including building a barbeque in the back where we would cook steaks for dinner parties.

Venetia was now attending a local public school, where she was in the first grade. Nanny took her there every morning and picked her up in the afternoon. But Venetia was not happy. When Bob and Frances—they were now married—came on Saturday to take both girls to their Brentwood home for the weekend, Venetia would complain on her return, "Why can't I live with Daddy? He has such a beautiful house, and there's a swimming pool."

George became angry when he heard this. "If my house isn't good enough for her, let the little brat live with her father. I don't give a damn."

I must admit I had noticed that recently, every time Venetia was naughty or did something to displease George, he would slap her... hard. One day I noticed scratches on her arm. I asked her what had happened. "George pushed me into a rose bush," she said. She started to wet her bed. I was worried. So much for George's "ready-made family."

I knew the disruption of my divorce and living with a stepfather would be unsettling for the girls, but I had no idea it would come to this. When Nanny said, "I can't think what's happening to the Captain. It's not like him to behave like this. I think he's sick. But," and here Nanny was right, "until things improve, it would be better for Venetia to live with Mr. Stevenson. For a little while at least."

So I lost my Venetia. I was heartbroken, but I knew she would be happier with Bob. I did, however, arrange for Nanny to go with her so that there would be some stability. I also knew that Nanny would report to me how things were going.

Robert enrolled Venetia in the prestigious Chadwick School in Palos Verdes. Her roommate for a short period was Christina Crawford, Joan Crawford's adopted daughter who, years later, wrote the damning *Mommie Dearest*.

Caroline missed her sister. Fortunately, she was soon caught up in her interest in horses, which would become a life-long passion. There used to be a riding ring at La Cienega and Beverly Boulevards where the Beverly Center is now. I would take her to ride the ponies. She told me, "I'm going to be a cowboy when I grow up, Mummie." The cowboy part didn't happen, but her love of horses has provided her with a successful profession.

A letter arrived from my old friend, Gar Davidson, who had returned to West Point. He was coming to Los Angeles a visit one of his former officers. "I don't have your phone number," he wrote, "but I will drop by your house on Saturday morning and hope that you will be home."

The day arrived. Watching from a window, I saw a car pull up. There was Gar, tall and handsome as ever. I longed to invite him inside and talk to him. But the specter of George coming home unexpectedly and finding a man in the house was frightening. His jealousy had now reached the point of insanity, and I hardly dared even to talk to a man.

Gar rang the doorbell. I watched as he rang again and again. Then he returned to the car.

I often wonder why I put up with George's jealousy for so long. We had been so much in love and still were at times. But he was becoming more and more difficult to live with.

George began to have terrible headaches and was unable to sleep. A friend of his, Jim Harding, who worked with him at the car agency, called me.

"Mrs. Stafford, I don't want to worry you, but I think George should see a doctor. He's obviously not well, and yesterday he insulted a customer. Fortunately, I was the only one who knew about it." He cautioned, "If it gets back to the boss, there will be trouble. I've given him the name of my own doctor who may be able to help with his headaches."

I thanked him for his interest. I made an appointment with the doctor, and surprisingly, George did not object. The doctor suggested that George should see a psychologist.

George reacted as I expected. "Hell, no. I'm not going to see a bloody shrink," was his response to the doctor's referral.

With Jim's help, I persuaded him to see Dr. Siegal. The meeting was not a success. George punched the doctor in the nose and charged out of the office, swearing.

The following day, I called the doctor to apologize.

"Don't worry, Mrs. Stafford. It's happened to me before. However, I would like to see *you* alone."

Later, as I sat stiff-backed in the doctor's office, he explained to me what I should have known. "Your husband is not actually a sick man. But he could be if we don't so something and now. I've seen many cases like this—men who have served in the military during the war, commanding others and used to being obeyed. Now they find themselves having to take orders from those who are now their superiors. But George has another problem that I want to talk to you about," he continued. "He tells me that he hates California and will never be happy until he can live in Texas again. I realize that this would mean giving up your career. If you were my daughter, I would advise you to put an end to the marriage and start life afresh before things get worse."

"I love him," I said as much in defiance to the doctor's suggestion as to reassure myself. "I married him 'for better or for worse, in sickness and in health.' I'm sure that if I'm patient, he will get better."

I would never admit that I had been wrong to marry him, and once again, I ignored good advice from a caring individual.

Some time previously, Hedda Hopper had written in her *Los Angeles Herald-Examiner* column something like, "...Anna Lee has left her brilliant English husband and will marry a raw-boned Texan. Another wartime marriage that will never last...."

I was determined to prove her wrong. I *would* make this marriage last.

Goodbye, Hollywood;
Hello, Texas

I put off making the decision about moving to Texas because my career was in full swing again.

Of all the films I made in Hollywood, *Bedlam* remains my favorite. Set in 1761, the film takes place in St. Mary's of Bethlehem's Asylum (known colloquially as "Bedlam"). Boris Karloff gave a wonderful performance as Mr. Sims, the Apothecary General of the asylum. It was wonderful to work with him again... and we continued our line-by-line poetry challenges.

"*Bedlam* is not a horror film," Boris would say when anyone referred to it by its other title, *Chamber of Horrors*. "It's a historical melodrama."

Writer-producer Val Lewton, with whom Boris had worked several times before (*Isle of the Dead* and *The Body Snatcher*), was a perfectionist. The look he wanted was based on the drawings of William Hogarth, in particular, *The Rake's Progress*. The film, directed by Mark Robson, was made at RKO in 1946. Cinematographer Nicholas Musuraca created a stunning, atmospheric look.

I played Nell Bowen, an actress, who is the mistress of a nobleman. Mr. Sims persuades her to visit the asylum "to see the loonies in their cages." She is so overcome with the horror of what she sees that she begs her patron, Lord Mortimer (Billy House), to help the inmates and reform the asylum. Sims informs her that it will cost him a lot of money, and Lord Mortimer tells her he must refuse. Nell becomes angry, and Sims has her thrown into Bedlam. Here, she gives loving care to the inmates and finally regains her freedom.

Since the film had a miniscule budget, very little was spent on my wardrobe. Walter Plunkett, best known for his costumes for *Gone with the Wind*, helped his friend, costumer Edward Stevenson (no relation to Robert), who was assigned to the picture. Plunkett found a dress that had been worn by Hedy Lamarr, which I wore in the scene at Lord Mortimer's ball. The riding habit I wore was supposedly made of the same green velvet material that was used to make the famous "drapery dress" worn by Vivien Leigh in *Gone with the Wind*.

Despite it being my favorite Hollywood film, *Bedlam* was not a critical or financial success. Poor Val never seemed to recover from the failure and produced just three more films. He died less than a half dozen years later at 46.

A film that perhaps should have resonated more strongly with me than it did was *G.I. War Brides*, also made in 1946. It is the story of an English girl who takes the place of a friend who has married a GI, but realizes she no longer loves him. She stows away on a ship to meet her husband-to-be in San Francisco. When she arrives, he decides he doesn't want to go through with the marriage.

Although it is billed as a marriage-go-round comedy, I found something sad about it. Years later I realized that, although fiction, this film was all too true regarding the number of wartime marriages that were mistakes. Mine included.

We had a real war bride as "technical advisor" on the production. She had married a GI and defended the American soldiers from the accusation of being "overpaid, overdressed, and oversexed." In an article in the *Citizen News* in April 1946, she said, "It ... was not fault of the GIs that they were paid more than our boys.... Neither do I think the American[s] ... were overdressed.... And as for the last item... you should have seen some of our English boys."

I certainly had fallen for one of the Americans!

I also read one of the roles (I cannot remember which) in a radio adaptation of the 1935 Clark Gable film, *China Sea*. Gable actually played the same role as he did in the film. It aired on CBS. How I wish I could have made a film with Gable... any film!

In early 1947, 20th Century-Fox sent me a script for *The Ghost and Mrs. Muir*. Rex Harrison and Gene Tierney were set as the stars. It is a romantic story, adapted from the novel by R.A. Dick by my old friend Philip Dunne.

Gull Cottage, on the coast in a remote part of England, is bought by a young widow, Mrs. Muir. She finds it is haunted by an irascible sea captain played by Harrison, who tries to frighten away any prospective owners of his former home. But Mrs. Muir is not easily scared—and she even falls in love with the ghost.

I loved the script. But the role I was offered was so small that it took

George Stafford, still in uniform, visits me, now Mrs. George Stafford, on the set of *Bedlam*.

up less than two pages and would require only one or two days' work at most. True, it was a good dramatic scene, but I hesitated to play such a minor role. Joe Mankiewicz thought I was just what he needed to play the prim but kind-hearted Englishwoman, Mrs. Fairley, whose own husband (George Sanders, again) has betrayed Mrs. Muir.

"They really want you," said my agent. "They're willing to offer you a fantastic deal: $2,000 a day with a four-day guarantee. You'll get $8,000 for a few hours' work."

It was too good to refuse, and I would have the opportunity to work with director Joe Mankiewicz, whose work I admired.

Among the others in the cast were Edna Best (Herbert Marshall's former wife), who played the housekeeper; Robert Coote, an old friend from England; and eight-year-old Natalie Wood.

On my first day, I was in the makeup room having the finishing touches put on my face when the door opened and one of the assistant directors walked in.

"Miss Lee," he said, "you can go home. Miss Tierney has had an accident and won't be able to work for several days. We'll let you know when we need you." Gene had fallen down some stairs and had broken her ankle.

I drove home with the pleasant feeling that I would receive $2,000 for doing nothing that day. It would, in fact, be several weeks before we had our scene together.

The role of Mrs. Fairley may have been one of my smallest parts, but it was more lucrative than any other film I did in Hollywood, based on the number of days I actually worked.

The film still makes me cry when I listen to the score by Bernard Herrmann, certainly one of the most haunting of all film scores.

Dear Gene! Although we only had that one short scene together, I felt a deep affection for her. There was tragedy behind those beautiful eyes. At the time we worked together, she was married to designer, Oleg Cassini, who did her costumes for the picture.

I knew that their daughter, Daria, had been born mentally retarded due to an incident when Gene, then pregnant, had been volunteering at the Hollywood Canteen. An ardent fan embraced her warmly. A few weeks later, Gene developed measles, resulting in the baby's retardation. Years later that the same woman met Gene again and told her how she had been under quarantine with measles but had managed to get to the Canteen that evening to see the star she so admired.

Gene and Cassini divorced in 1952. She did find lasting happiness when she married Texas oilman Howard Lee, to whom she was married for more than 20 years.

In *High Conquest*, I played the unlikely role of a mountain climber who, with four others, attempts to conquer the Matterhorn. Gilbert Roland, with whom I had worked in *My Life with Caroline*, played the role of lead mountaineer. Several second unit location shots were filmed near Zermatt, close to the Matterhorn. My climbing sequences were shot in California, near Arrowhead and Big Bear. I loved scrambling up and down the rocks even though my hands often bled from trying to hold onto the sharp stones. In Switzerland, a famous woman mountaineer doubled my character. In the finished film, I look very professional.

During the making of these pictures, I thought about the advice that the doctor had given me. I came to the conclusion that the only way I could save my marriage was to leave California and live in Texas. It meant more than leaving Hollywood; it meant leaving Venetia (Caroline would accompany me), my friends, and my career. Could I give up all that?

Before I made the final decision, in 1948 I worked again with John Ford. *Fort Apache* is considered one of his finest films, as well as one of the best of the Western genre and the first of his "cavalry trilogy." The others are *She Wore a Yellow Ribbon* and *Rio Grande*.

On meeting him again, he barked orders, as usual. "Darken your hair," he said, "and tone down that Limey accent."

We filmed in Ford's favorite location: Monument Valley, Utah, with its amazing rock monoliths. During the day, the temperature was seldom below 100 degrees. Fortunately, the actors were housed in Goulding's Lodge, which was air conditioned. The crew slept in tents... not air conditioned.

Henry Fonda plays Lieutenant Colonel Owen Thursday, the newly appointed commanding officer. John Wayne plays Captain Kirby York, his adjutant. Colonel Thursday's daughter, Philadelphia, is played by then-19-year-old Shirley Temple, in one of her first grown-up roles. She still had the same chubby face and enchanting smile that had won the heart of America more than a decade earlier. At the time, she was married to actor John Agar, who plays her sweetheart in the film.

My role is as Shirley's Aunt Emily, the wife of Captain Collingwood (George O'Brien). He is awaiting orders to report to West Point.

The first scene we shot on location is the one in which the regiment leaves the fort to seek Apaches who have left the reservation and are causing trouble.

Irene Rich, as the wife of the Sergeant-Major O'Rourke (Ward Bond, one of the Ford stock company), Shirley, and I were standing watching the regiment move into formation. The hot sun beat down on us; the heat was unbearable. I was wearing a tightly-laced corset under my costume. I started to feel ill. While Pappy lined up the camera and the assistant director changed the arrangement of the troops according to the director's wishes, we waited.

I grabbed Irene's arm. "I think I'm going to faint."

"Hold on, dear," she said.

The next thing I knew, John Wayne was carrying me into a dressing room.

Ford came charging in, obviously irritated.

"Anna Lee, are you pregnant again?" he demanded.

"No, sir. It's just the heat, and my corset is too tight."

"Well, get the hell out of it, and when you're feeling better, get on your mark. We have a scene to do."

That was the only time I ever fainted.

A day or so later, we were completing the same scene. The last of the troop is leaving the fort, riding away into the distance. Suddenly a messenger comes rushes in and places a paper in my hand: the transfer order my husband has been waiting for. I could call him back, but I refuse. "He's no coward. He'll want to be with the others," I say as I look into the distance where a cloud of dust obscures the departing soldiers.

My next line is, "I can't see him. All I can see is flags."

At that point, Shirley's voice rang out. "Mr. Ford," she called, "I think the line should be, 'All I can see *are* flags.'"

Ford's face was impassive, but his eyes gleamed dangerously. "Thanks to the institutes of higher learning for women, Miss Temple has found our script to be grammatically incorrect," he said.

The line remains as the writers had written it.

Another memorable sequence takes place toward the end of the film. Although I was not involved in it, it is an example of a filmic moment that only John Ford could create. Colonel Thursday and the remaining men in his command are kneeling behind their wagons, awaiting the Indians' charge. There is absolute silence. Then, from far away in the distance, comes the sound of horses' hooves. The sound becomes louder and louder as the Indians gallop towards the men, shouting their war cries. Then, another moment of silence. The scene ends with a shot of the bodies of Colonel Thursday and his men.

Ford could work magic.

I had recently not only converted to Catholicism, which gave me an emotional and psychological comfort I had felt lacking for some time, but

Opposite: **Shirley Temple (*left*) and Irene Rich (*right*) share my anxiety in a climactic scene from Fort Apache.**

also I made up my mind to move to Texas. If it would help George—and our marriage—I was ready to try anything.

I went to say goodbye to Ford and tell him about my plans. He went into a rage and yelled at me. "Have you gone stark raving mad? You can't do this. You're an actor with a career! You belong here. You can't shut your-

self away in a two-bit country town in Texas." He continued his tirade, say-ing, "For God's sake, be sensible."

For some reason, I apologized. "I'm sorry. It's all arranged."

John Ford had never liked George and didn't hesitate to say so. "That God-damned Texan!" he ranted. "I knew he would come to no good. Well, go to Texas. In six months, you'll be screaming to come back. And don't expect *me* to bail you out!" With that, he spat into a large brass spittoon, which was beside his desk.

Had I only listened to him.

The following week, we left for Texas.

J.W. had found us a ranch near Ruske Highway, about fifteen miles from Palestine. It was large enough to run 200 head of white-faced cattle. A Brahma bull, an enormous beast, was also on the property, but I was deter-mined not to be afraid of it. At one point, I even managed to climb on its back while one of the ranch hands took a photograph, which I still have and intend to show it to my grandchildren and great-grandchildren. I enrolled Caroline in the local convent school.

For a time, it looked as if our lives would settle into a comfortable routine.

I was anxious for George to meet my family, and we decided to make my long-anticipated visit to England. It was 1947. With the war over, I didn't need a visa. We took Caroline with us; Venetia was in London with her father who was making a film, so I was able to see her as well.

We stayed with Ruth and Peter at Sparepenny Cottage. My mother was still living close by. They were all really in a bad way financially; food was still in short supply as was everything else.

George had insisted that we ship over our Cadillac, which was the height of arrogance considering the situation in Britain. What a contrast that car was compared with Ruth and Peter's run-down Austin 7. It certainly didn't endear George to the locals.

One day, George announced he wanted ice cream. Where he thought we could get some, I don't know, and even if we had been able to obtain some, there was no place to store it. Ruth had no refrigerator.

Ruth's husband, Peter, and George didn't get on very well. George gave Peter the impression that *he*, with a little help from America, had won the war. This did not go down well with Peter, who had been in the thick of things as an RAF Wing Commander. Peter saw George's wartime duty flying celebrities around as having nothing to do with the war effort. Because of the conflict between Peter and George, as well as the cottage being too cramped, we moved to a hotel in Henley-on-Thames, leaving Caroline with my sister for a few days.

When we came to pick up Caroline, Ruth told me that their dog, Randolph, had tried to bite Caroline. How could that be? She loved animals and they loved her. Then I found out that Caroline had tried to eat the dog's food!

I still had quite a bit of money that I'd earned during my time with Gaumont-British and Ealing, which was in my account at the Westminster Bank in London. I was shocked by their answer to my request to have it transferred to my account in California: "I'm sorry, madam, but no English currency is allowed to leave Great Britain."

This was the first time I had heard of the new currency regulations. My fifteen thousand pounds could be spent there, but not a penny of it could be sent to America. When we finally left England, all I was allowed to take with me were ten pounds for expenses at the airport.

John came up with an excellent idea. "Joan," he said, "you can't take cash out of England, but there's nothing to prevent you from buying antiques. Anything over a hundred years old is considered an antique and can be shipped to America duty free. Why don't you buy something like old silver?" he suggested. "You could sell it in America, and I bet you will get twice the money you pay for it here."

George and I drove all around England and Scotland, visiting every antique shop we could find. In Yorkshire, we bought a magnificent sterling silver George III coffee pot, which had once belonged to Sir James Lavery, the artist who designed the ten-pound note. In Scotland, we found a silver cake basket, which still stands on my sideboard. So began my collection of Georgian silver. One of the oddities I also acquired was a blunderbuss used in the Battle of Trafalgar. It hung over the fireplace in the ranch house.

Some pieces I loved too much to sell, but, later, when I was going through financial difficulties, I had to sell some.

After at least a month in England, we returned to Texas. We began to renovate the old ranch house, which had good-sized rooms and a steep wooden staircase leading to the second floor. It was more a plantation-like property than a ranch house. I called the house Sevenoaks after the village of my childhood. I was looking forward to painting the house and filling it with our furniture, which we had already shipped from California. The silver from England would be just the finishing touch.

I was delighted to discover I was pregnant. George *had* changed, just as the doctor in Beverly Hills predicted. He was now loving and considerate and looking forward to the arrival of our baby, who was due in early January 1949.

The months passed quickly; by Christmas, the house was looking the way I had imagined. At Christmas dinner, 1948, after eating Christmas pudding and drinking a large quantity of eggnog, my pains began. We had arranged with the local doctor to have the baby delivered at Palestine Hospital. George telephoned him, but he was out, probably enjoying Christmas dinner with friends and family.

With the pains becoming intense, we drove directly to the hospital, only to find there was no room. There was an epidemic of chicken pox, and every bed was filled.

We were instructed to go to a small clinic used mostly for dentistry. There we would await the arrival of Dr. Roberts.

My pain was now unbearable. I asked the only available nurse if she could give me something for it.

"I'm sorry, ma'm," she said, "the only thing I have is aspirin. We're not used to delivering babies here."

Dr. Roberts, a former Army doctor, finally arrived. He seemed more used to dealing with rough and tough combat personnel than pregnant women. He certainly had no bedside manner.

I had a difficult, painful delivery. The doctor laughed and said, "Well, that's a good job over with. Like to see the afterbirth?" And he held out a kidney-shaped bowl filled with some bloody substance that made me feel sick.

But I was filled with joy: I had a son.

I stayed in the clinic for the next 24 hours, and then we drove back to the ranch house where Caroline and our housekeeper, Ira, were waiting to see the baby. We no longer had a nanny for Caroline. George disapproved of anyone helping to raise children. She had been dismissed, but I was able to find her a position with a friend back in Los Angeles.

We baptized our son John Winnifrith, after my brother. What a bright and happy baby. To make the family complete, we bought a dog, a Great Dane we called Prince. He would be the first of a number of Great Danes that I owned.

When John was five months old, I received an offer from Columbia Pictures for a small role in *Best Man Wins*. What fun, I thought, to take John with me and show him off to my friends in Los Angeles.

Of course, I was delighted to have an opportunity to resume my career. I felt comfortable enough about our situation to enroll Caroline as a boarder at St. Mary's Convent School, about four miles from the ranch. Ira would see to George.

Before leaving for California, I put the English silver in the bank. It was the custom in England to put one's valuables in the bank before leaving home for any period of time. I packed it all up in a carton and took it to the Palestine Bank.

George and his friends laughed at me. "What you doin' hidin' that in the bank?" they asked. "No one's goin' to steal stuff like that, and you've got a big ol' dog takin' care of everything."

"Well, it doesn't cost anything, and I'll feel a lot happier," I explained.

John and I boarded the train for the two-day journey to Los Angeles where Tom McDowall met us. Roddy's mother was John's godmother and insisted that we stay with them. She looked after John while I was working.

John Sturges, whose filmography would later include such memorable films as *Bad Day at Black Rock, The Magnificent Seven,* and *The Great Escape,* directed this picture. Why he took on this dreary story, I'll never know. I could hardly wait to complete it.

Although I was scheduled to return to Palestine just days after the completion of the picture, I decided to stay on to visit friends. I moved to an apartment in Beverly Hills that belonged to two friends of mine, Ivis Goulding, the sister of director Edmund Goulding, and Shan Jukes, an old friend. While I was in Los Angeles, she did her best to persuade me to return to California permanently, "where you belong," as she put it.

After I returned from work one evening, probably in early September, I was having a drink with Ivis and Shan. The phone rang. "It's for you, Anna," said Ivis, "someone with a Texas accent."

A voice that sounded like gravel said, "Mrs. Stafford, ma'm, your house is burnin' down."

"What do you mean?" I cried. "Where's my husband? Why isn't he calling me?"

"We think he's at Red Lake at a barbeque. We're all lookin' for him. Mr. J.W. thought I should call you right away. No one was in the house at the time. Someone's lookin' after the dog. Your horse, Tiptoes, was rescued. So things could be much worse!"

I hung up in a state of shock. This couldn't be happening. "I think I need a drink," I said.

"What you need is champagne!" said Ivis. "Fortunately, I have three bottles in the fridge."

So Shan, Ivis, and another visitor, June Lady Iverclyde, and I drank champagne until the phone rang about half an hour later.

It was George.

"Is it true?" I asked. "And what about Caroline?"

"I'm afraid so, darling, but at least we have insurance. We can rebuild. Caroline was at the convent. I went over to see her, and she told me all the children were leaning out of the windows watching the smoke and flames in the distance." George continued the story. "Because it was an old house, they think it was faulty wiring in the kitchen. The firemen said the well went dry before they could douse the top floor!"

John and I left for Texas the next morning.

When I arrived and saw what remained of our home, I was completely overcome. I'll never forget the sight of two tall chimneys standing among a pile of ashes and rubble. There had been two fireplaces; now one stood above the ruins; the other had collapsed.

I especially recall the skeleton of what was my mother's satinwood Bechstein grand piano; it lay on its back with the legs pointing to the sky. I could just make out the metal parts from what was the Trafalgar blunderbuss. Caroline's favorite toy, a rocking horse, ironically named Smokey, was nothing but ashes; just the melted wheels and rack that was used to push it were visible.

I spent the next two days sifting through the ashes, searching for anything. There was nothing left of my collection of Japanese dolls, which had been on stands and each displayed in their own glass dome. My collection of first editions... gone. So many things from my past... gone.

The firemen told me they had been lucky enough to rescue a roll of barbed wire and two saddles from the outhouse. I thought, "To hell with the barbed wire and two saddles! Why can't I find a few books and some pictures?"

Louella Parsons wrote about the fire: [Anna Lee] lost [her] wedding gown, the furniture [she] had brought from England, [her] collection of first editions as well as a book [she] was writing. (I don't even recall what *that* was!)

I did find the Chinese mandarin statue, with a head that bobbed up and down, that I remember sitting on the mantelpiece in my mother's bedroom when I was a child. How I loved to play with it. The bright yellow and green paint had not faded; it was just slightly singed.

At least I had the silver I had purchased in England. Neither George nor his friends, who had laughed when I placed it in the bank, were laughing now.

George began to talk about rebuilding the house. "The insurance will cover it, and this time we can make sure there's no faulty wiring." I think he was truly devastated by the destruction of the house. Here he was, a hero back from the war, married to a glamorous movie star living in a beautiful house. He wanted to regain the status, which he believed he'd earned.

"No, George. No!" I said more firmly than I had ever spoken to him. "I hate Texas. I want to get away from here. As far away as possible." I pleaded, "Can't we find a ranch somewhere else? Somewhere like Virginia or Georgia or even Kentucky?"

"That settles it then," said George, as calmly as I'd ever heard him speak. "We'll forget about trying to find a ranch for the time being and concentrate on looking for a home where we can all live and be happy."

We finally rented a house in Silver Spring, Maryland, which had a stable. In the tack room was the head of a Rocky Mountain goat, which the owner had shot. I remember that Caroline climbed up to it and cut off its beard! We had to pay handsomely for her indiscretion.

Finally George suggested with a tinge of sarcasm, "Let's try Connecticut. It's in *New* England so that should warm your British blood."

We found a lovely home in Darien on Christie Hill Road; it was almost a hundred years old but in very good condition. It had large rooms with windows that looked out on a lovely garden and beautiful lawns. Since we had lost so much in the fire, we began buying furniture in the local stores. We found a furniture maker who specialized in pickled pine. He made me a four-poster bed with carved posts, which I still sleep on. I added a canopy of pale blue and white muslin.

We bought a carved oak cradle, which I have in my dining room; now it's filled with plants instead of a baby.

I loved the Christie Hill house. I was so much happier there than I had ever been in the ranch house in Texas. And I was pregnant again.

George still wouldn't get a proper job. He finally decided he would be a realtor, but I don't remember him showing a home to anyone. Despite his promise, he began talking about finding another ranch. He was also becoming verbally and physically abusive.

My second son, Stephen, was born at St. Joseph's Hospital in Stamford on February 18, 1950. The hospital was run by an order of nuns, one of whom, Sister Mary Ann, became a good friend. I saw a great deal of her during my time in Darien, but one day she "climbed over the wall," and went to live in Iowa.

We found a young woman, Elizabeth Smith, to take care of Caroline, John, and Stephen. She stayed with us for several years. I enrolled Caroline in the local grammar school, Holmes Elementary School.

My film career was on hold. Very few films were being made in New York in the late '40s and early '50s because television was taking over. I could see television antennae rising from almost every home when I drove down Christie Road.

The new world of the television anthology series was born. Robert Montgomery was one of the first of the Hollywood actors to produce his own television show, *Robert Montgomery Presents Your Lucky Strike Theatre*, an hour-long show on NBC. I was asked to play in the television version of *The Citadel*, from the book by A. J. Cronin. Another British actress, Angela

Lansbury, was also in the cast. We became friends during the production, and she spent the weekend with me in Darien. I had worked with her mother, Moyna McGill, in London, and I remember her grandfather, George Lansbury, the fiery leader of the British Labour Party in the 1930s. We had a lot to talk about.

Robert Montgomery had an odd work ethic. He never attended the daily working rehearsals but had his stand-in play the part for him and only appeared at dress rehearsal... a little confusing for the rest of the cast. He was a good actor, though, and *The Citadel* was a success when it aired on June 19, 1950.

Of course, in those days, it was *live*, very different from the way it is done now. First, we would rehearse for five or six days before the performance. The rehearsal hall was a large, empty room in one of the run-down buildings on the west side of New York. The "sets," which we would not see until the morning of the dress rehearsal, were mapped out on the floor with white tape, showing the position of the doors and windows. We had to step gingerly from one "set" to another.

One of the problems working on a live dramatic show was the wardrobe. Sometimes I would have three or four changes in one hour; there was no time to run back and forth to the dressing room. Screens were erected to protect our modesty. The wardrobe girl would peel off one dress, and I'd slip into another.

Then the shoes! I remember one night when one was missing. I had to hobble on stage, rather like Cinderella, with just one shoe!

In those days, the program titles included the name of the sponsors, such as *Magnavox Theatre*, *Ford Theatre Hour*, *Kraft Television Theatre*, *Armstrong Circle Theatre*, *Pepsi-Cola Playhouse*, among others. Actors, most of whom were from the theatre, were needed, actors who could memorize more than a line of dialogue at a time. Many of these actors, who subsequently became famous in films, appeared in these shows: Grace Kelly, Rod Steiger, Walter Matthau, Anthony Quinn, Hume Cronyn and Burgess Meredith; even film stars from the earliest days of the medium—Dorothy and Lillian Gish—worked in these anthology shows. Paul Muni played in an early dramatic episode as did Buster Crabbe.

During this period, I was very busy. I ran from one studio to another. I wasn't out of work for more than three days at a time. Who needed films?

I appeared in a show called *The Web*, in a segment titled "Mirror of Delusion" with newcomer, Grace Kelly. Vincent Price and I co-starred in March 1951 in an adaptation of *Monsieur Beaucaire*.

In those early days, I never knew who would return to play other roles with me. A good example is a segment of *Kraft Television Theatre*. Patricia

Crowley played my daughter in the November 8, 1950, airing of "Sixteen." Not long after, Pat would again come back into my life as my "daughter."

Shortly after completing *The Citadel*, I was invited to Ogunquit, Maine, to play in a summer stock production of a play called *Miranda!*, beginning July 3, 1950. We had six performances, typical for summer stock. Playing opposite me was a young actor, John Newland, tall and handsome. In one scene, he wore shorts, and I noticed what good-looking legs he had. From then on, I called him "Legs Newland." I would love to have had a longer run.

The best part of the summer was my reunion with Venetia who I hadn't seen in a year. She was becoming a beautiful young lady.

I appeared in summer stock again in late summer 1953 at the Westport Country Playhouse in Westport, Connecticut. *Comin' Thro' the Rye* ran for a week. All I can remember is that it was excruciatingly hot in the theatre, and I had to wear a heavy green velvet cloak; I *almost* fainted.

In between these two summer productions, I received a call from a theatrical agent in New York to say that CBS' *Ford Theatre* was preparing an adaptation of Nathaniel Hawthorne's novel *The Marble Faun* and asked if I would like to play Miriam, the feminine lead. A young actor, Alan Shayne, would play Donatello, the marble faun.

I seldom fell in love with my leading man, but I felt a strong physical attraction for Alan. Following a rehearsal one day, he invited me to his apartment in Greenwich Village. At the last minute, I panicked and didn't go. What if George found out!

I loved *The Marble Faun*, and it received moderately good notices when it aired on October 6, 1950. I remember the *Variety* review said, "It fails to achieve maximum impact because of a few production miscues." That was putting it mildly.

The dress rehearsal went perfectly, which in theatrical parlance is unlucky. The day it aired live, something happened that remains very clear in my memory: in the final scene of the last act, Donatello pushes the villain off the edge of a cliff to his death on the rocks below. A mattress had been laid on the floor at the point where the actor would fall. During dress rehearsal, he hit the mattress perfectly.

On the air, the actor playing the villain missed the mattress and struck his head on the floor eight feet below. Alan and I watched in horror as blood gushed from his head. We had to continue our dialogue as if nothing had happened.

The reviewer did have some nice words for me: "Miss Lee turned in an exceedingly good characterization of the tortured Miriam, who twice committed murder indirectly by failing to act to prevent the crimes...."

Years later, however, I read in *Daily Variety* that the new president of Warner Bros. Television was Alan Shayne. I called the studio and spoke with his secretary. I asked her to give him a message: "Ask him if he was ever 'a marble faun.'"

Hardly a moment passed, and he was on the line. "Anna, where are you, and what are you doing?"

We had lunch together. It was wonderful seeing him again. Although we never saw each other after that, I did keep up with his career. He became a well-respected casting director for such films as *All the President's Men*, *The Day of the Dolphin*, and *Catch-22*, and produced a number of made-for-television movies.

I appeared twice more on the Montgomery series: "The Truth About Blayds," by A. A. Milne, which aired on April 28, 1952, and "Ringmaster," which aired on May 26, 1952, with Paul Lukas and Vincent Price.

I also appeared on several game shows. The first was *We Take Your Word*, which was an intellectual challenge about the origin of words. I appeared as part of the rotating panel five times in 1951.

Live television was like nothing else I've ever done. Those memories have not faded!

18

"The First Lady of Television"

As an aspiring actress in England, I had appeared in print advertisements while I was between acting assignments to bring in extra income. Why, I asked myself, couldn't I do the same now? By the 1950s, television commercials were the name of the money game. So I reinvented the career I'd had years before.

These commercials were, like the shows, live! On-screen talent had to be prepared for any emergency. I often found it took more acting ability to represent a product than any role in film or television!

One of the first commercials I did was for Lincoln automobiles. It was a particularly good opportunity because it was shown during *The Ed Sullivan Show*—known then as *Toast of the Town*—on Sunday nights, so I had a lot of exposure.

I sat in the front seat of a mock-up Lincoln, confidently holding the steering wheel while I spoke eloquently about the features of the car. Then, in order to demonstrate its flexibility, I turned the wheel... and the entire mechanism came away in my hands!

Too surprised to improvise, I sat and stared at the camera while interminable silent seconds ticking by.

Needless to say, Lincoln did not hire me again. Julia Meade became their spokeswoman.

I did receive another assignment. This one for Simmons Hide-a-Bed with a Beautyrest mattress. All I had to do was explain the reason that their bed was superior to its competitors. Not only were the coils inserted at a different angle, but it was easy to operate. Seated comfortably on the sofa,

I would gracefully rise, pull a lever, and the mattress would spring forward and voila! A bed.

"So simple, even a child could do it!" I said, smiling.

I was their spokesperson for almost two years.

Other products I was associated with were cereals and coffee. I remember having a nasty accident while shooting a spot for Sanka coffee. In order to make the coffee appear as if it were steaming hot, the property man had added dry ice.

I had been warned not to sip the coffee, but one evening, I became overly enthusiastic about the delicious taste, took a sip, and burned by tongue very badly. This time, however, I had learned enough to ad lib, and I finished the script to the end.

In November 1954, General Foods sponsored an hour-and-a-half program about Rodgers and Hammerstein. General Foods hired me to promote a number of their products. In his March 28, 1954, column in the *New Yorker*, Philip Hamburger wrote:

> ...a personable young lady called Anna Lee put in several firm and forceful appearances. Miss Lee did not sing or dance.... Her mind was on General Foods products, and on a party she said General Foods intended to throw ... after the show.... Before Miss Lee got down to discussing the actual victuals to be served, she described some of the table arrangements—party favors in the form of surreys with fringes on top, and specially designed table cloths bearing extracts from the musical scores of all the Rodgers and Hammerstein shows. "And after the party," she said, "the tablecloths are going to be given away as souvenirs."

I continued to serve up words of praise for the entire menu, including Birds Eye Chicken Pie and Minute Rice with sautéed mushrooms. The anniversary cakes were made "without the slightest trouble, thanks to the new Swans Down Cake Mix," I said in all seriousness. They were iced with Baker's Premium Chocolate, which "just can't be beat for texture, tenderness, and good eating," I smiled. Other General Foods products I mentioned as the camera panned included Kool-Aid, Minute Tapioca, Calumet Baking Powder, and, of all things, Gaines Dog Food. My final words were that these products are "contributing to better, easier and more economical living." I don't think I said a word about the contributions of Messrs. Rodgers and Hammerstein.

Looking at Mr. Hamburger's column today, it seems that there was hardly time for the cast (Mary Martin, Ezio Pinza, Yul Brynner, Patricia Morison, and Jack Benny as well as Rodgers and Hammerstein) to sing and chat in between my product pitches.

These commercials and the television anthologies on which I appeared paid our living expenses. George was still dabbling in real estate. We had heard that oil had been found on property near our Texas ranch. Could we be so lucky? We weren't.

Once I became a Catholic, I found the rituals, the ceremonies, the Mass in Latin were just what I needed in both good and bad times. I had been raised in a religious environment, and I knew that faith could help in so many situations. I may have become rather too ardent a Catholic. We didn't eat meat on Fridays. I went to Mass regularly. And, like my mother, I felt that maintaining the family as a unit was very important. Later, I had to make a decision that contradicted this basic tenet, which affected all those I loved.

In 1951, Aileen Leslie wrote a radio show called *A Date with Judy*. It proved to be very popular, and when Aileen decided to produce it on television, ABC bought it. I played Dora Foster, mother to Judy. Here I was at 40, playing an All-American mother, Dora, to the lively Patricia Crowley. The first episode was televised on Saturday morning, June 2, 1951. This was the first of two incarnations of the show. My role ran until February 23, 1952, and then the entire cast changed when it began its second run in the summer of 1952.

The story was about the Foster family. Along with Pat, with whom I had appeared on a *Kraft Television Theatre* in 1950, there was Jimmie Sommer as Judy's boyfriend, Oogie; Gene O'Donnell was Melvin, her father. When Venetia came to the set with me on one of her visits East, Jimmie was her first real boyfriend.

PATRICIA CROWLEY: I'm sure Anna was as surprised as anybody that she was playing the most All-American mother that ever was. Here was this elegant British woman with this beautiful accent. She was so adorable, and it seemed to work.

As with other live shows, there was no time to make corrections if something went wrong. On each of the episodes, much of the time was spent running from set to set: the living room to the bedroom, back to the living room, then to the kitchen and to the front porch.

We did the blocking with the cameras—three of them; then a dress rehearsal; and then the show. We didn't have an audience. It was live, and, of course, if anything went wrong, we just carried on.

PATRICIA CROWLEY: The tension began when they did the countdown. I was a kid, and I thought it was funny that everybody was so nervous. But Anna was totally professional.

It was a happy show to work on. Pat Crowley and I became great friends, and she would remain an integral part of my life from then on.

I don't know how Pat and her sister, Ann, and her mother and father managed. They all lived in a one-room apartment with a tiny bathroom and a kitchenette at 11 Riverside Drive, in a building called the Schwab House. Ann was appearing in *Seventeen* at the same time Pat was doing our show.

Ann later left show business, married a doctor, and raised a family in Maryland. Pat is now married to television producer Andy Friendly, son of Fred, former president of CBS News.

I found a newspaper article in which I described Pat as "playing my daughter so many times on television I've come to think of her as my own. She's the most talented young ingénue I've ever met apart from being completely unspoiled...." And it was true.

One of the most popular panel shows was *It's News to Me*, created by Mark Goodson and Bill Todman, which aired on CBS, first on Friday evenings and then on Mondays. The show was sponsored by Alcoa and aired from July 1951 to August 1954.

The contestant was told a story or shown a picture. The panelists would give the "details" behind it. We would do our best to confuse him by either claiming that we knew the story but would explain it in such a way that it would sound phony. Or, we offered another version that was actually the correct answer. The contestant was given $20 in $5 bills. Each time he or she guessed correctly, he won an additional $5! If he guessed incorrectly, John Daly took $5 from him. If he guessed correctly every time, he could walk away with the princely sum of $30. It was all a game of bluff, and I became good at it.

I auditioned for the program and soon became the sole permanent panelist. The first master of ceremonies was John Daly who always introduced me as "Our own delightful Anna Lee." Years later, when I would phone him, I would say, "This is your own delightful Anna Lee."

When John left after the first year, Walter Cronkite replaced him. My "lying" colleagues were Quentin Reynolds, June Lockhart (whose father, Gene, had played the villain in *Hangmen Also Die*), Nina Foch, Martha Scott (who was then appearing on Broadway in *The Male Animal*), and John Henry Faulk, an author and charming raconteur, who was dismissed by CBS just a few years later when he was blacklisted. I had no idea about his political leanings. When we talked, it was never about anything political. Martha was also later blacklisted.

Occasionally other panelists included Kitty Carlisle and Mel Allen.

According to one published article about my participation in the show, I was once asked about a piece of cheese. "'Sure I recognize that cheese," [I said]. It's the cheese for which a Wisconsin dairy farmer won a blue ribbon at the Chicago fair.... It won ... because it has no fat content....' "As Anna

I enjoy a laugh with *It's News to Me* panelists *(left to right)* John Henry Faulk, host John Daly, and Quentin Reynolds. (CBS/Photofest)

Lee ... recited her fable, the studio visitor saw no guile ... and like the usual eight out of 10 contestants, fell for her story...."

I loved the show, and since I have always enjoyed reading the news, I would scan the pages of magazines and newspapers, especially the *New York Times.* Also I tried to use the names of real people. In one instance I referred to a Mr. Pat Crowley. I knew that if Pat phoned, she'd have been watching the show.

The show also featured people who had witnessed or participated in a famous historical event. For instance, one gentleman had witnessed the burning of the *Hindenburg* on May 6, 1937; another had witnessed the signing of the Peace Treaty at Versailles on June 28, 1919.

I occasionally took Caroline to the set of *It's News to Me* and introduced her to some my fellow panelists. During the show, she sat on a stool right by the curtain where she could see everything. She once met one of the men who was in Joe Rosenthal's famous flag-raising photograph on Iwo Jima, who was the evening's guest eyewitness to an historical event.

At the same time I was appearing on the show, I gave a lecture in Philadelphia at a convent entitled, "Modesty in TV Wardrobe." One clipping I saved says, "But lest it be said that Miss Lee does not practice what she preaches, [we want to] report that her neckline has not slipped even once.... On the beautiful Miss Lee the high neckline looks good." Looking at the photos that accompany several articles about the show, I notice that I was not wearing a "high neckline" in any of them.

One evening, I was sitting in my dressing room at the CBS Studios on 42nd Street. There was a knock at the door. Mark Goodson walked in.

"Anna," he said nervously, "I have to ask you something, and I feel embarrassed because I am sure I know the answer."

"Go ahead and ask, Mark," I said.

"The question is: Are you now or have you ever been a member of the Communist Party?"

I started to laugh. "Mark," I said, "is this some kind of a joke? I'm a practicing Catholic, and you can't be a Catholic and a Communist too."

He wasn't laughing.

"No, Anna, it's not a joke. We've had several letters from people asking us to remove you from the panel because you are listed in a publication called *Red Channels*."

I was stunned. "I've never been involved in American politics. I'm ashamed to say I don't even know the name of the congressman for New York. In England, I was known as a Churchill Conservative, and I suppose I still am."

My explanation continued. "If I ever met a Communist, I would spit in his eye rather than have anything to do with 'the party.'"

Mark put his arm around me. "Don't worry," he assured me. "We have no intention of removing you. You are far too valuable to us. But with all these nuts around, we have to follow up every letter. I was sure it was wrong information."

So that was the end of that, I thought.

Mark told his side of the story in an article in *This World*, on January 27, 1991.

...I received a call from the agency [Young & Rubicam] requesting we drop Lee at once. I had long become inured to off-the-wall blacklistings—but this one was simply too wild. "Anna Lee? Impossible. She's never been touched by any list. What's going on?" The caller was guarded: 'You know we don't talk about those things. I'm sure you can find a good reason to unbook her.'

I then did something that in those days was *verboten*. I had lunch with Lee. I probed tentatively about her politics. She seemed nonplussed but told me she was not political, except she voted Conservative in England.

"What about your husband?"

"He's a Texas Republican," she responded. "Why do you ask?" I said there was some sort of mix-up and finished the lunch. I went right several [agency] executives.... "Gentlemen this one is crazy. Anna Lee is about as leftist as Herbert Hoover."

"Yes, we know. We did a little more checking and it turned out that there is a different Anna Lee who sometimes writes for the *Daily Worker*."

...Then came the zinger: "We're sorry, but we're going to have to drop Anna Lee anyway. We're already starting to get mail and we can't let the sponsor be involved with protests."

...I said the demand was outrageous and they were free to cancel the show if they wanted to, but I was not about to kill Lee because she was guilty of having the same name as someone else.

...Lee stayed on. The show stayed on. But so did the blacklisting...

I will always admire Mark for his strength of character and his belief in me; in those days when Senator Joseph McCarthy and his minions in the HUAC held unbelievable power, it was a very courageous move.

As it turned out the whole situation was due to a typographical error. The woman who should have been listed was *Ann* Lee, and had apparently written a letter to Harry Bridges, head of the Longshoremen's and Ware-housemen's Union, who *was* a Communist. The only Bridges *I* knew was Lloyd Bridges.

Working four days a week on *A Date with Judy*, once a week on *It's News to Me*, and rehearsing in between for a dramatic television show, I found the commute from Darien each day too difficult. We sold the house on Christie Hill Road and found an apartment in New York on Riverside Drive overlooking the Hudson River and a park. I had only a short bus ride to the television studios.

Venetia was still living with her father, and Caroline was boarding at Mary Immaculate School in Ossining, New York. When I had a weekend off, she would come into New York and I would meet her at Grand Central Station and spend time with her.

CAROLINE STEVENSON: Mom had brilliant red hair at the time and a beau-tiful complexion, and she would usually wear a blue or green cape coat. She was like something out of a magazine, drop-dead gorgeous. People would stop her and ask for her autograph. I was very proud of her. My biggest treat then would be when she would take me to F.A.O. Schwarz and buy me a stuffed animal. Then we'd buy chocolate éclairs and then to a play. I saw the original *Peter Pan* with Mary Martin; *South Pacific* with Ezio Pinza; *Oklahoma*. Those were my happiest times with my mother.

As I was preparing breakfast for the boys one morning in 1952 and get-ting ready to go to one of the studios, the telephone rang. The voice said, "This is Richard Rodgers."

I was so surprised that I could only stammer, "You mean *the* Richard Rodgers?"

The man on the other end laughed. "I didn't know there was more than one of me." It really was *the* man himself. He told me, "I watched you on television last night in a production of a play called *The Truth About Blayds*." That was flattering. "As you may know," he said, "I have a play running called *The King and I*, which I'm sending to London. I'm looking for an actress to play the English governess, Anna Leonowens, and you look just right for the part."

My heart was racing.

"By the way, do you sing?" he asked.

"Well, not really. I sang to the troops overseas during the war, but they were a captive audience," I explained.

"Well, I'd like you to audition for me. See the play tonight. I'll have tickets waiting for you at the box office of the St. James Theatre. Then be at the theatre tomorrow morning at 10 o'clock. Bring some music with you. I'll have an accompanist there."

I saw the musical that night and adored it. The part of Miss Anna, then played by Gertrude Lawrence, seemed exactly right for me. I couldn't wait to meet Mr. Rodgers. When I arrived backstage at the theatre, my enthusiasm evaporated. I was asked to stand on that bare stage beneath a single, swinging work light. It reminded me of my audition for the Central School so many years ago.

I squinted over the footlights into the dark theatre where I could just make out three figures: Richard Rodgers, his lyricist Oscar Hammerstein, and director John Van Druten.

A friendly man named Jack was introduced to me as the accompanist. I told him I would sing "The Rose of Tralee," and I asked, "Would you play it in the lowest possible key?" I was hoping that all those "ning-ning" and lessons with Uncle Sasha would pay off now!

I started to sing. It was as though my entire voice disappeared down a deep rabbit hole. The vast auditorium seemed to swallow up every note.

When I finished, the three figures from the audience approached the stage.

"It's a pretty little voice," said Mr. Rodgers as kindly as he could, "but it needs fortissimo. Can you sing louder?"

"Perhaps if I practice, it will get stronger."

"Do you have a singing teacher?"

I shook my head.

Mr. Rodgers obviously wasn't giving up on me yet. "I want you to go see Madam Zepilli." He handed me a card. "She has helped many of the actors who have worked with me, and you will like her. Work with her for a few weeks, and then come back and see me. We all agree that you look just right for the part of Miss Anna. Now, if you can only produce a voice...."

For the next few weeks, I worked with Madam Zepilli in her studio in the Steinway Building. She was Russian, spoke with a strong accent, and loved vodka, which, she said, helps lubricate the vocal cords. We practiced scales together. My voice was getting a little stronger. I practiced "Hello, Young Lovers" and "Getting to Know You," two of Miss Anna's songs in the show.

I phoned Mr. Rodgers and told him I was ready for him to hear me again.

I auditioned again at the St. James. In the long run, I had to agree with Mr. Rodgers. The show was going to play at London's famed Drury Lane Theatre, and I knew that my voice just wasn't strong enough to fill that vast auditorium. If it had been today, when all the actors wear microphones, I probably could have managed, but then...

I think Mr. Rodgers truly wanted me to play Anna. I begged him to remember me if he ever produced a show with a part for me that did not require singing. That I had the opportunity to meet the composer, that he had even considered me for the role was something I shall never forget.

The play opened in London in 1953 with Valerie Hobson as Anna.

Although my career was as good as it could get, on a personal level, my life with George was fragile at best. I realize now that I made many mistakes during my marriage to George, especially when it came to my daughters. One of the worst was that I had brought up Caroline to believe that George was her father. It was a terrible error on my part, but I had the best of intentions at the time. So she'd had grown up idolizing him. After one of my more bitter arguments with George—probably about his inability to find a stable job—I lost control and blurted out to Caroline, who was about 12 years old, that George was not her father, that Robert Stevenson was her real father, and that Venetia was her sister.

From that time on, George disowned Caroline. She was blamed for everything that went wrong. She couldn't do anything right. Fortunately, she was in boarding school and was, for the most part, out of harm's way.

Then, George announced that he wanted to resume his search for a cattle ranch. He didn't like New York, he said, and I think he resented the fact that I was doing so well while he could only find employment selling used cars from a lot on 59th Street.

As much as George hated New York, I loved it. I loved the city's tall buildings and green parks, the view of the Hudson River from our apartment window, and the wonderful, invigorating energy that surged through the streets.

I also loved being busy with my career again.

George, however, was very persuasive. "It will be much better for the children to be raised in the country," he told me. In one of his rare, generous moments, he told Caroline she could have her own pony. He also promised the boys that they could learn to drive a tractor.

I consoled myself by thinking that it would be a long time before he found his perfect ranch. Unfortunately, it didn't take him very long once he left New York, me, and the children and went in search of his Utopia.

"I've found the ranch," he shouted to me on the telephone some weeks later. He was exuberant. "I bought it yesterday."

"What do you mean you bought it yesterday?" I asked. "What did you do for money?"

"I wrote a check for it. All that lovely money you made in New York. I got it cheap. It's in Montana, and it belonged to an elderly couple who want to spend their final years in Florida." I was overcome with a variety of emotions: anger, frustration, fear.

"Six thousand acres of great cattle country," he continued with enthusiasm, which I could hardly share. "The ranch house needs some fixing up, and you know how you love to fix things up. It has indoor plumbing and running water."

"If it's going to be our home and paid for with my money, I would like to have seen it first," I admonished him, knowing that it wouldn't make a difference. "Is it close to a school? Caroline will be in the eighth grade. And the boys need a school. What about a church? How far is it from a grocery store?" I doubt he had considered anyone but himself when he used *my* money to pay for the ranch.

"No problem," he said. "It's near a small town called Melrose; there is a school for the kids in Dillon; and the ranch is only forty miles from Butte." Forty miles? "I'm sure there's a church somewhere nearby. We'll be able to take possession in about six weeks. So start packing."

"Six weeks?" I asked, stunned. I thought about uprooting the children again. What about my career? Without it, he wouldn't have been able to buy an outhouse.

He continued with a rush of words. "When we get there, I'll have to start buying cattle, about 2,000 head, I think."

And with whose money? I thought.

I told the children about the exciting adventure that we were going to have.

If only I had believed my own words.

Goodbye, New York;
Hello, Montana

On a cold morning in January 1954, we left New York. Our furniture and other possessions had already been loaded into a van and left for Montana some days earlier. It would meet us in Melrose. George, the children, and I headed West in our green Cadillac. A light flurry of snow was falling as we crossed the George Washington Bridge and saw the skyscrapers of Manhattan disappear behind us.

It's News to Me had ended in late November, and I had said a sad goodbye to all my friends in the theatre world. Some of them were envious of me. They thought it was exciting and wonderful to be leaving the city and going to live in what they called "the Wild West."

I tried to lessen my concern by listening to the happy chatter of the children. They were talking about tractors and horses and all the things they would do on the ranch. For them it was going to be a great adventure.

I still hadn't convinced myself.

Our journey west was a long and tiring one. At night, we slept in a motel. If there wasn't one available, we slept by the roadside in the car.

I held the map. I wasn't the best co-pilot George ever had! Once, he asked me how far it was to the next town. Not really knowing how to read a map, I took a careful look and announced, "About two-and-a-half inches." George didn't think that was funny and berated me. It wasn't supposed to be funny. Of course, I hadn't looked at the scale of inches to miles. I had never had to before.

Among the stops we made, one that John particularly enjoyed was at the Custer House at Fort Abraham Lincoln in Mandan, North Dakota. On display at the museum was George Armstrong Custer's uniform, along with his sword and some other artifacts. John, who was a history buff even as a youngster, was fascinated by it. Mummie," he asked, "is General Custer in Purgatory?"

"No, darling. I'm sure he is happy in Heaven," I assured him.

"Then I shall pray for him," John said in a matter-of-fact tone. He bought a color postcard of Custer and for many years kept it by his bed. Much later, when we were in London, he bought a bronze bust of Abraham Lincoln, which was one of his most precious possessions, along with a framed picture of Robert E. Lee.

I sometimes wonder if he was looking for a father figure. He certainly didn't have one in his own father. George disapproved of his love for the Civil War heroes and teased him about it. "He should be out there playing football instead of reading about dead generals," he'd complain.

Poor Caroline was either sick with migraines or throwing up from the moment we left Manhattan until we arrived at the ranch. She was miserable for the entire trip.

Eventually, we arrived in Butte. I tried to persuade George to spend the night in a local hotel, but he insisted on driving to Melrose. By the time we arrived, it was getting dark. All I could see of the town was one narrow, snow-covered street with three bars and a single grocery store. There was no sign of a church or school.

The truck with our furniture was already there. The driver, Jim, was having a beer in one of the bars.

"Don't care much for this climate," he said. "Nothing but snow. No wonder people don't want to live here. Only saw two ranches all the way from Butte," he commented.

We piled back in the car and stopped at a gas station to ask for directions to Hairpin Ranch, our new home.

"Better not try to reach it tonight," was the attendant's warning. "There's a big snowstorm coming on. You won't be able to see more than a few feet in front of you, and it's a steep mountain road with a sheer drop on one side. Better wait in town 'til the storm's passed."

George would have none of it. "I want to get there before it gets too dark," he said. "C'mon. Let's get started." He told Jim his plans.

"Not me," Jim protested from the cab of the van. "I'm not risking my van turning over on a mountain road in this storm. I'll meet you there in the morning if the weather clears."

He waved to us as George started up the car and turned onto the Melrose highway. We began the steep climb up hill called Dead Horse Gully.

"Not a very refined address to put on my notepaper," I said. "Hairpin

Ranch, Dead Horse Gully, Jackson, Montana!" I remembered the elegant-sounding address of my childhood: The Rectory, Ightham, Kent.

Heavy snow was falling now, and it was difficult to see ahead, but I did see far below a river clambering over dark rocks, shining in the dark. On the near side was a steep cliff. I wondered what would happen if we met another car. But George drove slowly and cautiously; I'll give him that. Finally, we reached the crest of the hill. There was nothing but a vast expanse of snow, no sign of a tree or *any* kind of vegetation. Somewhere in the dark was Hairpin Ranch!

I had pictured a small, neat farmhouse, surrounded by a white picket fence, like the ones in Hollywood movies. All I could see was a building with two chimneys covered with snow. There was smoke coming from one of them.

"Good," I thought. "There will be a warm log fire waiting for us."

The children and I tumbled out of the car and headed for the warmth of the house. A man stood at the door and introduced himself as Buck. He said he had worked for the people who sold George the ranch.

"They thought as how you might need me to help you find some good ranch hands," he explained. "So I've been squatting here. Hope you don't mind." I've lit a fire, and there's soup on. You'll find a couple of old mattresses and some blankets in one of the rooms."

No romantic log fire. Instead, there was a large, black potbellied stove in what was called the "mud room." It sat in the middle of the room and was the ugliest thing I had ever seen. It was the only source of heat on the ground floor. The floor was covered with linoleum. I climbed a flight of rickety stairs to the main bedroom. It was large and had two small cracked windows that looked out over the snow-covered property. The room was intensely cold. There was no heat upstairs, and no bathroom, just a washbasin.

I bundled the children in blankets and put them next to the stove. George and I huddled together.

The next morning—still bitterly cold, but no more snowfall—Jim arrived with the furniture, and he and Buck began to unload. They had great difficulty carrying my four-poster bed up the stairs. The posters were too high, and in the end, they had to saw several inches off the legs.

We had even brought the rolls of carpet from the Riverside Drive apartment. The carpet never made it inside the ranch house. The beautiful beige shag, along with its padding, was nailed to the siding on the calving barn for warmth. "Now we will have the only barn with wall-to-wall carpeting," George laughed. I was not amused.

The children went out to play in the snow. Of course, they had seen snow in the East, but this was Wild West snow!

I began to explore the buildings around the main house. There was a large shed near the kitchen door. Inside was a tractor and other farm equipment. The remains of a moose head were nailed to the door. What a horrible relic! Blood had dripped from its mouth and onto the snow. I made a mental note to have Buck remove it.

At the far end of the yard was another building where the ranch hands were housed.

Snow began to fall again, and it looked as though it would be a big storm. Jim asked George if he could spend the night. "I don't want to drive my van down that icy mountain road. It's just too dangerous."

George offered, "Stay here until the weather clears. You can help Mrs. Stafford move the furniture around. Buck and I need to discuss finding some ranch hands."

From what I understood, getting ranch hands was not easy. The young men preferred to work in the copper mines in Anaconda where the pay was better. The ranch hands who eventually worked for us were mostly elderly alcoholics. George found them in one of the Melrose bars, sobered them up with black coffee, and brought them back to the ranch. They would work for a week or so and then leave and get drunk again.

One morning, Buck came into the kitchen looking quite ill.

"Buck," I said, "you don't look well. What's the matter?"

"Mrs. Stafford, ma'm, I need to get a shot. Can I take the jeep into Melrose? It won't take long, and I'll be back soon."

"Of course," I replied. "Go ahead. You might be getting the flu."

When George came in some time later and asked where Buck and the jeep were, I told him. "Buck wasn't feeling well," I explained. "He said he needed to get a shot. He's gone to the doctor in Melrose."

"You idiot!" he shouted. "Don't you know what he means by 'a shot'? It's a shot of whiskey or gin, and now he won't be back for at least a week and neither will the jeep." By the time he finished his tirade, his face was red.

Buck did come back, but as George had predicted, it was several days later. I never fell for that story again.

We were running about eight hundred head of white-faced Herefords and with ten bulls; that number would increase with the arrival of the calves.

With six ranch hands who lived in the building at the end of the yard, my chores meant not only feeding them, but also doing their laundry. They had a routine: they changed their underwear once every two weeks. The smell of stale sweat and urine was horrible. With as much dignity as I could muster, I would dump the underwear into the boiler and stir it around with a wooden broom handle. It was an odious chore.

Although George was an excellent cook, I was the one who prepared the meals for the hands. Initially, my cooking chores went unappreciated. One of the first meals I prepared was a large chicken salad. When I placed it on the kitchen table, the hands looked at it curiously and poked at it with little enthusiasm.

Buck explained. "Mrs. Stafford, ma'm, we don't much care for this green stuff. What we would all like is a mess of beans with some biscuits."

I had no idea what a "mess of beans" could be, but with Buck as my *sous chef*, I prepared the unsavory dish. When I was through with the preparation, I thought it looked unappetizing and unhealthy. The ranch hands thought it was delicious.

It was bitterly cold that winter. In spite of stoking up the wood stove every few hours, icy air penetrated into every corner of the house. In order to keep warm, I went to bed at six o'clock in the evening after tucking the children in. I wrapped myself in as many blankets as I could find. George would join me later, and we would huddle together beneath the covers and watch the snow seep through the cracked windowpane.

More often than not, the loud mooing of a cow in the pasture would awaken us. This meant that a calf had been born and was lying out somewhere in the snow. It had to be brought inside as soon as possible so it wouldn't freeze.

George would jump out of bed and call over his shoulder, "Follow me, and bring the blankets." Buck would already be in the kitchen, having carried the calf in from the pasture. We would throw the blankets around it and rub it until it seemed out of danger.

A few weeks after its birth, the calf would be branded. After I saw a branding for first time, I couldn't bear to watch, as each of the new calves would be led, one by one, into a small enclosure. A coal fire burned nearby with the branding iron plunged deep into the fire. Just as the iron became white hot, George took charge and picked up the iron and pressed it against the calf's side. I could smell the burning hair and hear a cry of pain from the young animal.

Once was enough.

"Why do they have to be branded?" I asked. It never occurred to me why this seemingly barbaric action had to be taken.

"To stop them from being stolen by other ranchers," George told me.

I saw many things during that first year on the ranch. I watched as cattle were dehorned and castrated, as well as branded.

Years later, when I was working in Hollywood, I was told that I looked too small and delicate to be cast in any role in a Western. Little did they know what I had seen and done.

Three times, I escaped from ranch life and returned to civilization in New York. The first time was for the Fifth Annual Corporate Communion Breakfast for employees and friends of the *New York Herald Tribune* at the Hotel New Yorker. As the keynote speaker, I observed, "Catholic women in show business have a great responsibility to uphold the dignity of womanhood by the clothes they wear before the television cameras and by their public behavior." I wonder if *anyone* had seen the gowns I wore on *It's News to Me*.

Two months later, I was back in New York, again for a Catholic event; this one was the third annual Mother-Daughter Communion Breakfast, held in the Astor Gallery of the Waldorf-Astoria. Again, I was the keynote speaker.

I was again the keynote speaker at another Catholic-sponsored event. My topic at Fordham University was "Communication for Christ."

Each trip away from the ranch made each return to the ranch more difficult.

I wanted to make the ranch experience as positive as possible for the children. So, Caroline, John, and Stephen each had their own horse.

George, playing the good father, allowed Stephen to drive the jeep. When he was behind the wheel, I was mad with worry. Buck acted as tour guide for the children and took them on outings to the nearby ghost towns. John, especially, liked the history behind the towns.

I enrolled the children in school. Caroline attended Baggerly Junior High, her first coeducational school. In her other schools, she had had to wear a uniform, so she only had a few ordinary school clothes. She had also been taught to stand up when answering a question and had been taught to address the instructor as "Sister" or "Mother." I can't imagine what her first male teacher thought when she called him "Sister" or "Mother" when she stood up to answer a question.

Every morning, I drove her down from the ranch on the rough mountain road in the red Ford pickup to catch the school bus, which would pick her up and drive 35 miles to the school. At the end of the day, I would collect her at the pickup spot. More than once I drove the pickup into a ditch, and George would have to bring a tractor to haul it out. So Caroline often missed the bus to school.

One day, I was in the pickup with John beside me when I saw a car coming up the hill towards us. The road was covered with ice, and, like an idiot, I jammed on the brakes. The pickup skidded to a stop with its front wheels embedded in a pile of rocks.

My left arm hurt, and so did my neck. John had bumped his head against the windshield. No seatbelts then. The car that we hit was intact. After checking to see how we were, the driver went on to the ranch to let

George know what had happened. When he arrived, my husband was more concerned about the damage to the pickup than the injuries we might have had. Fortunately, we weren't seriously hurt, but we were sore for the next few days. John had quite a bump on his head.

I must admit that the country was beautiful. Despite that, I became increasingly depressed over the next several months. I was desperately unhappy. Nothing seemed to break the monotony of our life; I missed the excitement of New York, my friends, and my career.

The only social event that I recall is a Fourth of July picnic when I met our neighbors for the first time. The local ranchers and their families gathered in a small park high up in the summer grazing land. The women were friendly and kind, but their conversation was limited to exchanging recipes for goat's milk custard and corn fritters. They were obviously not concerned with the way they looked. One woman wore blue jeans held together by safety pins where they were torn. I mentioned something about this to George. He laughed and said, "That family is worth almost a million dollars. They don't need to be fashion plates."

How much longer could I go on being a rancher's wife? Whatever happened to those golden days in England and Hollywood and New York? Why did I marry this man? George was entirely different from the person with whom I had fallen in love. We still slept in the same bed, and when we made love, it was often in a rough and often painful way.

Each week, I drove to Butte to shop for groceries. One day, after a particularly unpleasant quarrel with George, I put everything in the pickup and decided to treat myself to a drink in the bar at one of the hotels. I parked outside the largest hotel, locked up the groceries, and went in. At that time in the afternoon, the place was deserted except for a one man sitting at the bar staring into a glass.

He smiled at me as I pulled the stool up to the bar. "Come and sit over here. You look as though you need a friend."

I didn't realize my emotional state showed on my face. I thought I was concealing it. After all, I was an actress.

The light was dim, and it was difficult to see his face. But there was something familiar about him. I couldn't place it. Perhaps he just reminded me of someone I had met long ago in London or New York or Hollywood.

"Let me buy you a drink," he offered and called to the bartender. "Give the lady a vodka and tonic. We don't want to get her drunk too early in the day."

The drink burned as it slid down my throat. It felt deliciously warm. After just one drink, I was relaxing for the first time in... how long?

"Now, tell me the story of your life," said my new friend.

The vodka unleashed my tongue, and before I could control it, I had poured out my heart to this stranger, telling him how unhappy I was.

"I think I can make you feel a little better," he said. "Come upstairs with me. We can talk better there."

"Why not?" I thought as I slipped from the stool and followed him. George had always accused me of sleeping with someone, whether it had been his Army Air Corps pilot friend, or, more recently, Jim, the young truck driver. I had never been unfaithful to him, but now perhaps it was time to change that.

My new friend was not a great lover, but compared with George he was kind and gentle.

"Who are you?" I asked as we lay in bed together. "Have we met before?"

"No names," he admonished. "That would spoil everything. Can I give you some advice?" I nodded. "You must leave this man. He sounds like a bastard, and you will never be able to change him. Take the children. Go back to New York or some place where you can resume your career."

Later that afternoon, we said goodbye. We never did exchange names, but many years later, I saw his picture in a magazine and realized who he was: one of the great movie swashbucklers of all time. But no names!

George was standing outside the ranch house when I drove up. I had hardly turned off the motor when he said, in his usual accusatory manner, "You're late. I suppose the clerk in the grocery store was making love to you."

I ignored him. I felt strangely happy. I knew what I had to do. I only needed validation from someone who would give me an objective opinion. It had been offered—with no strings.

For the next several weeks, I planned my escape. New York, I knew would be very cold. I still had friends in California, though.

George must have sensed something because he was much more solic-itous toward me. "You'll never be able to change him," were words that I kept telling myself.

Then I discovered I was pregnant. Of course, George was pleased... with himself. He insisted that I see a doctor in Butte to make sure every-thing was all right.

The doctor was pleasant enough. At the conclusion of the examina-tion, he opened a desk drawer and handed me a pamphlet entitled, "How to Deliver Your Own Baby." I remember the first line: "Early in your preg-nancy, begin collecting newspapers"!

"Why newspapers?" I asked the doctor.

He explained that the bed linens in some of the ranch homes were so soiled that it was more hygienic to cover them with clean newspapers.

"That finishes it!" I said to myself. "I'm not having my child delivered on *The Butte Bugle* or whatever the name of the local paper is." And I made a pact with myself: "I'm going back to California."

When I made the pronouncement to George, his response was, "I can't come with you. The cows are due to calve in February."

"Well, I'm due to calve in November. So, I'll go alone... and I'm taking the children." In mid–September 1955, I piled Caroline, John, and Stephen into the pickup, and we left.

Goodbye, Montana;
Hello, Hollywood—Again

I was seven months pregnant, and it was very difficult for me to sit behind the wheel of the pickup. It wasn't easy keeping on the right road. I couldn't drive and look at the map. Caroline sat beside me, holding the map and giving me directions. At times we lost our way. At night, we would pull into a motel.

Finally, we arrived! It had been some time since I had been to Los Angeles. Everything had changed. Even the streets seemed different. How was I going to find Beverly Hills or Brentwood or any of the places I had known?

"The ocean will still be in the same place," I told myself. "Find the ocean, and Santa Monica will be there."

We found Santa Monica and took a room at the William Tell Motel, which would be our home for some time.

I began making phone calls the next morning. I was delighted to find so many of my old friends. At least *they* were in the same place. They were equally happy to hear from me. I spoke with Pat Crowley and her mother; Ruth Roberts; and Rita Edelman.

Everyone was so thoughtful, so kind, so giving.

Pat asked where I was going to have the baby. I told her that George had given me $500 to pay for the hospital and lodging to get here. Most of that was gone, so that I would probably have to go to some clinic nearby.

"You'll do nothing of the sort," she said. "My sister is married to one of the doctors on staff at St. John's, not far from where you're staying. He'll find you a good doctor who won't charge more than you can afford."

Meta Sterne, John Ford's secretary, came to see me. She brought an envelope from him. Inside was $500 in cash.

I was astonished at his generosity. "You have to promise," she cautioned, "that you will never thank him for it or tell anyone he gave it to you."

I had always had a somewhat sour feeling about Hollywood and what it can do to friendships. But in that situation, I have never known such loving kindness in all my life. People seemed to sense that I was in trouble, although only a very few knew the truth. People I hardly knew—such as Jan Clayton—sent me things for the baby, the children, and myself.

Rita Edelman, whom I had kept in touch with, was very sensitive to my plight. She came to the motel with bags of groceries and, if I remember correctly, a bicycle for the children.

All this was just what I needed to get back my faith in human nature. I enrolled the children in local schools and began to see what I could do to keep the wolf from the door.

I was obviously too pregnant to work. There weren't any parts for pregnant women at the moment, my agent told me.

Ruth Roberts, now a producer with *The Loretta Young Show*, suggested that I try my hand at writing a script for the show.

"All you have to do is make sure the plot ends with Loretta doing something noble. You know that she is very religious and wants her stories to end on a positive note," she advised.

I rented a typewriter—no computers then—and spent the next few days writing a teleplay for the show. I called it "Far Away Island." Loretta liked it. It went into production with Loretta and John "Legs" Newland and aired much later, in January 26, 1958. I was encouraged by the reception to my first script, and I wrote another for her, which I thought was even better than the first.

It was turned down, as were two others that I submitted.

Beginner's luck, I assumed, until I asked Ruth why I had received the rejections.

"Anna, dear," she said, "it wasn't the scripts. But if I tell you the reason, you must swear not to tell anyone I told you." What she told me was frightening. "The producers of Loretta's show found your name in *Red Channels*, which means you have some association with the Communist Party. I'm sure it's not true, but you're on the blacklist. No one in film or television will hire you."

I was stunned. I couldn't believe she was telling me this. I thought the entire situation had been cleared up before I left New York. It had followed me to California. I was devastated. What was I to do?

At the same time this professional problem re-emerged, I was having problems with Caroline. Although she says she doesn't remember, I recall that she was going through a rebellious teenage stage, doing everything she could to annoy me. Although she spent her days at St. Monica's School, she said she felt cooped up living in one small room, as we all did. I decided I should remove her from this environment and told Ivy Wilson how worried I was about my daughter.

Ivy suggested that Caroline move in with her son, Douglas Crane, who wrote for *The Playgoer*, and his wife, Andrea. This would be, I rationalized to myself, a temporary solution to the problem... at least until the baby was born. Caroline moved in with the Cranes, their children, and their boxer, Abelard.

Ivy was the Hollywood correspondent for the London *Star*. She became a sort of godmother to Caroline and took her everywhere, to premieres and previews, and introduced Caroline to Hollywood glitz and glamour. Caroline liked the Crane home at the top of Mulholland. Unfortunately, some personal misfortune occurred at the Crane home—I was never sure what— and I had to find another place for Caroline.

A friend of the Edelmans, the well-known actor Leo Carrillo, had a ranch near the beach, and his family agreed to look after Caroline. It was not the happy experience she had with the Cranes. The Carrillos had German shepherds who were very territorial and, as Caroline told me, they wouldn't let her out of the bedroom. She was terrified, and I had to find yet another place for her.

Through the Knights of Columbus, I found a place for her in Portuguese Bend, south of Los Angeles, a home where there were horses for her to ride. Again, it was a nightmare for my daughter. The first night there, they left her with a newborn baby.

One of the stories she remembers about this period is about a pair of brown and white saddle shoes.

CAROLINE STEVENSON: For some reason, I didn't have shoelaces for these shoes. I used string to tie them. I remember hearing people whispering, "You'd think that a movie star could get her kid shoelaces."

At another point she lived in Tarzana in the San Fernando Valley with actor Rand Brooks and his wife. Brooks had appeared as Charles Hamilton in *Gone With the Wind*.

It all sounds rather sordid. With all this turmoil, Caroline bore these indignities with grace beyond her years.

CAROLINE STEVENSON: Decades later, I can be objective about this period in my life. I never really held anything against my mother about it. I felt it was just my lot in life and accepted it. There were times when I called my mother and said, "You've got to get me out of here." I think I actually ran away from a couple of the homes, but I didn't run far. Mom would come and get me and hide me out in one of her friend's houses. I decided very early that I would be a survivor and not a victim. I have no regrets. I truly feel that everything in life is a learning experience, and you can either learn the good things or the bad.

Venetia's life was very different. She had been living with her father and was surrounded by the film industry all her young life. Bob often took her with him to the sets of the films he was directing. In the late '40s and early '50s, she remembers being on the sets of *Dishonored Lady*, starring Hedy Lamarr, and *My Forbidden Past*, with Ava Gardner.

I never thought, though, that she would follow in my footsteps and become an actress.

VENETIA STEVENSON: I became an actress almost accidentally. It just sort of happened. I used to hang out at Malibu Beach. Photographer Peter Gowland, who supposedly invented "the California girl" look, started taking pictures of me. Soon I was on the cover of *Esquire* and *Look*. In fact, I was on the cover of a lot of magazines. Somebody saw one of the covers and put me under contract to RKO. When it shut down, I moved to Warners. In 1957, I was voted The Most Photogenic Girl in the World by *Popular Photography Magazine*. On the basis of that, I was invited to appear on *The Ed Sullivan Show* to accept the award. Performing on the show that night were the Everly Brothers. That was my first meeting with Don Everly.

Elvis Presley was part of Venetia's crowd. It was rumored that she was in love with the singing sensation. I was not an admirer of Elvis and would not have approved of the marriage. When Elvis joined the Army in 1957, they lost touch.

VENETIA STEVENSON: When I appeared on *The Ed Sullivan Show*, Elvis phoned and asked me to visit him in Memphis on my way home. I met his mother at that time. She was just the kind of mother I would like to have had: she stayed home and baked cookies. When I told my mother about this, she became very jealous.

I had spoken to George several times since I'd left the ranch. Things were going badly. More than a hundred calves had died, and George was becoming disenchanted with his life as a cattle rancher. It was obvious that this enterprise was not proving to be the great financial or personal success that he had expected.

"I think I'll sell the damn place and move back to California—at least the weather is better there," he told me more than once when we spoke.

As concerned as I was about his coming to California, I was more concerned bout the impending birth of my fifth child.

On the Saturday before I was to give birth, George called. Since the only phone was in Melrose—and it was a party line—our conversation was limited. He managed to tell me that he hadn't been able to sell the ranch and decided to let it go into foreclosure, which meant we lost a lot of money. Or rather, *I* lost a lot of money, as it was my money that had been used to purchase the property. He did sell the cattle, the hay, and the farm machinery, bringing in some badly needed cash. His last words before he hung up were, "I'm coming out to Los Angeles. I'll be there in a few days." I couldn't believe this was happening.

The following Monday, after sending John and Stephen off to school, I planned to check myself into the hospital. They told me as they were leaving, "We'll miss you, Mummie. Be sure to bring back a boy. We don't want any more girls in the family!"

I must have been quite a sight: a very pregnant woman with a suitcase walking along Santa Monica Blvd. toward the hospital.

I was so pleased that Venetia came to be with me, and she took charge of everything. At 17, she was quite the independent young lady.

Although I had been due in early November 1955, the birth didn't happen until the end of the month. The doctor who Ann Crowley's husband referred me to called it a "lazy baby" and seemed to have no desire to be born. I was miserably uncomfortable. The doctor decided that labor would have to be induced.

Finally, in the early hours of November 28, my third son was born, a healthy 7 pounds, 8 ounces. I couldn't have been more thrilled, and neither could his older brothers. Unfortunately, I was having a negative reaction to the spinal block I had been given and was having the most agonizing headaches.

Ever the dutiful wife, I sent a telegram to George in Melrose to tell him about the birth of our son, but he had already left, and no one knew where he was. I finally located his attorney in Bozeman, and he traced him to Las Vegas. There he was, happily gambling away what little money he had made from the sale of the ranch items.

It all sounded like a soap opera. (Little did I know!)

George turned up unexpectedly at the hospital a day or two later. He was quite drunk. When I asked him if he would like to see his son, he said, "Not just yet. All I want to do is sleep," and he threw himself down on the empty bed in my room.

When I offered an excuse to the nurse, she said, "Don't worry, dear. A lot of new fathers get drunk when they're going to see their baby for the

A family portrait of *(left to right)* Caroline, baby Timothy on my lap, me, John, and Stephen. They were all growing up so fast.

first time. I remember one who was so tipsy that he fell down the stairs and broke his leg. He was in the hospital longer than the mother and baby!" She was very thoughtful.

I think I had reached the point then that nothing he could do to me could ever hurt me again. I was still asking myself how I could have been such an idiot to take him back. I thought it out carefully: I did still love him in a strange kind of way, not like I used to but enough to make it worthwhile. In spite of what he might believe himself, I think he still needs me. And he is the father of my three sons.

The second reason I gave myself was one of faith: I had no alternative but to try to make it work. I could not marry again and stay in the Church, and the thought of leaving it was intolerable. I could never have come through this time without my faith. I realized that it was more important to me than George or anything else, except, of course, the children.

My son was baptized Timothy Paul Stafford in St. Monica's Church on New Year's Day 1956. His godparents are Ann Crowley and John Ford.

Because Ann and her husband were unable to attend the ceremony, Pat stood in for them.

I had always loved the name Timothy, and for many years he was known as "Little Timmy." He legally changed his name to Jeffrey Byron when he was 18.

Despite being the father of three wonderful boys, George was still unhappy, especially about having to return to Los Angeles. So we decided to move—again. This time to San Francisco. We found a charming house at 31 Sylvan Drive in the suburb of Stonestown. I loved the area and the house. Caroline, John, and Stephen were able to walk to school, our neighbors were very nice, and George, in another attempt to be a good provider, was working as a salesman at a Cadillac agency.

Although I thought this move would change our lives, it didn't. George and Caroline just did not get along. I knew had I had to again get her away. All the boarding schools I contacted were far too expensive for our budget. The local priest suggested that I send her to St. Joseph's Catholic Orphanage, just a few miles away.

Place my daughter in an orphanage? The word was a dagger in my heart, but what option did I have?

I spoke with the Mother Superior and told her how I hated to think of my daughter being called an "orphan." She said, "My dear Mrs. Stafford, only a very few of the children in our care are actually orphans. A great many of them are here because they have had problems with someone in the family." That assuaged my feelings... somewhat.

I sent Caroline to live at the Mount St. Joseph Roman Catholic Orphan Asylum. Since the asylum—I hate *that* word, too—was only a boarding facility, she enrolled in the day school at the Immaculate Conception Academy.

George essentially wanted me to disown Caroline and not to see her. That wasn't going to happen. I was, however, getting closer to disowning *him*!

Fortunately, I had a wonderful neighbor, Betty Scanlon, who would bring Caroline home when I was certain George was downtown. That way, we could have time together.

One of the brighter events for Caroline during that bleak time was her meeting actor Tab Hunter. Tab was a great horseman and competed in horse shows. Venetia and Tab shared an interest in horses. They also shared an agent, Dick Clayton. One time, Venetia and Tab were in San Francisco for a horse show at the Cow Palace. Tab and Dick came to Caroline's school and asked the sisters if she could accompany them to the show. The nuns agreed, and off she went. For Caroline, it was an afternoon away from the anxiety of her personal life.

In 1958, on the set of *Gideon's Day* with *(left to right)* Jack Hawkins, John Ford, me, Anna Massey, and John Wayne, who was visiting his great friend, "Pappy" Ford.

Horses have played an important role in all our lives, and we have made some of our best and long-lasting friendships because of these wonderful animals.

I loved San Francisco—the flower stalls along the sidewalks, the beaches, the magnificent Golden Gate Bridge, our house. Everything was a delight, except George. Again, he was not happy selling used cars. He heard from a friend in Los Angeles that Casa de Cadillac, a San Fernando Valley Cadillac dealership, needed a salesman.

"As much as I hate the idea of being in Los Angeles again, at least I'd be selling *new* cars instead of the flea-bitten contraptions I have to peddle here," he said.

Back we went to Los Angeles. We found a house on a hilltop in Sherman Oaks. To the delight of the children, it had a pool, and they were soon swimming like fish. Of course, they were enrolled in yet another school.

Now that I was back in L.A., I thought of trying to re-start my career, but I still had the blacklist hanging over my head. I contacted my wonderful friend, John Ford, who took matters into his formidable hands. He had connections in Washington, and without telling me any of the details, he cleared my name. I was able to seek work again. I will always be grateful to him.

It was Mr. Ford who gave me my first job after being removed from the blacklist. He was going to make a film in England, *Gideon of Scotland Yard*, also known as *Gideon's Day*. I was offered the role of Mrs. Gideon, opposite Jack Hawkins, the eminent British actor.

The occasion to work abroad was just what I needed. It would give me some time away from George and time to think. I decided to take the boys.

Tim was only about eighteen months old. On the flight over, he was restless and cranky, and I couldn't get him to sleep, much to the annoyance of the other passengers. A young man in a Royal Air Force uniform was sitting behind us and was aware of my difficulties. He opened a bottle of beer and handed it to me, saying, "Put a few drops of this in his bottle. It usually works like a charm."

It did. Tim slept the rest of the way to London, as did his brothers.

My brother John met us at Heathrow Airport. He and his family were still living in Chelsea, and we stayed with them. How wonderful it was to be with my favorite brother again. The boys, especially Stephen, had an opportunity to visit with their uncle and their grandmother.

STEPHEN STAFFORD: Uncle John, who was Secretary of Agriculture, took me around in his MG. We went to all the farms. I also visited antique shops with my grandmother. She was a lot of fun, a very outgoing, loving person.

On August 10, 1957, *The Star* published an article about my visit and featured a photograph of me with the boys in top hats. I had mentioned in a radio interview that they were eager to see what the hats were like. Within days, listeners sent more opera hats than I could have used in a lifetime.

Although the article mentioned the boys, the reporter failed to mention that I also had two daughters. Caroline, especially, was hurt by the omission.

The visit abroad provided a happy respite. It was wonderful to be working with Pappy again. Jack Hawkins was a delight, and my old friend, John Loder, was also in the cast.

The production took place at Columbia's British studios at Elstree. One day, John Wayne, who was in London, came to our set to visit his great

Mummie comes to say goodbye to us after I complete *Gideon's Day*, with *(left to right)* John, holding his beloved bust of Abraham Lincoln, baby Timothy in my arms, and Stephen.

friend, John Ford. He and I had a few minutes to reminisce about the old days and our films together.

John Loder told me he was having difficulty finding work.

"John, why don't you go back to Hollywood?" I suggested. "There's plenty of work there."

Venetia's wedding to Russ Tamblyn on February 14, 1956, at the Wayfarers Chapel, Portuguese Bend, in Rancho Palos Verdes, south of Los Angeles. (Collection of Venetia Stevenson)

"Anna," he said sadly, "I shall never be able to return to Hollywood. Hedy would be waiting for me, and the moment I step on American soil, she will sue me for money she claims I owe her for back alimony and child support."

Hedy Lamarr had been his third wife and was bitter over their divorce.

Although we had known each other for decades and worked closely in several films, John and I never had a love affair. We remained friends until his death in 1988 at 90. In one of his obituaries, the reporter wrote, "He was once described by ... Anna Lee as 'the most beautiful man I've ever seen.'"

He certainly was one of them.

While I was in London, I did some shopping. I remember buying a Harris tweed jacket for Stephen while we were in London. Decades later, Stephen's son, Ian, wore the same jacket, proving the durability of the fabric. Stephen tells me that it still hangs in a closet in his Ojai home.

As production came to a close, I found myself dreading the return to America for two reasons: I didn't know when I would see my beloved England again, and I wasn't at all sure about my relationship with George. I wept throughout the entire flight across the Atlantic, much to the bewilderment of John and Stephen.

Pappy Ford dried my tears and again came to my rescue by offering me a part in *The Last Hurrah*. His friendship was stronger than ever, and he never once said, "I told you so." When anyone became a member of the Ford stock company, they became family, and he looked after each one.

Although my role was small in the film, what made it all worthwhile was the scene I had with Spencer Tracy. Spencer must have guessed that I was nervous about playing opposite him. He was kind and helpful, and the scene went well. He was by far the best actor with whom I ever worked. He never seemed to be acting. It was so natural.

Several members of the Ford family had roles in the film: Donald Crisp, who had starred in *How Green Was My Valley*; Maureen O'Hara's brother, Charles B. FitzSimons; handsome Jeffrey Hunter, who had starred opposite John Wayne in *The Searchers* the previous year; and a member of Ford's real family, Ken Curtis, who, at the time, was married to Mr. Ford's daughter, Barbara.

Katharine Hepburn, with whom Spencer Tracy had been living for some time, came to visit him on the set. They were devoted to each other, but Mrs. Tracy was a devout Catholic and refused to give Spencer a divorce. Despite the fact that their affair would have made big headlines, the press treated them with respect and never badgered them, as they would today. Years later, I attended Spencer's funeral. Katharine was not there.

Although Venetia was not living with me and had her own life, I was able to keep up with her comings and goings. I knew she had been seeing Clyde Kennedy, one of the finest horse trainers in the country, on a personal and professional level. It was through Tab Hunter that she met him. Hollywood columnists insisted that they were "just friends."

Caroline continued her infatuation with horses and was under the tutelage of Clyde for show competitions. She fell in love with him. *They* became engaged, and just before her seventeenth birthday in 1958, Caroline became Clyde's seventh wife. They were married at our home when we lived in Sherman Oaks. Actor Aldo Ray was best man, and his wife Johanna was matron of honor. Although Clyde was a successful horse trainer, he evidently was not as successful as a husband. The marriage was annulled three months later.

After her breakup with Clyde, Caroline fell in love again, this time with Tim Burant, another horseman, who was about 50 years older than she was. He was known as the "Galloping Grandfather" because of his fame for riding in the Grand National three times, the last when he was 70 years old.

When this relationship dissolved, she leased stables in La Tuna Canyon, horse country in the Los Angeles area, and opened a riding school.

Venetia fell in love with actor Russ Tamblyn. They were married on Valentine's Day 1956 at the Wayfarers Chapel in Portuguese Bend. I didn't remember attending the ceremony, but Venetia showed me photographs in which I appeared. But I can't remember being there. The marriage ended the following year on the same date. By then, Venetia's acting career was well under way, and she appeared in several television series, including *Playhouse 90*, several episodes of *Sugarfoot* with Will Hutchins, and *77 Sunset Strip*.

Several years later at Tab Hunter's house in Burbank, she again met Don Everly. He was now divorced and had had a daughter, whom he named Venetia. Don and she became an "item," and in 1962 they were married. That marriage lasted eight years. They gave me my first grandchildren: Erin, Edan, and Stacy.

Caroline married a second time to Chuck Williams; their daughter, Sarah, carries on in the family tradition by competing in horse jumping shows, many of which I attended all over the country.

Back to Work
with a Vengeance

The year 1959 was a busy time for me—five films in a single year, as well as stage and television roles! My professional life was very fulfilling.

In *This Earth Is Mine*, I play Rock Hudson's mother, despite the fact that I was only twelve years older than he was. As Charlotte Rambeau, an invalid paralyzed from the waist down, I played all my scenes in a beautiful bed with lovely embroidered sheets and pillowcases. (Decades later, I wouldn't have to "play" the role of an invalid. When I became paralyzed, I refused to lie down.) The makeup people had to age me. Besides the lines in my face, Universal's hairdresser, Larry Germain, suggested that I should have silver streaks in my hair.

"Where on earth will I find someone who can do streaks?" I asked. This was many years before every hairdresser could do highlighting.

"There's a hairdresser we use who does a wonderful job," Larry told me. "Nick Cardinale's salon is on Canon Drive in Beverly Hills."

Off I went to have Nick do my streaks. Thus began a friendship that lasted more than forty years. Nick died in March 2003, and now his son, Rico, is my hairdresser.

This Earth Is Mine is about a family who owns a vast vineyard. We shot on location California's famous grape-growing area, the Napa Valley. At the conclusion of the film, the local growers association gave all the principal actors cases of wine.

I enjoyed working with Rock. He was warm and friendly, and when the picture was finished, we went to San Francisco together for publicity. We had a wonderful time riding the cable cars and exploring Chinatown.

1885-39

Although just a dozen years older than Rock Hudson, I played his invalid mother in *This Earth Is Mine* in 1959.

At the time, I had no idea he was gay. It wouldn't have made a bit of difference if I had known. He was a charming man and talented actor.

The film also starred dear Jean Simmons, velvet-voiced Claude Rains, and lovely Dorothy Maguire. I was in good company.

The Horse Soldiers was another John Ford–directed film, also starring John Wayne. His co-star was William Holden. It was the first major film for the beautiful Constance Towers.

CONSTANCE TOWERS: Anna had a heart-to-heart talk with me when we arrived on location in Mississippi. She told me about watching Ford all the time, explaining that when he was setting up a scene, he would go through the action. Later, he'd say to me or another actor, "Show me what you can do in this scene." Of course, if I were paying attention, I already knew what he wanted.

Connie became one of the Ford family, and Pappy became godfather to her children.

Connie told me the story about how she got the part of Hannah Hunter, the Southern belle, who eventually falls in love with the John Wayne character, a Union soldier. Her story is very different from the way I got my first role in a Ford film. It shows the way Ford worked and how he handled his actors.

CONSTANCE TOWERS: My agent at MCA told me to be at the Blessed Sacrament Church in Hollywood one afternoon. I was to sit in a pew in the middle of the church. I was told I would "get a message." I went there, thinking it was the craziest thing I'd ever done. I was the only one in the church. Finally, I heard footsteps, and someone sat down in the pew behind me. I heard the prayer rail being lowered. "Don't turn around," said a voice. "You've got the part." I knew John Ford's voice. I heard him get up. I admit I did kind of turn around just as he was going out the door.

I went home and called my agent and told him, "I got the message, and I'm sure it was Mr. Ford who told me."

"Yes," said my agent, "he wanted to tell you himself."

Mr. Ford really was a character.

Just over two decades later, Connie and I would play adversaries on *General Hospital*, she in the role of Helena Considine, a role created by Elizabeth Taylor, and I as Lila Quartermaine.

From Mississippi, we moved our location to Louisiana. One day, my driver picked me up a half hour late. I was beside myself with worry about arriving late on the set.

When I did arrive, Ford wouldn't listen to my excuses, but bawled me out in front of the unit. Only later did I found out that in the scene I was to play that morning, he wanted me in a frantic state, and he had arranged for the tardy pickup to assure my agitation. He certainly got the performance he wanted. That was the only time I bore the brunt of his scheming in all the times we worked together.

As a memento of the film, John Wayne gave me a coffee mug. On it is written "Anna from Duke. Just say 'Yo.'"

Sam Fuller, the GI who had written the letter to the magazine during World War II, contacted me years later, saying, "When I become a director, I'm not going to have you play those stupid good women you always do. I want you to play a really bad woman."

He gave me that chance in *The Crimson Kimono*, a murder mystery with an interracial overtone. It was one of the few Hollywood films that dealt with Japanese-American racism. Sam wrote, produced, and directed the film, and as a former crime reporter, he was able to include many seedy elements of the job in the film. Only Sam would use the color crimson in the title and then shoot the film in black and white.

As Mac, I play an alcoholic artist who wears a beret and scarf tied jauntily around my neck while I paint and smoke cigars. One day, we were shooting a very long scene in which I had to puff away on a large cigar. I asked Sam, "Why can't I rehearse with cigarettes?"

"No, no." He was adamant. "I want you to get used to these."

"These" were long stogies like Winston Churchill was famous for smoking. I could hear the crew discuss—and probably take bets—about how many puffs it would take until I passed out. I also had to drink whiskey, neat. Any other director would have had the actor drink strong tea. But, no, Sam wanted the real thing.

I became violently ill and was home for three days. I must have been allergic to the combination of whiskey and tobacco.

The critic for *The Hollywood Reporter* wrote, "...Anna Lee is good as the far-out artist...."

Venetia and I made our only two films together that year. Despite some personal problems between us (my conversion to Catholicism did not sit well with her, and my continuing marriage to George strained our relationship), I was thrilled to be able to work in the same movies, even though we didn't share any scenes together in either *The Big Night* or *Jet Over the Atlantic*. At least we shared credits on the films. Unfortunately, neither was a success.

> VENETIA STEVENSON: One thing I remember about *Jet*, which oddly was shot in Mexico City, was that George Raft, one of the other stars of the film, had a major crush on mother. They hung out together after hours.

George was playing some kind of law officer who was taking the Guy Madison character to stand trial. Of course, Madison is not only innocent of the crime with which he charged but he also saves the day.

The original title of the film was going to be *High Over the Atlantic*. Why it was changed, I don't know, especially because the aircraft we were supposed to be on wasn't even a jet; it was a four-motor plane.

In the story, the George Macready character plants a gas bomb on board, and the various passengers try to deal with the problem. A romance springs up between Venetia's character and Brett Halsey, who plays a millionaire.

Late in 1959, I was fortunate enough to work in two Civic Theatre Foundation productions at the Ritz Theatre on Wilshire Boulevard in Los Angeles. The first part was as the Irish charwoman in *The Plow and the Stars* by Sean O'Casey; the second was a role in *The Would-Be Gentleman* by Molière. Because the plays would run back-to-back, I rehearsed the O'Casey play during the day and in the evening, played in the other. It was, to say the least, a challenging and exciting experience. I enjoyed being in front of a live audience; it's very different from film and even live television. As an actor, I get an immediate response from the audience and am able to play off that. Every performance is different. It's invigorating for an actor.

Just before the opening of *The Plough and the Stars*, I received a number of Western Union telegrams from family, friends, and fans.

One particularly touching one came from my youngest daughter: "I'd send you flowers but I am broke. Much love and luck, Caroline."

Over the next few years, there were also television series, including: *Hawaiian Eye, Wagon Train, The Loretta Young Show, The Alfred Hitchcock Hour, Maverick,* and *77 Sunset Strip.*

John Ford was well aware of my family situation. As part of his "reel" family, he arranged for me to appear in as many of his films as possible. I was invited to play a small role in his *Two Rode Together* with James Stewart and Richard Widmark. Many of Ford's company were in Texas for the film: Woody Strode, Olive Carey, Harry Carey, Jr., Henry Brandon, Andy Devine, and Ken Curtis.

I also had an uncredited role in *The Man Who Shot Liberty Valance.*

Ford kept me busy and out of harm's way.

As Mrs. Bates, the nosy neighbor, in *Whatever Happened to Baby Jane?* directed by Robert Aldrich in 1962, I had the opportunity to see two of Hollywood's Golden Era actresses at work... and at each other's throats. I was thrilled that I was going to work with Bette Davis and Joan Crawford at Warner Bros.

There was a role in the film for a young actress to play my daughter. Caroline read for the role and actually got the part and was even sent for costume fittings.

CAROLINE STEVENSON: Robert Aldrich called me himself and said, "I'm sure you've heard the term 'pulling a Hollywood.'" There was an embarrassing pause on his end of the line. "Well, I hate to tell you, but I have to pull a Hollywood. We would love you to be in the film, but Bette got wind of the part, and she wants her daughter to play it." So B.D. Merrill plays Liza Bates.

B.D. was the daughter of Bette's third husband, William Grant Sherry, but Gary Merrill, Bette's fourth husband, had adopted her. When B.D. was older, she changed her name back to that of her biological father.

Bette's dressing room was to the left of mine, Joan's to the right. Obviously, the production team knew better than to put them next to each other. I got all the vibes from both, and there were plenty. Bette used to swear like a trooper and always said what she thought. Joan was always genteel and elegant and always had an entourage with her.

Bette was by far the better actress, and I liked her much more as a person. I always knew where I stood with her. She would tell you straight to your face. I never felt I could believe what Joan said.

It was fascinating playing with them because everyone on the set knew how much they hated each other. They tried to conceal it as much as possible, though.

On my first day on the set, my scene was with Bette. I was very, very nervous. In the scene, I take flowers to her to give to Joan, who plays her crippled sister. It was about a two-and-a-half minute scene. After it was over, I was anxious to know how she felt about my performance.

The director came up to me afterwards and told me, "You've got it made. Bette said to me, 'Thank God you've got a pro in Anna Lee.'" That was an award itself. I was proud to be called a "pro" by Bette Davis.

One day I brought Stephen and John to the set. I introduced them to Joan, who asked, "Would you boys like something to drink?"

Stephen said, "Yes, I would like a Coke."

"Oh," she replied rather annoyed, "there is no such thing. There is only *Pepsi*-Cola!" At the time she was married to her fifth husband, Alfred Steele, who was CEO of Pepsi. Stephen settled for a Pepsi, which he took from the cooler Joan kept outside her dressing room.

Now seven years old, my son Timmy expressed an interest in acting. We made our first movie together in 1962. Entitled *Bearheart of the Great Northwest*, also known as *Legend of the Northwest*, it was written, produced, and directed by Rand Brooks. The film about a boy and his dog not only cost Rand his personal fortune, but also probably brought about the end of his first marriage to Lois Laurel, daughter of Stan Laurel. Creditors prevented the film from being released until some fifteen years later.

Just as there had been a Ford in my future, there was a Ford in Tim's future. Pappy Ford asked me to bring Tim to Paramount. He wanted to consider him for a role in *Donovan's Reef*, a film he was going to direct in Kauai with John Wayne and Lee Marvin.

Ford looked Tim up and down and said, "Yeah, but we'll have to do some makeup tests." Tim was going to play Luki, who is half Hawaiian. He eventually had to have his hair dyed and wear dark makeup.

Because I was in the midst of shooting *Baby Jane*, I couldn't accompany Tim to the islands. I decided to send John and Stephen with him for moral support. Ford would be their temporary guardian.

TIM STAFFORD/JEFFREY BYRON: From the moment I arrived in Hawaii, I was homesick. I transferred that feeling into a crush on Elizabeth Allen, who was playing the love interest in the movie. In one scene with Elizabeth and Cesar Romero, I was placed between them in a jeep. They were both dressed in white. Just as the jeep started to move and the camera was rolling, I knew I was going to vomit. Whether it was sunstroke or something I'd had for lunch, I don't know. I looked at Elizabeth and thought, "I love her too much; I can't throw up on her." So I turned and threw up all over Cesar.

Pappy Ford, the sternest, toughest son-of-a-gun anyone ever worked with, broke out in hysterical laughter. "Cut. That's it for the day," he called. I was rushed off to the hospital. Ford came to visit me and said he was one of the great joys of his filmmaking career to see me throw up on Cesar. Elegant Cesar, however, was not amused, but forgave me, eventually. In fact, Cesar became a great friend of the family.

When Tim returned home, he confided his love of Elizabeth Allen to me. I arranged a "date," and Elizabeth took him miniature golfing.

Tim was a successful child actor for several years. By the time he was in his early teens and attending St. Cyril's in Sherman Oaks, he decided he wanted to be a "normal kid." He was interested in sports and wanted to attend school on a regular basis. He came to me one day and very bluntly told me, "Mom, I don't want to do this any more." I didn't object.

My two older boys were enrolled in the prestigious Chaminade College Preparatory School in Canoga Park.

With three boys in private school and a husband who wasn't contributing much to the family's finances, I was having difficulty making ends meet. I arranged for Tim to live at a friend's home. His surrogate godmother, Patricia Barry, had a sister, Priscilla. She and her husband Lloyd Dunn lived in Encino near Portola Junior High, and Tim lived with them for two years.

My next co-star was quite different from Bette and Joan. The old saying that actors should never play opposite children or animals came true for me in *Jack the Giant Killer* in 1962.

As the villain Lady Constance, I have a scene with a raven, which looked simple on paper. But when the trainer arrived on the set with the bird and I saw him wearing a thick glove on which the bird was perched, I began to have second thoughts. Then there were those scratches on the trainer's face. He assured me that the bird was perfectly trained.

In the scene, the bird is perched on my wrist. I carry it to a window where it flies off. We were ready for the first take. As the camera began to roll, the bird pounced on the stone in the ring I wear as part of my costume and pulled it from its setting!

Take two: the bird is again on my wrist, and I am looking at the actor with whom I am playing the scene. The bird obviously hadn't read the script. Instead of flying out the window, it flapped its wings, flew at my face, and bit my lip. Blood was everywhere. The crew was in turmoil.

I was rushed to the hospital and given a tetanus shot.

We finally did get the shot, but I wouldn't want to co-star with a raven again. Never more!

This film followed director Nathan Juran's far superior *Seventh Voyage of Sinbad*, with some of the same actors. But the special effects in *Jack*, although credited to the great Jim Danforth, were not up to the quality of the previous film. Juran had been one of the art directors on *How Green Was My Valley* and had moved into directing.

George still couldn't settle into a permanent job. He now had the notion that he would like to open a restaurant. We bought property in the San Fernando Valley and built a restaurant, using my earnings once again. At the time, the corner of Vanowen and Platt was in the middle of farms and ranches.

I accepted it as another challenge and actually enjoyed designing and decorating the interior. George was going to cook.

STEPHEN STAFFORD: My mother picked out the tables and chairs and had a friend paint a mural. Mother also had a lot to do with the menu. George was more the kitchen guy. I remember him as a fantastic cook. The restaurant was on the order of a diner. His specialty was something called "broasted chicken." I was one of the busboys and worked the cash register.

The *Valley News and Green Sheet* (now the *Daily News*) restaurant reviewer Larry Lipson wrote about us in his "Valley Ramblings" column.

...A few weeks ago Anna Lee and her husband George Stafford, wondering how green the Valley really is, opened what they call a "refreshingly different restaurant" in Canoga Park.

The Valley Pantry is predominantly a self-service operation with lush green vines and a splashing fountain setting off an Italian courtyard.

The restaurant is already prospering and has a still small but very devoted clientele ... from as far away as Beverly Hills and Santa Monica ... for take-home food!...

"It's strictly a family project," Anna said. "My husband is owner-manager and also cooks when we're rushed. I take all the telephone orders and do the bookkeeping. The boys [help out] when they're not in school."

The restaurant kept George's interest for about two years. Then he wanted to do something else.

Not long after the closing of the restaurant, George and I separated. One night, when we weren't living together—he had moved into an apartment—he called me very late. "I'm coming over," he announced. I asked him not to as I had an early call. He said, "You're not going to work any more because I'm coming over to kill you."

I frantically phoned a friend who called him and managed to quiet everything down. He never did come over. He wasn't drunk then, just nasty.

How did I manage with the children, a career, and this man?

There was a time when he actually did get his fingers around my throat and left marks. When I got to the studio the following day, the makeup girl gasped, "What have you done to yourself?"

"Oh," I said, laughing it off, "it's just my husband."

Fortunately, one of the loveliest films with which I was ever associated, *The Sound of Music* took my mind off my problems. William Wyler was originally set to direct, but whether it was studio politics or scheduling, the film was re-assigned to

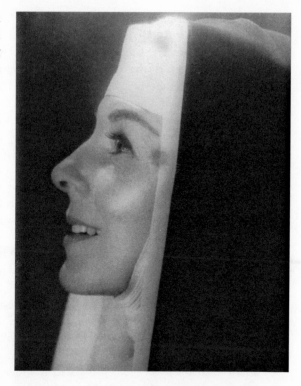

My role as Sister Margaretta, "the nice nun," in *The Sound of Music* is remembered fondly by many of my fans. It was one of three times I played a nun.

Robert Wise. He had edited *Citizen Kane*; directed the famous science fiction film, *The Day the Earth Stood Still*; and had also directed the Academy Award-winning *West Side Story*.

My agent suggested that I might like to play the baroness. When I talked with Mr. Wise, he told me that role had already been cast. But he asked, "How would you like to play a nun?"

I had played nuns before on stage and television, and I told him I'd come from a long line of nuns. I'm very glad I was able to play Sister Margaretta, the nun who says about Maria (Julie Andrews), "She makes me laugh."

George was not happy about my going abroad to work. But that didn't prevent me from having a glorious experience. I stayed at the Hotel Bristol, along with many of the other cast members.

In an opening scene, several of us nuns sing, "How Do You Solve a

Problem Like Maria?" I finally got to sing a Rodgers and Hammerstein song and even a few solo bars.

The only scene I had directly with Julie Andrews is the one where she is called in front of the Mother Abbess (Peggy Wood), and I say, "You may go in now, Maria."

Salzburg was a heavenly city. Peggy and I had a wonderful time seeing the sights, walking and walking and walking. We visited all the churches and went to so many concerts.

The film premiered at the Rivoli in New York on March 2, 1965. The Los Angeles premiere was held on March 10 at the Fox Wilshire Theatre on Wilshire Boulevard, near La Cienega. The stars of the film, Julie Andrews and Christopher Plummer, attended. And so did many other actors: Doris Day, Agnes Moorehead, Hugh O'Brian, Gregory Peck, Robert Stack, Cesar Romero, James Coburn... and my former son-in-law Russ Tamblyn. It was such an important event that the ceremonies were broadcast on local television.

Although my role as Sister Margaretta was small, many fans remember it fondly.

The film won five Academy Awards: Best Picture, Best Director, Best Adaptation Scoring, Best Editing, and Best Sound. Julie Andrews was nominated as Best Actress but lost to Julie Christie in Darling.

After such a happy time, I reached a point in my life where I decided I had to divorce George. I just hated the idea of divorce. I'd been through it before. But I couldn't bear George's abuse any longer. I think my decision was made when, just before Christmas, John and Stephen came to me. "Do you know what we want for Christmas?" they asked.

"No, darlings. What do you want?"

"We want you to divorce our father." I think they saw how he had been treating me for a long time.

The papers were filed, and it was a matter of waiting. When I went to court for the final decree in 1964, Caroline came with me. The judge ordered George to pay me the ridiculous sum of $10 a month. For a long time after that, he would stall and stall about the alimony. I'd have to go and pick up the check from him.

But it was finally over. I could get on with my life.

Just after my divorce, my old friend Ronnie Neame came to Hollywood. He was staying at the Sunset Towers. Because George was stalking me when I visited Ronnie, I wore a disguise, a red wig and dark glasses, parked my car on a side street, and dashed into the hotel. It was comforting to have him as a friend during this difficult time. When Ronnie married his second wife in Santa Barbara, I was a tiny bit jealous because he and I had spent a weekend there.

Roles on television series kept me moderately solvent. I took everything I could, from *McHale's Navy* to *Dr. Kildare*, from *Bob Hope Presents the Chrysler Theatre* to *Combat*.

I even made a commercial for Listerine. We shot it on location at Caroline's La Tuna Canyon horse ranch and used her horse, Boomer, a lovely chestnut with white legs and face.

I was outfitted in a full riding habit as Lady So-and-So. The regalia, rented from Western Costume Company, included a frock coat, breeches, and top hat... but someone forgot to hire boots for me.

Fortunately, Caroline said I could borrow hers. The only problem was that my daughter is much taller than I, her legs are longer, and her feet are larger. When I put on the boots, they came up over my knees. I couldn't walk in them or bend my knees to get on the horse.

The crew tried to get me up by using a ladder. That didn't work. Caroline came over to give me a "leg up," like they do for racehorse riders. With the extra push and with my legs unable to bend, I belly flopped over the saddle and hung upside down, false eyelashes, chignon, hat, everything askew. I was like a board with these boots on.

By the time everyone got me upright, one of the eyelashes was half way down my cheek, and my makeup was running.

Caroline, the crew, and I were in hysterics.

Finally, the crew built a stairway of apple boxes, and I was hoisted onto the horse. Caroline had to crouch down out of camera range and keep the horse standing perfectly still. We couldn't even look at each other because we'd start laughing.

As a reminder of the day, Caroline renamed the horse "Listerine."

Over the years, we've shared a lot of laughs remembering that day.

22

A New Life,
Personally and Professionally

My beloved mother died on December 24, 1966. For the last few years, she had been living in a nursing home in Tunbridge Wells. The last time I saw her, just the year before, I remember her saying, "Look, Joan, there goes your father in his canonicals. He must be going to the new church." She was convinced she saw him. She is buried next to my father at his church.

Financial problems made it impossible for me to return to England for her funeral; I was devastated at not being there. It was comforting to know that John and Ruth took care of all the arrangements.

Late in 1964, *The Hollywood Reporter* noted that I had been signed for a co-starring role in John Ford's next production, *The Chinese Finale*. He was set to begin production at MGM early in 1965. Production didn't begin until much later, and the film title was changed to *7 Women* when it was released in 1966.

Patricia Neal had been set to star, but when she suffered a stroke just a few days into filming, Anne Bancroft replaced her.

Most people say that Ford was a man's director. On this film he had seven women and one man, Eddie Albert. Everyone said Ford was going to be a brute, but he was charming and polite to all of us. He knew we were all professionals, and we wouldn't give him any problems. He wasn't polite to Eddie, however. There was always a whipping boy on a Ford movie, and in this case it was Eddie.

In response to a fan's letter about *7 Women*, Ford wrote:

...*7 Women* is *my* favorite picture directorially. The Commie critics treated it harshly but abroad it is highly successful. I am afraid American audiences want sex, more sex, and sex mixed with violence. That is not my métier. I prefer Americana.

The film did not receive the best of reviews. It may not have been one of Pappy's best, but it was a strong film.

My boys were growing up so fast. I tried my best to attend school functions, sports games, and other family-oriented events. Sometimes work interfered, though.

On June 11, 1967, John graduated from Chaminade. Stephen would graduate the following year. Tim transferred from Notre Dame High School to Chaminade and graduated two years later. It didn't seem possible that all my children were now out of school.

When he first transferred to Chaminade in the tenth grade, Tim boarded there. Because of his interest in sports, he became very attached to one of his coaches. One day, Tim came to me and told us how unhappy he was as a boarder. "Would you consider paying Coach Orlando and his wife Claudette for me to live with them?" he asked. He evidently had worked this all out in advance. I agreed. For the next three years he lived in Reseda with them and came home on weekends. To this day, Craig Orlando is one of Tim's best friends, and they talk on the phone almost every day.

Patricia Barry and her husband, producer Philip Barry, Jr., came into my life in the early '60s. Their daughter's nanny was a friend of Roddy McDowall's mother. Patricia and I became great friends. She and Philip bought the former Charlie Chaplin home on Beverly Drive at Carmelita in Beverly Hills.

Patricia is probably best known for her role as Adelaide "Addie" Horton Williams on the daytime drama, *Days of Our Lives*. She also later appeared on *All My Children*, *As the World Turns*, and *The Guiding Light*. She would, unbeknownst to me at the time, play an important role in my professional life.

Sometime in 1966, I played in *Picture Mommy Dead*, which was originally titled *Color Me Dead*. I have no memory of the film at all. The reviews ran the gamut from "wretched thriller" (*Los Angeles Times*) to "first rate psychological shocker" (*Los Angeles Herald-Examiner*).

In another example of "pulling a Hollywood," the director cast his own daughter in the lead. The whole film is probably best forgotten.

In 1967, I was signed to appear in *In Like Flint*, a follow-up to the previous, and successful, *Our Man Flint*. They were both send-ups of the James Bond films with James Coburn as the Bond-like character.

Just before I was to leave for location in Jamaica, I was in a bad car accident. Jeffrey was in the car, but didn't suffer any serious injuries. I had stitches in my thigh, cracked ribs, a broken wrist, which also needed stitches, and whiplash. I explained to the emergency room doctor that I couldn't possibly be admitted as I was due to leave for location in days. He told me that if I could walk down the hospital corridor without assistance, he would *consider* discharging me. Two days later, I gritted my teeth and walked the length of the hall.

By the time I boarded the plane, I was under the influence of pain-killers. I had a few cocktails en route; when I landed, I wasn't feeling much pain.

The only person who discovered my plight was the wardrobe lady. I swore her to secrecy.

Several days into filming, I found I couldn't move my right hand very well. I couldn't even turn a doorknob. I also knew that I had to have the stitches removed; otherwise, according to the doctor, I would be in serious danger of gangrene. I bore all the pain until I knew they had too much footage in the can to replace me. Then I had a doctor on location look after me.

With my second unsuccessful marriage over, I had no thoughts of another one. I was, after all, 55 years old. But one never knows what's in the future.

Money was still a problem, and I was working two jobs—besides the acting ones. I was a hostess at a restaurant where I saw many of my indus-try peers, and I was a salesperson at David Orgell's, the silver shop in Bev-erly Hills. I made a combined salary of about $85 a week.

PATRICIA BARRY: Anna was having financial difficulties. She was working at Orgell's, so whenever I needed anything, I'd go there to give her busi-ness. She was *the* greatest salesperson. Even now, I can see her behind the counter and hear her say, "This is just the perfect thing...." She knew a lot of people who came into the store, and she carried it off like she owned the place. David wanted her to feel like she was the hostess. She had the bearing and the appearance and that British accent. At the end of the day, she'd come to my house. One time, I was painting the interior, and she'd leap up on the ladder and get to work. The molding in the breakfast room is her "artwork." It's still there today. She was a real pro. Then she'd change her clothes and go off to her job as hostess at the restaurant.

Besides working at Orgell's and the restaurant six days a week, I also was selling Christmas cards from home, just to make additional money.

In December 1969, I attended a party that John and Mary Ford hosted for their daughter. A gentleman approached me from across the crowded room. He introduced himself. We strolled to the buffet, and then wandered into Ford's den where we sat and talked and talked and talked. We found out that we were born on the same day, January 2. Kismet! We were both born under the sign of Capricorn.

When the Fords were closing up the house for the night, they found us still talking at 2 a.m.

The gentleman was Robert Nathan, whom I knew as the poet and novelist. After all, I had known about his poem "Dunkirk: A Ballad" during the war and was very moved by it then. Even though I had read his poetry, I had never read any of his books, even his two most famous, *Portrait of Jennie* and *The Bishop's Wife*, which had both been made into successful films.

He told me that he liked *The Bishop's Wife*, which had been made in 1947. Although he hadn't written the screenplay, he had had made significant contributions to it. Originally, David Niven was cast as the bishop, and Cary Grant was to have been the angel. Robert approved of the reversal of roles.

He wasn't as pleased with the version of *Jennie* in 1948. He felt that producer David O. Selznick had skewed it away from the original tone.

Robert told me he only knew of me through, of all things, my Listerine commercial.

His background was very impressive: schooled at Phillips Exeter Academy, then Harvard, class of 1916, where he studied law, not literature. He was a fine pianist and sang German *lieder*. He was known for arriving at friends' homes in a beret and cape.

Robert had been married six times. He was a great romantic and thought if he kissed a girl, he had to marry her.

Our first date was a Seder at Jean and Irving Stone's, his great friends. Robert was a non-practicing Jew. In fact, he said he didn't even know what to do. We followed along in the Haggadah, drank many glasses of wine, and generally had a wonderful evening.

By December 1969, we were engaged. I was still living at 15063 Del Gado Drive, Sherman Oaks. I wrote to Ruth and her husband to tell them the news.

Dear Ruth and Peter,
   Christmas came rather late for us this year but it was the happiest one I have spent since I can remember!... [I have some] startling news... I am marrying Robert Nathan: writer, poet, musician, bon vivant, etc., etc. I am very much in love with him and wildly and deliriously happy! It all happened so fast that I am still in shock and have great difficulty in believing it all really happened...
   Anyway, it was spontaneous combustion for both of us even though he is 20 years older than I am. It doesn't seem to make any difference, and I am madly in love with him. I hope you have read at least one of his books: *Portrait of Jennie* or *The Bishop's Wife* because then you will understand why I love him. I'm mailing you a copy of his poem *Dunkirk* which I think you will like...

John Ford walks me down "the aisle" for my marriage to Robert Nathan, April 5, 1970.

Anyway, I shall keep you informed and the lovely part is that I shall actually see you this spring or summer.

I am no longer working at Orgell's as Robert insisted that I leave... Now I have a "job" doing "research" for his next book...

With much love to you all,

Joan

Everyone on the other side of the Atlantic still calls me Joan.

On April 5, 1970, I became the seventh Mrs. Robert Nathan. John Ford gave me away. Robert assured me that his previous marriages were just bad rehearsals! We honeymooned in Santa Barbara.

Our life together was going to be far different from my previous marriages. I was very happy.

Robert hadn't been to England since 1928, so we decided to make a visit as part of our honeymoon. By the middle of May, we were in England. We stayed with Ruth and Peter in Sevenoaks.

When we returned, we decided to sell my house in Sherman Oaks and make our home in Robert's house, a lovely cottage built in 1936, on Doheny Drive, just off the Sunset Strip.

Although there was a bit of television work—*Mission: Impossible, The Bold Ones: The Senator*—the phone wasn't ringing with acting offers so I put my career aside again while I established my new home.

My character voices paid a few bills in 1972 when I took part in *The ABC Saturday Superstar Movie*, "Oliver and the Artful Dodger." It was a two-parter in which I played several characters.

Roles came in dribs and drabs: On *The Streets of San Francisco*, I play Mrs. Claridge in an episode titled, "Deadline." The show, which starred Karl Malden and Michael Douglas, featured a number of my former and future acting compatriots: Pat Crowley from *A Date with Judy*, and Leslie Charleson and Anthony Geary, who would become part of *General Hospital* in a few years. I made a Movie of the Week, *My Darling Daughters' Anniversary* with Robert Young, Ruth Hussey, and Raymond Massey, and I appeared on an episode of *The FBI*.

We had a full house at the end of February that year, with John home from his various travels, and Andrew, Peter and Ruth's youngest son.

On April 8, 1973, Robert was honored with a tribute by the Los Angeles Library Association at the Century Plaza Hotel. Among the distinguished writers who attended the event were Irving Stone, Irving Wallace, Leonard Wibberley, Ariel and Will Durant, and Jack Smith. Joseph Cotten, Anne Baxter, and I, read from Robert's novels and sonnets.

In his acceptance speech, Robert said,

> If this were an Oscar ... I'd thank my producers, Mr. and Mrs. Harold Nathan, and my wonderful director, Anna Lee... [I remember teaching] Stephen Vincent Benet fencing in the basement of a little apartment I had in an old brownstone house near Madison Avenue. I used to give parties there—we all gave parties because it was Prohibition, and one drank whatever and wherever one could. You'd expect me to have a lot of memories ... of Dos Passos, of e.e. cummings, of Scott Fitzgerald ...

George S. Kaufman and Dorothy Parker ... but memory is a queer thing. And the only things I can remember anybody saying to me were "Hello!" and "Which way to the bathroom?"

...I've thought a lot about [art]; and I've come to believe that art is a communication informing man of his own dignity, and of the value of his life, whether in joy or grief, whether in laughter or indignation, beauty or terror... Man needs the comfort of his own dignity. And that's what the artist is for. To give him that comfort...

President Richard Nixon sent a tribute, as did Senator Alan Cranston.

I heard that John Ford was seriously ill, and I wanted to visit him. I drove to his home in Palm Desert on August 29, 1973. His first words to me were, "Anna, we're going to make another picture. I'm going to do the story of James Dolittle, and you're to play his wife." His next project was always on his mind.

Although his sarcasm and vindictiveness were legendary, only on *The Horse Soldiers* did he ever do anything to me. I had forgiven him, of course. It was all about the scene.

He told me once, "I can always spot a trouper a mile off. As long as you know your lines and where to stand and don't fool around, we'll get along." We always did. My association with Mr. Ford had been a long and happy one. He was all that a great friend should be: loyal, loving, and lasting. John Ford died just two days after I saw him.

When he turned 18, Tim decided to change his name because, as he told me, he had become "disconnected" from his father.

TIMOTHY STAFFORD/JEFFREY BYRON: When my brother Stephen and I were both trying to get jobs as actors, agents would confuse the two of us, even though there was an age difference. I'd be sent on his audition; he'd be sent on mine. Robert had come up with a pet name for me: Lord Byron. It meant a lot to me that it came from him. I thought it would make a good last name.

Very typical of Mom, she had gone to a numerologist who had given her different names to choose from. One of them was Jeffrey, allegedly a name she had wanted to call me when I was born because she was a friend of actor Jeffrey Hunter. I legally changed my name to Jeffrey Byron.

But there was another reason.

Years before, with Tim's movie earnings, George and I had bought property in my son's name. Because he was a minor, we put the property in George's name. The property was his college fund. Some time after our divorce, I received a notice that the property had been sold because of failure to pay taxes on it. Whether George did this on purpose or just forgot, we'll never know. I think this may have been the "disconnect" between Jeffrey and his father.

Robert would be celebrating his 80th birthday on January 2, 1974. I wanted to do something for this important milestone, something other than just a big party.

He wrote to Ruth insisting he didn't want anything special.

> I [am begging] Anna not to hire a dance band or to set off a train of fireworks.... And finally, I had to put my foot down very firmly on a salute of 21 cannon. I am being honored by the city again, another plaque, this time from the mayor. I intend to be buried like a Crusader with the plaques covering the sepulcher, with my crossed feet resting on my poodle or possibly a hot water bottle....

I was driving along Sunset Blvd. when the idea came to me: there were billboards proclaiming the attributes of the latest rock star or promoting a radio station or new film. If a rock star could appear on a billboard, why not Robert whose writings had brought happiness to lives of so many people?

There was a billboard on the corner of Sunset and Doheny (in fact, it's still there), and I found out that it would cost several hundred dollars for just one day. So I started writing to all our friends as well as Robert's publisher, Alfred Knopf, explaining that instead of the usual birthday card, could they make a contribution to pay for this giant card. Of course, I cautioned secrecy and asked them to mail their contribution to John D. Weaver, a writer and friend of ours.

The response was overwhelming. More than one hundred people contributed, including Joan Crawford, Greer Garson, Ingrid Bergman, Richard Chamberlain, and Lotte Lehmann.

The billboard would read: "Happy Birthday, Robert Nathan," followed by the names of the people who sent greetings. The picture of Robert by Honor Earl would complete the billboard.

On January 2, we were scheduled to be at City Hall in the early morning for Robert to receive a citation from Mayor Tom Bradley. As we headed East on Sunset, I furtively looked up at the billboard. It was blank. I prayed all the way to downtown that the "card" would be there on our return. After the ceremony, we lunched at Scandia. I drove slowly up Sunset to Doheny and looked up.

There it was! I pulled the car to the curb and asked Robert, "Darling, would you get out and see if there is something wrong with the right rear wheel?"

Mystified, he did as he was asked. "No, nothing is amiss," he said,

"Now, darling," I said, "look up there, above the liquor store."

Robert's expressions were unbelievable: astonishment, shock, horror, then finally, amusement and joy.

My favorite photograph with my erudite husband Robert Nathan.

The news services had been tipped off and came running with their cameras.

That evening, we had an enormous party at the home of our dear friends, Patricia and Philip Barry, Jr. It was only when the birthday cake was wheeled in inscribed, "Happy Birthday, Robert and Anna," that I suddenly realized that it was my birthday too, my 61st.

Jobs were still scarce, whether they were in films, television, or theatre.

But in 1975, I had the opportunity to appear on stage, an opportunity I couldn't turn down. I was offered the second lead in *The Opening of a Door*, an adaptation Jerome Chodorov wrote of his famous play *Kind Lady*, which would run at the Westwood Playhouse, now the Geffen. Cathleen Nesbitt, my old friend from *The Passing of the Third Floor Back*, was the star. She was 87 at the time. We shared a dressing room, and while we were putting on our makeup or dressing, she would tell me about her romance with poet Rupert Brooke. She was terribly crippled with arthritis then, but once she was on stage, no one ever knew. She moved so beautifully.

Probably the television work that I'm most proud of is *Eleanor and Franklin* in 1976, and then the following year, *Eleanor and Franklin: The White House Years*. I play Laura Delano. Every aspect of these television movies is impeccable. Every actor, from stars Edward Herrmann and Jane Alexander, to supporting actors Lilia Skala and Irene Tedrow, contribute to the authenticity and dramatic story.

My oldest son John joined the Navy in 1968 and served for four years, perhaps trying to emulate his godfather, John Ford. He was stationed aboard the USS *White Plains*, a support ship off Vietnam. He thought that this structured environment would help him find his way. As usual, he wrote letters to me, explaining that he wasn't comfortable in the service but would finish his stint.

JEFFREY BYRON: There is a story that John rose to the rank of Chief Petty Officer faster than anyone had ever done to that time. For whatever reason, he never got off the ship he was assigned to. But here he was, finally going to accomplish something, but he threw it all away when he got in to a skirmish with a subordinate and was demoted. We were never able to substantiate the story, but he did receive an honorable discharge.

Just a year later, 1969, Stephen joined the Marine Corps, but was never sent overseas. After he was discharged, he continued working as an actor and trying to get into the cameraman's union.

JEFFREY BYRON: John turned to Stephen, who had broken into the camera side of the movie industry and worked at a camera rental facility. The whole reason for anyone working at this place was so they could go out with the cameras as an assistant; each day they were out would count toward days required for union membership.

Stephen was able to get John a job there. John really took over, totally reorganized the place and was working his way up. John was there for some time and had only three or four days left to be eligible for his union card. But he sabotaged that effort.

It seems that he was asked to do an errand and buy something for the staff. He was told to take some money from petty cash, but over the previous few weeks, there hadn't been any cash and he had been paying for everything himself. Of course, at some point he would have submitted the receipts and been reimbursed. But, no, John allegedly blew up at the owner's wife. He was fired.

Caroline was busy with her horses, and Venetia was designing and manufacturing a line of children's clothes. Jeffrey, who had returned to acting, was in Dallas shooting *Seniors* with Dennis Quaid.

At the end of 1976, John was in Canada, working at a hotel in Campbell River, British Columbia. He said he was hoping to get a job in one of the lumber mills where the pay was better and that he would be leaving for England later in the year.

I wrote to Ruth.

[John] plans to travel around on his moped buying up small antiques which he can then sell when he returns to Canada. He's planning to spend Christmas in a hotel—alone! He wrote me that he does not want to "inflict" himself on any of my family because he feels he would be "in the way"! Of course, this is nonsense. If you have room for him, would you be a darling and invite him for Christmas? ...I can't bear to think of him spending it all alone in some seedy hotel. But he will only come if he is "invited," so would you be an angel and write him a note?
Your loving sister,
Joan

My son was a lost soul. On occasion, he would come home to Doheny Drive, stay with Robert and me for several weeks, and then be off again to heaven knows where. He was very good about writing letters. I kept them all. Unfortunately, they were all destroyed in a fire years later.

Robert was writing every day in his little study. I had to find something to occupy me in between acting assignments. Being a staunch Maid of Kent, even after all these years, I thought I would like to do something to support the National Trust in some way, especially because of my brother's association with the group.

Much of 1976 was taken up with organizing The Royal Oak Foundation of California. Our first meeting was at our home on June 2, 1976. I was named Chairman of the Board/Assistant Secretary. We scheduled our first event as a fundraiser on May 6, 1977, to save the White Cliffs of Dover. This iconic symbol of England was being threatened with what is euphemistically called "development." Hotels, theme parks, and vacation homes were planned for the area but would destroy this historic site.

The program featured a number of articles, including "A Dissenting View," by Norman Corwin. He wrote a humorous piece in the guise of a fictional developer about why not to save the White Cliffs, including such arguments as: "...When you see one white cliff, [you've seen] them all..." and '[There are proposals to erect] fine, well-built condominiums and high-rise apartments ... which would have such fitting names as Channel-Vue Arms, Shangri-Dover, and Cliffside Park Towers."

My old friend Charles Bennett contributed "Those White Cliffs...," in which he recalls his love of the area. I asked Robert to compose a special poem for the occasion. He graciously agreed. The result was:

The White Cliffs

Here, from these cliffs that face upon the sea,
They watched the Roman galleys, many-tiered,
Sweep through the pages of their history,
Where once the sails of Tyre had appeared
Low in the west a thousand years before.
Later, the dragon ships. And from these heights
They saw the Spaniard pass and heard the roar
Of distant cannonades on bygone nights.
You shining cliffs of Dover, rising bare
Against invasion and world of foes,
Indomitable in the English air,
Fortress and keep of kings—as daylight goes,
Stand yet awhile, invincible and white,
Against the gathered armies of the night.

Mel Torme, a kind and generous talent, was a great supporter of our efforts, and entertained the guests, along with Shani Wallis. Toasts were made by Tom Aston, British Consul General in Los Angeles, and then-Mayor Tom Bradley. This was followed by an auction, a raffle, and a screening of *The White Cliffs of Dover*, the 1944 film starring Peter Lawford and Irene Dunne.

The Royal Oak Ball netted $23,000, which we gave to the National Trust's White Cliffs of Dover fund to purchase 17 miles of coastline.

Later that year, I had another car accident, this one at the corner of Wilshire and Santa Monica Boulevards. Someone broadsided me. I was not seriously injured, but I was badly shaken. It just happened that Jeffrey, who was living in Westwood at the time, happened to be driving by, saw my car, me on a stretcher, and pulled over. Jeffrey attributes my later problems to the fact that I was not properly treated for any neck trauma. I'll never know. What's past is past.

I was becoming anxious about my career. I had made *Beasts Are on the Streets*, a television movie that aired in May on NBC. Another film that's best forgotten.

Not long after my return, my agent, Maggie Henderson of the Henderson/Hogan Agency, called. I couldn't help but hold my breath about what my next role would be.

"The producer of *General Hospital* would like to see you about a role on the soap opera," she said.

"What's a soap opera?" I asked.

She explained that it is a series of programs that began on the radio and were sponsored by soap companies, therefore the "soap." The "opera" part comes in the multi-threaded, convoluted story lines, just as in the music

My original *General Hospital* family *(left to right)*: David Lewis
("Edward the First"), me, still standing upright, Stuart Damon (Alan
Quartermaine) and Leslie Charleson (Monica Quartermaine). (Col-
lection of Leslie Charleson)

version. The stories are open-ended melodramas and have several plots running at one time. *General Hospital* was, I found out, one of the grandfathers
of all television soaps. It had been on television since 1963.

It sounded very confusing to me. "Oh, all right," I agreed. "I'll go to
the interview."

I thought I would be meeting with Executive Producer Gloria Monty
who had recently come to the show and was charged with bringing viewers
back to the show; ratings had slipped dramatically. But the person who interviewed me was Judy Lewis, Loretta Young's daughter, who was associated
with the drama for a period of time.

Judy explained my character, Lila Morgan Quartermaine. She is the
matriarch of the Quartermaine family and lives in a mansion at the fictional
address of 66 Harbor View Road, Port Charles, New York. She had been

married before. She is now married to Edward, owner of the family business, ELQ. They have two adult children, Alan (Stuart Damon), a doctor, who, like his father, is a philanderer, and is married to Monica (Leslie Charleson), herself a philanderer. Daughter Tracy (Jane Elliot) is a much-married schemer and blackmailer. Lila is the voice of reason and sanity in this dysfunctional family unit. She is a gentle person who dispenses worldly advice to her family and others who seek and appreciate her wisdom. She is loved, admired, and respected by everyone in town.

But, Judy told me, Lila has a "past." My past and the secret that Edward and I have concealed for years is revealed much, much later.

There is probably more of a back story to Lila than any other character I had ever played.

But I was still skeptical. I told Judy, "Let me try it for three or four days, and I'll see."

By the end of the third day, I was hooked. For 25 years, I have been working fairly steadily on *General Hospital*. My television family has become as close as my real family: especially Leslie and Stuart, and much later, John Ingle as Edward.

The series in those days, revolved around the traumatic situations—accidents, births, deaths, and such—that took place at the Port Charles hospital, hence the title *General Hospital*. We Quartermaines were characters around whom many of the storylines revolved. We really never seemed to have a storyline of our own.

SHELLEY CURTIS (Consulting Producer and Director): Gloria Monty brought the show from a half hour to 45 minutes, [sharing a 90-minute block with *Days of Our Lives* and] reinventing the show which was almost canceled to an Emmy-winning one. The stories broke all boundaries with storylines.... There was an AIDS story, a heart transplant story, and one with Monica having breast cancer.

Gloria didn't wait to have the stories dictated by the audience. She gave the fans surprises all the time. Gloria would watch the movies from the '30s and '40s and style the show after them, especially the Quartermaines who were fashioned after the family in Lillian Hellman's *The Little Foxes*. She created the template for the Quartermaines. We felt we could do anything as long as we had the characters. We always had Lila and Edward.

Not long after my joining the show, David Lewis was cast as Edward, my husband.

PATRICIA BARRY: The casts and crews of the various soaps were always exchanging scuttlebutt about what was going on and what was coming up in the various shows. There was always gossip. I was working on *Days of Our Lives* when I heard that the Lila Quartermaine role was opening up. I called

Gloria Monty and recommended Anna for the role. I didn't say anything to Anna because I wasn't sure if anything would come of it, but I planted the thought in Gloria's mind. In the end, I never did say anything to Anna because I didn't want her to think I was in any way demeaning her, but I knew the financial difficulties she was in. Fortunately, it worked out.

What I found amusing in terms of the Lila character was that she had "a past." She apparently had lovers. "That sounds familiar," a cast member said to me. "Art imitating life." I just smiled.

I was able to film a television movie early in 1979. I play Lady Earl, in the Stephen J. Cannell production of *The Night Rider*. We shot on location in Louisiana. I was in a store buying cookies one day, and a lady came up to me. "Lila Quartermaine," she said, "whatcha all doin' down here?" she asked.

It was one of the first times that I realized how much the character had taken over. I was Lila to the fans, not Anna Lee.

The Royal Oak board and I had decided to hold another benefit.

The Anglo-American Heritage Ball was held at the Beverly Wilshire Hotel on April 20, 1979. This time the proceeds went to pay for restoration of Ightham Mote, one of the few remaining medieval houses with a moat.

The 42-page program featured a letter from Queen Elizabeth The Queen Mother, president of the National Trust. The highlight for me was a two-page photo spread of "This Sceptered Isle" by my son John. His glorious photographs of Wells Cathedral, Glastonbury, Salisbury Cathedral and other British sights were the centerfold of the program.

Our distinguished group of Honorary Patrons included Roddy McDowall and my brother, Sir John Winnifrith, KCB. Our patron was the Consul General Tom Aston, CMG.

Robert, ever supportive, wrote another poem:

Heritage

There stands the royal oak, beneath whose spread
Lie the green meadows where the seasons pass.
How many armies by their captains led
Have swept like winter storms across that grass!
How many children through a thousand Mays
Have played their common games among these stones,
Living and loving, singing out their days
Above their fathers' bleached and buried bones.
Still stands the oak, thrust upward to the sky.
How deep its roots, and from what sunless earth
It lifts its branches on which you and I
Open like leaves but newly come to birth:
Two separate entities, and yet as one
From the same earth drawn upward to the sun.

General Hospital gave me time off to fly to England to lunch with Queen Elizabeth The Queen Mother at Clarence House on June 16, 1979. I had been invited to attend in honor of my work for the Royal Oak Foundation.

Before I left, Roddy McDowall asked, "If you happen to meet Princess Margaret, will you please give her my regards? And tell her that I'm coming over later this year."

Just before lunch, in came the Princess. I approached her, curtsied, and said, "Your Royal Highness, I have a message for you from Roddy."

Her face lit up. "Is he here? Has he come back?" she asked. "He said he'd let me know as soon as he returned from Scotland."

I suddenly realized we were talking about two different Roddys. I said, "No, ma'm. I mean Roddy *McDowall*."

Her smile turned to a terrible scowl, and she said, "Oh, *that* Roddy." She turned her back to me and walked away.

I remembered, too late, that she had been seeing a young man whose name was, coincidentally, Roddy.

Just two months later, on August 27, 1979, the Queen's cousin, Louis, Earl Mountbatten of Burma, and last Viceroy of India, was assassinated by the IRA. I was so incensed by this deed that I put a placard outside the house that read, "God Save the Queen: Death to the IRA." Because of that I had a lot of trouble. A busload of IRA supporters came by and rang the doorbell. I didn't answer, but they had words with me through the door.

I felt so strongly about the murder of this wonderful man that I wrote a letter to the editor of the *Los Angeles Times*, which appeared on September 2.

The entire civilized world is appalled by this atrocious act.

And the IRA Provisionals, who so proudly boasted of the "execution," have only succeeded in making Ireland one of the most hated countries on the face of the map... We mourn the death of Lord Mountbatten. Throughout my life he was a legendary figure—a combination of Sir Galahad, Admiral Lord Nelson and St. George.

One of the great heroes of World War II, he himself did more to promote the cause of human rights than the entire population of the Irish Republic....

He was also a great human being. It is interesting to note that India was the first country to declare a week of national mourning to express their love for the former viceroy. So much for the fallacy of "brutal, oppressive British rule."

We can only hope that this infamous deed has succeeded in disgusting those Irish-Americans who have been persuaded to contribute money to the IRA for weapons and explosives... under the misguided assumption that they were adding the cause of human rights and "liberation."

Nothing could be further from the truth.

Anna Lee Nathan

Los Angeles

23

General Hospital

Having some place to go on a regular—but not daily—basis was a blessing. *General Hospital* was even better than I had expected. This was no hurry-up-and-wait process like films. Shooting soap operas, which air daily, is a rapid procedure, even though we shoot an episode that might not air for ten days. We're always scrambling. It was such fun. Working during the early days of live television was the best training I could have had for this type of fast-paced production.

Robert, my erudite, sophisticated, literary husband, immediately became a fan of *General Hospital*. From the day my first episode aired, he watched every one. In fact, he became addicted to it. I think he rejoiced in my new career and shared my interest and excitement in being able to work again.

At one point, I asked Robert to write a poem for a *General Hospital* fan club publication. His poem is as close to doggerel as anything he ever wrote:

> I've had my ups; I've had my downs.
> No street was ever named for me;
> I never got to be as great
> As everybody hopes to be.
> And when I walk around the town,
> No one says, "Oh, look! That's he!"
> None rush to take my photograph
> Or ask me for an autograph—
> But though my face is rather plain
> I have not lived my life in vain:
> I married "Lila Quartermaine"!

Then, in February 1980, *General Hospital* laid me off for a month. The Quartermaine storyline would be on hiatus. It was the right time, I felt, to have a little surgery on my eyes. Nothing serious, just some minor cosmetic work to raise my droopy lids and appease my vanity. I had to keep up my appearances, after all.

Also, I had shot *Scruples*, which aired that month. So I was able to fill in some monetary gaps.

When I returned to *General Hospital*, the Cassadine family—the nemesis of the Quartermaines—had a new character, Helena. None other than the legendary Elizabeth Taylor, a great fan of the show, played the role for about six months. Then the character disappeared. In 1997, my friend Constance Towers took over the role.

I wanted to return to England for my annual visit, but unfortunately, Robert's health was too uncertain. I didn't want to leave him. He was slowing down and didn't get around much. Our excitement for the year was our tenth wedding anniversary.

Caroline had visited us late the previous year with my granddaughter, Sarah. They were living in New Mexico. Caroline was going through a difficult second divorce, but it seems that throughout her life, adversity has made her stronger.

John was working at a travel agency and attending night classes at UCLA, hoping to become a film editor. Stephen was a first assistant cameraman on the television program *CHiPs*. And Jeffrey was rekindling his acting career.

In late 1979, a friend wrote that my portrait by William Russell Flint had been auctioned for $37,000. I had always wondered what happened to that painting. So I wrote to Christie's auction house. Although they wouldn't reveal the buyer, they did tell me that a gentleman in Belgium had purchased it; they forwarded my letter to him. What would it be worth today considering the popularity of Flint's work!

In January 1981, I received a reply from the buyer.

Dear Mrs. Nathan:

...It is really a very pleasant and interesting surprise to discover that the fascinating lady of the painting ... exists. I ... bought the painting not only because I like Russell Flint, but mainly because I liked the subject. But I thought it was only a dream and imagination of the artist.

I am a businessman and collect paintings for my pleasure only.... I believe I can say the painting has a good home. If you happen to be in Europe, you are very welcome to visit my home and see the place where the painting is hanging.

I am often in the USA for business but only on the East coast.

If one day I have the opportunity to come to California I would very much like to meet you.

...Hoping to hear from you, I remain,
Sincerely,
Georges Evens

The letter was written on his business letterhead: Diamants Bruts and Tailles. Sadly, I never returned to Europe to see where my portrait was hanging.

Early that year I developed a weakness in my left leg and went lame. My daily ritual of three-mile runs was no longer possible.

The doctors first thought that it was a vascular condition, and I was sent to the hospital for various tests. They didn't prove anything except that my veins were in excellent condition, and there was nothing wrong with my circulation. I was re-diagnosed as suffering from acute osteoarthritis of the hips and knees stemming from old back trouble, an auto accident, and a fall from a horse years ago. More tests: three brain scans and a CT. The worst of all the tests was the myelogram. Whoever invented it must have had a medieval torture device in mind. I was strapped to a board. My spinal fluid was drained and replaced with some disgusting dye. I was tipped up and down, back and forth. Just thinking about it makes me nauseous.

Nothing to do for my pain, they concluded, except take two aspirin in the morning and two at night. If I could have gotten to London, I could have had an injection of U.S.-banned Gerovital, which might have lessened the pain. That wasn't going to be possible. I worked out on a stationary bicycle hoping that would help. It didn't.

Of additional concern was that the storyline on *General Hospital* was no longer focused on the Quartermaines. That was very worrying because it affected my income.

My health continued to deteriorate. Months passed and there was no improvement. Neurologists had given up on me. While I waited to decide what to do for a second opinion, I saw a chiropractor who assured me that he could do something. If that didn't work, Lourdes was the next step! Fortunately, I could still hobble around on a cane.

Fortunately, the *General Hospital* writers turned the storyline back to the Quartermaines. That kept me going professionally and personally.

Caroline and I hosted the U.S. Olympics equestrian team in April 1982 at the Equestrian Center in Burbank. The event was followed by a preview of the Disney film, *Dark Horse*.

Then in May, Venetia, her daughter Erin Everly, and John attended an awards banquet at the Variety Arts Center that honored me as the recipient of the first annual Jessie Matthews Memorial Award given to "a member of the Hollywood British community for career achievement and humanitarian services."

My health continued to deteriorate, and I had moved from using a cane, to a walker, and, finally, a wheelchair. After having been active and self-sufficient for so long, I was frustrated and maybe just a bit angry.

A heart attack in the fall slowed me down further. I recovered quickly and was right back a week later on *General Hospital* doing one or two shows a week. I was either propped up in a chair or walking with a cane, which I could just manage for a few minutes.

I decided that I had just one more Royal Oak event in me. In October, we took a booth at the Highland Games, and John baked 300 of his Macfarlane shortbreads, which sold for $5 each. After subtracting the cost of ingredients, he made about $1,200 for the Trust. I tithed ten percent of my *General Hospital* salary.

My left leg was still causing far more problems than I expected, and I was admitted to the hospital for another series of tests.

There was bad news: I was going to have to have back surgery. The "second opinion" neurologist said there was something wrong with my spinal cord. With two opinions, both indicating the same procedure, I resigned myself to the surgery.

To keep up my spirits prior to the surgery, I had a manicure and pedicure and had my hair done before I entered the hospital. I thought I should look my best. After all, I would be in an "operating theatre"!

On November 28, the night before the operation, I had second thoughts. Once I signed the consent form, I felt even more trapped. Of course, reading the form didn't help. What an intimidating document! First there was the description of the surgery and then a list of what could go wrong. I could be completely paralyzed; I could have another heart attack. They saved the worst for last: I could die.

I doubt I read every word. I picked up a pen, took a deep breath, and signed my name.

As I lay there in bed, I thought, "What am I doing having this surgery at almost 70 years of age?" I didn't feel it was really me lying in that bed at Cedars-Sinai Hospital. Up until just two years ago, I was active, energetic, and healthy. I was in top physical condition. What had happened? When did it all begin? Was it the fall from the horse years ago? Was it that car accident? Was it just old age?

As I thought back over the last two years, I realized that I had been to a neurologist who sent me to a neurosurgeon who sent me to an orthopedic surgeon who sent me to a vascular specialist. First I was told it was arthritis; then it was supposed to be brain tumor. After several brain scans, I was told I didn't have a tumor. I could have told them *that!* I'd seen too many movies where the heroine had a brain tumor. I didn't have any of those scripted symptoms.

Finally, after more doctors' appointments, I had taken matters into my own hands. Everything from acupressure to osteopaths, from kinesiologists to faith healers—I tried them all. Nothing helped. Ruth suggested—rather, she begged—that I come to England to see a famous neurologist. Why not, I thought. I bought the plane ticket and was already packing when... another heart attack in May 1982.

This was the final blow, I thought. Six more weeks in the hospital.

I had always had faith that kept me going. But was it deserting me now?

When I recovered, my cardiologist sent me to see Dr. Charles Carton, who had saved Patricia Neal's life when she had her stroke several years ago.

His diagnosis was a new one: a piece of bone was pressing on a nerve in my spinal cord... probably. He said he couldn't make any promises.

As the hours the night before my surgery slowly drifted by and I lay there recalling the nightmare of the past two years, my nurse came in. She chattered about this and that and mentioned that the last occupant of the room was Sammy Davis, Jr. Well, that was one bright spot and maybe a good omen: he had recently been a guest on *General Hospital*.

The nurse then proceeded to remove the pins from my hair. When I protested, she said, "You're lucky the doctor doesn't want to shave your head. Everything has to be hygienically clean." She not only washed my hair, but also removed the polish from my fingers and toes.

So much for wanting to look my best in the operating room!

She then gave me a sedative. My body was limp, but my mind was racing. I didn't want to die. I had so much to live for: my children; my wonderful husband; my grandchildren; the wonderful world of *General Hospital*. There was so much I still wanted to do.

It's not that I was afraid to die. I had already had an incredibly rich life. Of course, there had been good times and bad. It had been quite an adventure. I have always believed in an afterlife, which would be the ultimate adventure.

With my religious upbringing, I found prayer the ultimate foundation of my life. Now, not only was *I* praying, but also there were friends and fans all over the country praying for me. How lucky was I!

I dropped off and slept relatively peacefully.

The morning arrived. I was transferred to a gurney and wheeled down the hall and into the operating room. As I saw the double doors of the operating room ominously swing open, I murmured two prayers which were always reassuring and soothing: "This too shall pass" and "Let go and let God."

With the best doctors at my side, I slipped into the netherworld of sedation.

More than nine hours later, I awoke in recovery. "I made it!" was my first thought. I couldn't move my head as I was in a neck brace. But the only pain I had was in my hip where the doctor had taken a piece of bone and put it in my spine.

I was in ICU for several days and then moved into a private room. When I first saw all the flowers, I thought it was for my funeral. Masses of flowers from friends, strangers, colleagues on *General Hospital*. What was especially touching was an arrangement of freesia from the crew on the show. They had remembered that it was my favorite flower.

PATRICIA BARRY: When I came to visit Anna in the hospital, I couldn't find her room, and the nurses were less than helpful. Finally, I resorted to peeking into rooms. I came to one door and I heard a clicking sound. I opened the door, and there was Anna. She said, "Hello, dear, I think I'm having a heart attack. I'm ringing and ringing the bell, and no one's coming." I ran out into the hall and said, "You've got to come now." Fortunately, Anna came out of it. I'm sure I saved her life. Imagine, this was after the surgery!

The best "gift" was from *General Hospital*'s Gloria Monty. Before I left, she had assured me that I had a place in the Quartermaine family when I returned. She was true to her promise: the writers had already generated a storyline that Lila had been in a car accident on a visit to Palm Beach. The story played out that I was so seriously injured that when I returned, I would be in a wheelchair.

The network had already renewed my contract several times since I joined the show, and they continued to renew it. That in itself was enough to renew my health and spirits.

Just the thought of being able to return to all these wonderful friends who were counting on me did more to speed my recovery than all the medication and physical therapy in the world. I will always be grateful to Gloria Monty. She not only had the confidence that I would return; she also kept her word that I could return.

One disappointment when I did return three months later was that I could no longer run up and down that lovely staircase in the Quartermaine mansion. Some weeks later, still in the hospital, I had enough strength to write to Ruth and Peter:

Dear Ones,
...I am still in hospital but making giant strides. All the stitches are out and the incision healed. They carved out a big hunk of my hip to replace the vertebrae....

The only problem now is this infernal neck brace I have to wear until the spine fuses. It makes me look like the Man in the Iron Mask and it's very uncomfortable.

Meanwhile, I am working four hours a day with a physical therapist in order to get my leg muscles back in shape again.... The next step is a special section of the hospital where they do advanced therapy and work your tail off eight hours a day.

I shall be home for Christmas and ready to go back to work on *GH* by the first of January....

> With fondest love to you all,
> Joan

While I was recuperating, I received an enormous amount of fan mail. The fans have always been supportive. They have been an inspiration. I wouldn't disappoint them. I *would* return to the show.

I was back working on the show on March 3, 1983. Although the doctor said that there was little chance of regaining the full use of my left leg, I thought, "At least I can drive a car to work." For a period of time, I had to wear a leg brace and a pair of the ugliest shoes I ever saw. Within months I graduated to a cane. It would be some time before I was completely wheelchair-bound.

Queen Elizabeth II arrived in Los Angeles, and I was invited to the reception aboard the royal yacht, *Britannia*. ABC supplied me with a limousine and a gorgeous dress. I was still wearing the brace and funny shoes, so my curtsey was a little awkward. The Queen was very sympathetic. "Please, don't try," she said. Two large sailors hoisted me up and down the gangplank.

I have been truly fortunate. At least from the waist up, I am strong. I have my sight, my hearing, and my own teeth! I learned very quickly that the real key to survival is to maintain a sense of humor. I also retain my unshakable belief in God and the power of prayer.

If my legs weren't nimble, at least my hands are. I worked on a crewel piece for Robert for almost two years. It was a literary tree of all his books in 75 different colored wools. Today it hangs in our dining room.

A surprise letter from Buckingham Palace arrived informing me that I had been selected to receive an MBE (Most Excellent Order of the British Empire) in the 1983 Summer Honours. Nothing would keep me from the ceremony and accepting the honor in person from my Queen.

Jeffrey, Caroline, her 10-year-old daughter Sarah, and John accompanied me. Jeffrey had just torn his hamstring in a water skiing accident, so we were both in wheelchairs at the airports in Los Angeles and London.

Caroline, in full regalia—hat and gloves—John and Jeffrey in suit and tie—were able to accompany me to the ceremony at Buckingham Palace. Jeffrey was using a cane and sat in an aisle seat so he could stretch out his leg. Caroline sat next to him. Little Sarah had to wait outside the Palace under the watchful eye of a London bobby.

A family photograph with *(left to right)* including Tim (now called Jeffrey); me; Caroline; her daughter Sarah; and John. They all joined me in London when I was awarded the MBE, a glorious occasion. Jeffrey and I are both sporting walking sticks. (Collection of Caroline Stevenson)

The number of Honours to be handed out seemed endless. But finally it was my turn to approach Her Majesty. I was determined to use a cane... with great difficulty. I wasn't about to be wheeled up to Her Majesty. During my brief conversation with the Queen, I mentioned Jeffrey's accident and pointed toward him. The Queen looked in his direction. I'm sure that other members of the audience wondered what we could be chatting about.

By the time we returned to the hotel, The Athenaeum, there was a message from the Queen's doctor, Sir Something-or-Other. Despite all the details and all the people the Queen saw that day, she remembered my mentioning Jeffrey and had obviously referred the information to her private secretary who had the doctor phone.

The next day Jeffrey went off for treatment and did so for the next several days. Within a few days, he was walking as if nothing had happened. And people complain about British health care!

> CAROLINE STEVENSON: Mom traveled with lots of suitcases and paraphernalia. She was always losing a bag. "Where's my bag? Where's my bag?" she'd ask. I was the one in charge of taking her to places she wanted to visit, her sister in Sevenoaks and her brother, who was in the hospital with pneumonia. We took the train several places, and she'd always jump up from her wheelchair and say, "We've got to get ready to get off the train!" I finally said to her, "Mom, if you say that one more time, I'm going to throw you off the train." I was afraid she would fall, but she just kept getting up before the train slowed. I look back on it and laugh.

In January 1984, I was awarded a "Soapy" from *Soap Opera Digest* as Favorite Woman in a Mature Role. "Old" could have been substituted for "Mature"! I was presented the award on the Merv Griffin Show. Merv pointed out that the scenes between Edward and Lila were the warmest and most humorous on the show. "My regret," I said, "was that he and I don't have those lovely, sexy scenes [that the other characters have]."

Just before the Olympics came to Los Angeles in 1984, we were working on *General Hospital* six days a week, trying to get forty shows in the can before the Olympics staff took over our studio space and hordes of visitors descended on the city, making it difficult to get to and from the studio. We made it.

The storyline on the show at the time involved Alan Quartermaine (Stuart Damon) who had to get out of Port Charles because of some trouble.

> STUART DAMON: Gloria Monty thought it would be a good idea for me to sneak out of [Port Charles] in drag. So there I was in high heels, a dress, and a red wig. I'm almost 6' 6", and nobody was going to notice me! I sent a message to my family saying that I was leaving and that I wanted to say goodbye to them; they should meet me at the dock. They were all there,

and in I came in full drag. No one—not the actors, the crew, no one—had seen me before my appearance. I came out, and there was dead silence. Anna, as Lila, looked at me and, in all seriousness, says, "Alan, if you had a problem, you could have come to me." This was not in the script. When they called, "Cut," the entire floor just exploded in laughter.

Although Robert's health was deteriorating rapidly, he wrote almost every day in our study. He would wait until he had finished about half of whatever he was working on and then would ask me to read it. I was very flattered that he asked my opinion.

On May 25, 1985, Robert died. He was a very kind, gentle man, so very different from my second husband. I made sure that the details for his burial were just the way he wanted. According to his friend, John D. Weaver, who spoke at the service on June 8, 1985, "If any of us had ever suggested this memorial service to him ... he would have said, 'Who would come?'"

Of course, hundreds of his friends and admirers attended.

David Lewis read from *The Summer Meadows*, which Robert had written about me:

We had been walking in the rose garden, my wife, Cordelia, and I. It is her garden really... she is an Englishwoman who talks to flowers. They bloom under her care and never talk back, which makes it possible for her to express those opinions which I have begged her to hide from our friends.... [L]ike so many Victorians, she believes in love, which is a great comfort to me.... I hope that when I die, [my] sense of self will not disappear but that I shall take it with me, and I want it to be filled with joy.... As long as Cordelia is there with me at the end.

Leslie Charleson read an excerpt from his unpublished autobiography about his coming to Hollywood. His observations ring true even today.

I prepared for Hollywood: I engaged a secretary (my first), bought some clothes, a portable typewriter, and some paper and pencils.... In those days, the motion picture industry was third in the nation in wealth and influence; money was scarcely even counted, it was just there; influence could be summoned merely by picking up a telephone. The world's gods and goddesses lived in the hills above Sunset Boulevard; a nation's dreams centered on Hollywood and Vine. And the men who controlled all this were patriarchs... elderly, dictatorial, unread, unscrupulous, rapacious, afraid of their wives, surrounded by their concubines, sentimental, pious, uneasy, and without mercy. I got along with them very well.

Another friend, writer Turnley Walker, read a poem Robert had written about the enticements of Hollywood:

Who lets the lure of motion pictures blind him
Had better leave his ego far behind him.
To wealth he'll get in fairly close proximity—
Along with spiritual anonymity.

Robert is interred at Westwood Memorial Park, in the heart of Westwood.

My husband's death was not unexpected, but the death of my oldest son, John, at 36, was a terrible blow. My brother John was the one who phoned to tell me that John had died on November 29, 1985. He had collapsed and died of a heart attack in Scotland. John took care of the funeral arrangements and saw to it that he had a proper burial in Kilmarnock. My poor health and poorer financial condition prevented me from attending his funeral.

Also, that year, my first husband, Robert Stevenson, died in Santa Barbara. He had had a stroke some years before. He had divorced Frances and married Ursula. My marriage to him ended on a bitter note, but we did have, for a time, a wonderful union, which produced two lovely daughters.

I remember him very fondly, both personally and professionally. During his tenure at Disney, he had directed nineteen films, including *Mary Poppins*, *Bedknobs and Broomsticks*, *That Darned Cat*, and *The Love Bug*.

The novel he wrote while we were on hiatus in 1938 was never published in the U.S. Unfortunately, I've never been able to locate a copy of the book.

The Toronto Film Society hosted a retrospective for me in March 1987. There was a banquet in my honor and they screened two of my favorite films, *Bedlam* and *Summer Storm*. I knew that *General Hospital* was televised in Canada because people would stop me on the street and say, "Oh, it's Lila," or greet me like a long lost relative, "Oh, Lila, it's so wonderful to see you."

There was an event that recalled old Hollywood later that year when the famous Brown Derby restaurant honored me during their re-opening. Caricatures of stars who had dined there graced the walls. I was presented with my own caricature, which remained on the wall until the restaurant finally was finally demolished to make way for a parking lot!

My family attended, and I was delighted that many of my *General Hospital* family came as well. Jackie Zeman, Anne Jeffreys, Brad Maule, and Gloria Monty were among those who helped me celebrate.

Sometime about 1986, the writers created a storyline for the Quartermaines which is one of my favorites. Some machinations by Monica and one of her paramours somehow caused the family to lose all its money, resulting in our moving from our lovely mansion to rooms above a diner.

But all was not lost. Lila, ever the savior of the family, began her own business, making relish from a secret recipe. She called it Pickle-Lila. And she recouped the family fortune. How many bottles of this magic mixture she would have had to sell to amass enough money to regain the fortune is never revealed!

I remember my costume: an apron-cum-pinafore in blue and white checks. At that time, I seem to recall I was wearing a leg brace, which drove the sound man to distraction because it clicked when I walked.

At the January 18, 1988, 4th Annual Soap Opera Digest Awards, I was given the Best Supporting Actress award. It was very gratifying to receive a standing ovation as I hobbled to the podium at the Beverly Hilton Hotel ballroom. The award was handed to me by Ian Buchanan, Duke Lavery on *General Hospital.* I call him "my favorite Scot."

I was certain that I wouldn't win, so I hadn't prepared a speech. I did manage a few words. I had a list of who to thank in my head, just in case: *Soap Opera Digest,* ABC, the crew on the show. Then I decided to dedicate the award to two people who meant a lot to me but were no longer with me: Robert Nathan and my son, John Stafford.

Although I didn't know it at the time, my visit to England in May 1990 would be my final journey home. Jeffrey accompanied me. It would be the last time I saw my sister Ruth. But we speak on the phone every Sunday.

The children's careers were blossoming.

In his "Just for Variety" column in *Daily Variety,* Army Archerd wrote,

Venetia Stevenson produces "The Servants of Twilight" ... and Stephen Thomas Stafford is producer/director of "The Color of Evening," the script adapted from the novel by Stafford's stepfather, Robert Nathan....

Art in the blood is very thick.

General Hospital marked an historical event on August 9, 1990: the 7,000th episode aired. It became the longest-running daytime drama on ABC. (The others are *All My Children* and *One Life to Live.*)

Wendy Riche joined the show in 1991 as executive producer. Gloria Monty had remained with the show for years, but had left, and then returned. She left permanently in 1991.

WENDY RICHE: I met her on my first day. I came in to work, went down to the set, and Anna was there. I kneeled at her feet so that she would not have to strain to look at me. What I saw was wisdom and love and intelligence and a woman whom I knew I was going to like. She was a role model for everyone on the show. She was always a lady, which didn't mean she didn't ask for what she wanted and when she wanted it. Whether it was hair, makeup or wardrobe—if there was something that didn't sit well with her—she would speak up. She knew exactly how she wanted to look.

My second *General Hospital* family. I am in front with Sean Kanan
(A. J. Quartermaine). In back *(left to right)* are Stuart Damon (Alan
Quartermaine), Leslie Charleson (Monica Quartermaine), John Ingle
(my "Edward the Second"), and Steve Burton (Jason Quartermaine).
(Photograph by ©Craig Sjodin/American Broadcasting Companies,
Inc.)

I told Wendy I wanted to work more, and she made every effort to get me as much work as I could physically manage. She spoke to the writers, asking them to write me in two or three times a week.

WENDY RICHE: I told them that Lila is the matriarch of the show. She will work really well with the grandchildren. What greater opportunity for storytelling than to have the wise grandmother around who also has a sense of humor? Daytime television is a reflection of real life. Very few of us live without contact with other generations. With Anna, there was the opportunity to have somebody with a history. What an opportunity for storytelling!

The fan luncheons were a highlight of each year. I attended all of them. The continued love of the fans was very flattering. It was an effort for me to get prepared, but when I arrived at the restaurant, there was always a group from the show who would lift up me up to the stage in the wheelchair. I would give a little talk and then sign autographs. It was great fun.

I have great respect for the fans. They always showed consideration for my physical problems. Although they wanted to get near me, they never grabbed at me or made me feel uncomfortable.

The show went on location several times. I recall once we were shooting at the Bonaventure Hotel in downtown Los Angeles, and another time we used the Greystone Mansion as the exterior of the Quartermaine home.

LESLIE CHARLESON (Monica Quartermaine): We were on location at the Bonaventure. Anna was there along with Robert. We got our call late that night. She and I got in the elevator, and when we exited, we immediately got lost. When we got to the street, Anna asked some homeless person, "Excuse me. do you know where they're shooting?"' I was tugging at her— she was walking with a cane then—and trying to pull her away. When we finally arrived where we were supposed to be, we were hauled into a car, and Gloria referred to the two of us as the most unprofessional pair she'd ever worked with. All we did, in the end, was a ride-around in the car. I still laugh when I recall that we were the only two people in the entire crew who got lost, and here was Anna talking to this bum. Very egalitarian.

After many years, my wonderful Edward, David Lewis (he became known as Edward the First), became ill and, in 1989, he left the show. He was "killed off" in a plane crash. He was replaced for a short period by Les Tremayne. David returned in 1991 for about two years, but eventually, he told Wendy, "I don't think I can do this any more in a way that I will be proud of my work. I think it's time to go gracefully."

And so I was alone. I would occasionally have a scene in which I spoke to Edward's picture—and the image answered. It was always a sweet moment for the character and for me.

In 1993, Edward the Second joined the show. Out of an elevator came my wonderful "new" husband, John Ingle. We shared a television life for the next ten years.

Where David Lewis had been a more sedentary character, the new Edward was more active; he would go out on the town, drive cars, attend meetings. But he and I still had the same loving but confrontational relationship that David and I had. I could still tell him, "Put a sock in it, Edward," when I didn't agree with him.

David had been just two years younger than I. John, however, was 15 years younger than I. But in soap opera, real time doesn't exist.

I remember John's comment to me about the age difference, "Edward has been 'youthenized.'"

My secret past came to light after John became Edward. The story line reveals that I had been married before, to Crane Tolliver, obviously a bounder. He shows up in Port Charles to tell me we had never obtained a legal divorce and not only is my marriage to Edward invalid, but also that my children are illegitimate! To save the day, the writers kill him off, and Edward and I are wed again, making everything—and everyone—legal.

But that is the least of Lila's troubles. Lila decides to write her memoirs. (By then I was already well into my real story.) The story line reveals that Lila had a fiancé, who attacked her. To defend herself, she picked up a fireplace poker and walloped him. Lila had killed him! Edward, who wants to take responsibility for the death, marries Lila in his place. There were letters that Edward secreted about the incident which are discovered in the course of the story line.

Relationships on a daytime drama are not for the faint of heart!

24

A Pillar of Strength

After Robert's death, I had a series of part-time housekeepers-companions, but by the spring of 1992, I had to admit to myself that the time had come to have a full-time caregiver. Routine things that I had taken for granted for so long—preparing meals, bathing, and dressing—were becoming increasingly difficult for me.

I'd also had another driving accident; this one occurred on the studio lot. I thought my wonderful Honda Prelude car was in reverse; it was in drive. I drove through a wall and into somebody's office. The next day, Leslie Charleson, thoughtful as ever, sent me a racing helmet.

I phoned a local agency that provided caregivers. Most of those I interviewed didn't meet my requirements. The one who did was Zoraida Alvarez from Costa Rica. For the next several years—with one interruption—she was with me twenty-four hours a day.

Obviously, I needed to get to the studio, but now that I was permanently in a wheelchair, how was I to manage the transportation? Without my knowing, Jeffrey went to producer Joe Hardy, who had replaced Gloria Monty. Joe knew Jeffrey from having previously directed him in a TV movie, *Love's Savage Fury*.

JEFFREY BYRON: I spoke to Joe about two things. The first was about Mother, who was now permanently confined to a wheelchair. I explained how difficult it was for her to get to the studio, and I asked if he could arrange for a car to pick her up and bring her home. He thought it was a great idea. For about the next ten years, a car and driver came to the house on the mornings she had to be at the studio and brought her home in the evening.

The second thing was about the show's storyline. The writers, I said, seem to be hiding the fact that Mother is in a wheelchair. I suggested,

"Why not make it a part of the storyline? It would be inspirational to
see this woman in a wheelchair and how she gets around and it wouldn't
detract from Lila's elegant appearance or her being feisty." Joe responded
positively to the idea. Within weeks, the storyline included the fact that
Lila had fallen down a flight of stairs. From that point on, Anna Lee as
Lila became not only a spokesperson for the elderly but also for the handicapped. It added to the character's persona.

Late in December 1992, I received a script from Wheeler Winston
Dixon, a film professor and filmmaker at the University of Nebraska. His
script, *What Can I Do?*, is about a wealthy, elderly woman who lives in a New
York City apartment. She's so lonely that she hires five guests to come and
listen as she tells the story of her life. She reminisces about the things she's
done and the mistakes she's made. It was a wonderful study in loneliness.

The script is an 80-minute monologue; the guests don't say a word.
What a challenge for an actress, I thought, and immediately called Wheeler
and accepted his offer.

I invited the young writer-producer-director to my home on New Year's
Day 1993, and we discussed the project over lunch.

W. W. DIXON: I knew Anna from her films, but it was my wife who kept
telling me, "You have to see Anna Lee on *General Hospital*." So I watched
the show and knew right away she was the one. When I visited her just
prior to shooting, Anna said, "Well, I suppose you'd like to hear me read."
I listened to her, and she just blew me away by reciting from memory practically the whole damn script.

He told me had had submitted the script to a number of older actresses
who had turned him down. They told him, "You expect me to memorize 80
minutes of dialogue? I can't do that. Besides the story is too depressing, too
difficult, too complex."

The plan was for a car to call for me at 6 a.m. the following morning
to take me to the sound stage in Hollywood for the first of a three-day shoot.

What I hadn't told Wheeler was that I had received word earlier that
day that my brother John had died and would be buried at Appledore, where
he had lived for many years. I was distraught over the loss and knowing that
I would be unable to attend his funeral made it even more difficult for me.

I couldn't sleep that night thinking about John and about the commitment I had made to film *What Can I Do?* Late that night, I phoned Wheeler
to tell him of my loss.

W. W. DIXON: I thought at that point that the whole project was going to
collapse. Then she sort of brightened and said, "You know what? I'm
going to do it. I'm going to use it." What she meant, of course, was that

she was going to use the pain, saying, "There's nothing better than for me to come in to work." Despite her promise, I got on the phone to arrange some backup in case she folded.

I was up at 5 a.m. to be ready for the car. I remember that it was pouring rain and very, very grey. How appropriate, I thought, considering my emotional state and the role I was about to play. But it was my birthday, and what a celebration to be still working in my favorite medium at 80!

W. W. DIXON: We pre-lit Anna's shot, and I decided to do her close-up immediately because of the stress of both the role and her personal situation. I had told the crew about her brother's death, that she was totally in grief. Everything we did was for her. The crew was astounded.

During her close-up, we had a camera set up with four magazines of film at all times, instead of the usual two, so we could keep filming, stopping only to load a new magazine, which would take a matter of seconds.

We shot 96 minutes of film on her close-up, finishing at 10 a.m., which shows how few mistakes she made.

All the takes were ten minutes. We'd reload, slate it, and pick up where we left off, backing up two or three lines. That was even more phenomenal: she could just do it in her head. I'd say, "We'll take it from so-and-so." She'd say, "Yes. Yes." Then we followed up with side shots, dolly tracks, everything to cover. It became apparent that we were going to get the whole thing in one day, which was incredible. Lesser people would have folded, but she had this indomitable spirit. Anna was such a trouper....

Looking at the film, you can see that Anna captured the essence of the piece. She's endlessly sympathetic and gentle, but at the same time, ruthless. She managed to convey sympathy, empathy, pity, and steely resolve—all at once.

Wheeler told me the entire budget for the film was only $20,000. The film premiered at the Museum of Modern Art in New York in 1994 and is now in the Museum's film collection. Imagine, one of my films in their collection!

Looking back, I realize this was the most avant-garde film I had ever been associated with. It was a wonderful experience. It would my last feature.

The same month I made *What Can I Do?* I received a star on the Hollywood Walk of Fame. At the time, I was the oldest person to receive a star. My star, between those of Ingrid Bergman and Fran Allison, of the children's TV puppet show *Kukla, Fran and Ollie*, is located at 6757 Hollywood Blvd.

Fortunately, as it turned out, the ceremony had to be postponed because of rain, so I was able to participate in Wheeler's film.

John Baradino, Leslie Charleson, and Stuart Damon were among the *General Hospital* family who attended, along with Mel Torme and Cesar Romero, and my real family.

Johnny Grant, the honorary mayor of Hollywood, read the resolution prior to the unveiling of the star: "Therefore, let it be resolved that the Mayor and City of Los Angeles, by adopting this resolution, hereby congratulate Anna Lee on this well-deserved honor." The Mayor and the members of the City Council had signed the proclamation. Johnny added, "This is one time the Mayor and the entire Council could get together and agree on something." He then proclaimed "Anna Lee Day in Hollywood."

Having my star is just like being in the company of so many of those with whom I worked with when I first came out to Hollywood.

But I have to laugh when I think that dogs may have piddled on my star.

One of the most terrifying nights of my life occurred on December 9, 1994. I was sound asleep when I was awakened by someone pounding on the front door. My first thought was that someone was trying to break into the house. Zoraida was at my side in an instant. The next thing we heard was the front door being broken down. We were terrified. Someone ran into the house shouting, "Your house is on fire!"

Zoraida got me into the wheelchair and out the front door and, with the help of this guardian angel, we got to the lawn of our neighbors, musician Herbie Hancock and his wife Gigi. The fire trucks were just arriving. I couldn't believe I was living another house fire nightmare.

The name of this Good Samaritan was Milo. He just happened to be on his way home, further up the road, when he noticed the roof was on fire. If it hadn't been for him, who knows what would have happened!

JEFFREY BYRON: About midnight I received a page from Stephen, who had been called by a neighbor, probably Herbie Hancock. Stephen said to get to Mom's house right away, that the house was burning. As I sped toward Doheny Drive, all I could think was, "Is Mom all right? How did this happen?"

Stephen, who had driven in from his home in La Crescenta, saw the panic on my face when I drove up and rushed to the car. The first words out of his mouth were, "Mom's OK. She's looking pretty good under the circumstances." I expected her to be in shock and unable to speak. But not my mother.

"I'm fine," she said. "I'm worried about is my script, though. I have to work on Monday. Can you go through the rubble and find it?"

I found a hotel at Beverly Drive and Pico and got Mom and Zoraida a room. Then began my new full-time job: taking care of Mom, the insurance, and rebuilding the house.

The day after the fire, the insurance company inventoried everything. We were told what was salvageable and what wasn't and what it all was worth.

Much of Mom's book collection was in ashes, including her signed copy of *The Coming of the Fairies*, inscribed to her by Arthur Conan Doyle. Letters and other memorabilia were also gone, including letters from my brother John. Her scrapbooks from the beginning of her career were saved.

Unfortunately, Mom's homeowner's insurance stipulated only a specific amount and when that was gone... that was it.

Although Mom had a wonderful job, she was far from being rich. During the time she was married to Robert, he'd had many physical problems and no health insurance. So over the years, she had taken money out of the house to take care of these major medical bills, resulting in a huge mortgage.

Robert did leave Mom the house, which was worth a lot, and the rights to his works, but most of them had been out of print for years.

Between the day after the fire and just days before Christmas, I was going non-stop trying to find a house. It wasn't easy. January 1994 was the month of the big earthquake in Los Angeles, and rental housing was at a premium as people needed a place to live while their homes were being repaired. I finally found a handicapped-accessible house in Sherman Oaks. I had the finances to live in the house for about ten months. But the house was unfurnished, and there was no money to furnish it. I didn't want Mom to see the house until it was furnished.

About mid–December, I called *General Hospital* Executive Producer Wendy Riche. Would she consider letting us temporarily use the furniture from the sets that was in storage at the studio? She agreed immediately.

Just days before Christmas, a studio van pulled up. Not only did the network supply everything we needed for the house, but they also brought in a fully decorated Christmas tree and about fifty poinsettias! It was really a teary moment.

On Christmas day, Stephen and his wife and children came for dinner. Despite the traumas that we had all experienced in the previous weeks, we made it as festive as possible.

I knew Jeffrey hadn't been getting a lot of sleep over the previous few weeks. Caroline suggested that he visit her in Santa Fe for a few days' rest. It was a fine idea. Zoraida and I could manage. I asked my old friend Joyce Howard to stay the weekend and keep us company.

On December 27, Jeffrey left for Santa Fe.

JEFFREY BYRON: I hadn't been in Santa Fe for more than a few hours when I received a frantic phone call from Joyce. "Zoraida is gone," she told me. "She said she was going to mail a letter. She hasn't come back. It's been hours."

I made a quick turnaround and flew back to Los Angeles. I was immediately on the phone again trying to get another caregiver for Mom. It's difficult to find someone who has the skills to care for someone who is wheelchair-bound. And my mother was a handful to begin with. It was a comedy of errors. We hired someone; fired her; hired someone else; she left; then someone else, who lasted about three months.

In mid–June 1995, Zoraida called saying she wanted to return. Our best guess is that she suffered from post-traumatic stress syndrome due to the earthquake and had fled to Costa Rica. I think she had guilty feelings about abandoning me. She wanted to return. Jeffrey had a long conversation with her and making it very clear about the situation. "I don't know what happened or what you did or why you did it. It doesn't matter," he said. "But you'll have to promise you'll never do that again. If you want to leave again, you'll have to give me notice."

I always think of Zoraida as our Mary Poppins. She just popped into our lives. We never really knew anything about her. She never told us, and we never asked. When she did talk about her personal life, we were never sure it was the truth. But she was my pillar of strength.

After that, she was with me for years.

Jeffrey rebuilt the house so that I could navigate around in my wheelchair. There was a ramp from the driveway to the front door. Doorways and hallways were wider so I could glide up and down without bumping into the door frames. I could even ride into the shower.

JEFFREY BYRON: Because the insurance didn't cover rebuilding the house for handicapped access, I tried every angle I could think of. I called the president's office at Whirlpool and spoke to his secretary. As luck would have it, she was a great fan of General Hospital and Anna Lee. I explained about the fire, about Mom being under-insured, and that we were rebuilding the house. The result: Whirlpool gave me all their kitchen products at cost. Then I went to Kohler for their products, and so on.

Mom was no longer strong enough to move herself around in a regular wheelchair and wanted a motorized one that would give her some independence. Her insurance, which had been terrific, wouldn't pay more than $5,000 for the chair, which cost $25,000! I called every wheelchair company I could find, telling them, "She's Anna Lee. She's on General Hospital. It would be great public relations for you."

I finally found a company that gave us two wheelchairs, one for home and one to use at the studio. The one at home was a candy apple red. She had photographs taken in their chair, and they could use them in their printed materials. They also received credit every day she was on the air.

Stuart Damon recalls one of my first days on the set with my motorized wheelchair.

STUART DAMON (Alan Quartermaine): If Anna had to take a driver's test for the wheelchair, she would never have passed. She was hell on wheels.

She could have been in the NASCAR race. We would get hysterical watching her maneuver that thing. When she finished a scene in the chair, she turned to go out of the room, and she knocked over furniture, a lamp; she ran into the doorjamb. Then she drove over my foot. How we laughed. She didn't do it to call attention to herself. It was just how she drove.

Following in my daytime drama footsteps, Jeffrey got the role of Dr. Markham Boardman on the *General Hospital* spin-off, *Port Charles*. For three years, he played the villain. We even had one episode together on *Port Charles*. There is a short scene where Lila wheels herself into the hospital and accidentally runs into Dr. Boardman. He also appeared as Dr. Jeff Martin on *All My Children* and as Richard Abbott on *One Life to Live*, both produced in New York.

When ABC canceled my car and driver, citing budgetary problems, I had to find my own way to the studio. Jeffrey purchased a Honda minivan. My vanity plate reads, "Lila Q." Zoraida lifts me from the bed and carries me to the van. She drives me to the studio where she lifts me out of the van and into my wheelchair.

I still have dressing room number one, which I have decorated with film memorabilia. Just outside the door, I have a lobby card from *Non-Stop New York*. The hairdresser, Catherine Marcotte, knows exactly how I like my hair. The makeup artist, Donna Messina, knows the colors I like and what will coordinate with the colors of my caftan costume.

Just to make sure everything is the way I like it, I have my own mirror to double check.

DONNA MESSINA (Head of Makeup Department): Anna knew exactly what she wanted at all times. She always insisted on a particular color for her eyebrows; they had to be taupe. Her lashes had to be on *perfectly*, and they had to be a certain size: Maybelline 747. If anyone tried to sneak on a different size, she'd know every time! She always did her own lips—always—until the last couple of years when she couldn't use her hands very much. She loved pink. I'd try to get her into something peach or red, and she'd say, "No, darling, this is not the color. You've made a mistake."

Despite the aches and pains, I love my life. How lucky I am to have a wonderful career at my age. The cast and crew are joys to work with. At home and at the studio, I continue to receive fan mail, some of it is from the *General Hospital* audience. Some of it is from people who remember my early films. I even had a young man come out from Georgia pay his respects. I invited him to tea.

I was fortunate to be included in some of the *General Hospital* storylines, despite the writers moving in new directions.

The family celebrates my ninetieth birthday in January 2003. *Left to right, top row:* son Jeffrey Byron, grandchildren Ian and Samantha Stafford, great-grandson Eason Everly, granddaughter Erin Everly, son Stephen Stafford. *Left to right, middle row:* daughter Caroline Stevenson, great-granddaughter Eres Everly, daughter Venetia Stevenson, grandson Evan Stafford. *Left to right, front row:* granddaughter Sarah Williams, me, Stephen's wife, Tamara. Granddaughter Stacy Everly is not pictured.

WALLY KURTH (Ned Ashton): The storyline had me entering the Quartermaine kitchen carrying a guitar and singing. Anna's line was something like, "Oh, my favorite cowboy is Gene Autry." Now, Anna, who never asked to change a line, did *not* want to say that Autry was her favorite cowboy because John Wayne was! She just wouldn't say it. I can hear her saying, "Ge-e-ene Autry? He's *not* a cowboy." Production came to a stop while the director, the producer, everyone, came on the floor and tried to convince her to say the line. She finally agreed. It was the only time I ever saw her pout. When she finally had to say the line, she gave the name her own spin, and it was obvious that he wasn't her favorite cowboy!

My dear Roddy McDowall passed away in September 1998 at the age of 70. Now just Maureen and I are the last of the cast from *How Green Was My Valley.*

Three of my favorite ladies shared my birthday with me: *(left to right)* **Patricia Barry, Leslie Charleson, and Anne Jeffreys. (Photograph by Krista Dragna)**

In 2003, could it be that I was going to celebrate my 90th birthday? Jeffrey organized the most wonderful celebration. My entire family came from far and near to be with me. Venetia came from Atlanta, where she has lived since 1999. Venetia left the Hollywood scene long ago and is working with the Atlanta Police Department as a victims' advocate. Her children Erin, Stacy and Edan joined us. Caroline came from Santa Fe with Sarah. Stephen came from Ojai with his wife, Tamara, and their children, Evan, Samantha, and Ian. Jeffrey came from just across the patio from the guesthouse at the back of the property, where he has lived for the last few years.

My other "family" came to share the festivities: John Ingle, Stuart Damon, Leslie Charleson, Patricia Barry, Anne Jeffreys, and Wendy Riche; other guests included Tab Hunter, Pat Crowley, film critic Leonard Maltin, Joyce Howard, agent Dick Clayton, and my long-time publicist, Tommy Garrett, among others. Maureen O'Hara, looking stunning, gave a special toast.

The weather was beautiful, and the caterer set up the food outside. The

With my co-author, Barbara Roisman Cooper. (Photograph by Martin M. Cooper)

cake was a masterpiece of the baker's art: The names of all my films were written in icing.

Toward the end of the afternoon, I became very tired and had to be taken to bed. Guests continued to arrive, but I received them in bed. I certainly didn't mind welcoming them into my blue-and-white bedroom. And they understood.

> JACKIE ZEMAN (Bobbie Spencer): I went into her bedroom and saw the apparatus above the bed that she used to pull herself up. Seeing that apparatus hit me very hard because I suddenly realized just how spunky she was to be able to get up each morning and prepare herself to get to the studio. I was in awe of this woman who not only had something to contribute when things were going her way but also when things became difficult and the quality of life changed. It was an emotional moment for me.

In the spring of 2003, Zoraida told me she had to return to Costa Rica for surgery, but she assured me she would return. The day Zoraida left was a sad one. She gave us several phone numbers where we could contact her.

Then she was gone. We never heard from her again. Despite all Jeffrey's detective work, we never could find out what happened to her. To this day, we don't know.

After several misadventures with other caregivers, we found Lynn. She has been an excellent choice.

I still look forward to my ride to ABC. I work only rarely now, and I cannot deny the whole process has become more difficult.

Writing my story is more and more difficult, too. I used to be able to sit at my desk and peck away at my portable electric typewriter. I'm too old to learn how to manage a computer. Now I type sitting in bed with my "bed dog" Rickey, a Pomeranian, beside me. He's a lovely caramel-colored ball of fluff that keeps me company and makes me smile.

I still try to answer as much fan mail as possible. Signing photographs is all but impossible because my hand just can't hold a pen anymore.

My advice to all those who ask how I can endure the frailties of old age, I reply, "Nil *desperendum*—never give up. If you do, you'll end up in an armchair for the rest of your life."

Writing my story has enabled me to relive the good, the bad, the happy, and the sad parts of my life. I have had ninety-one years of exciting adventures.

I'm glad I've been able to tell my story.

Epilogue
by Jeffrey Byron

My mother, Anna Lee, passed away on May 14, 2004. What an extraordinary life she had!

Beginning at the ripe "young" age of 65, most of Mom's life took place in the make-believe world of the ABC soap opera, *General Hospital*, on which she played Lila Quartermaine for a quarter of a century. She was 88 years of age the last time the network renewed her contract for two years. She would be 90 when the agreement was up. Imagine!

The 25 years Mother spent on *General Hospital* were some of the happiest of her life. She often said that having this job "kept her around" and lent purpose to her life. For that her family is forever grateful.

Unfortunately, the very end of her tenure on *General Hospital* wasn't a happy time.

The last few years she was on the show, I had overseen Mom's business arrangements with ABC. A network business affairs representative would phone me, usually within six months of the current agreement being up, and say, "We'd love to renew your mother's contract." I would receive the paperwork for a two- or three-year deal. It was flattering for her to be wanted, considering her age and health issues.

Each renewal usually brought a salary increase. But by the mid-1990s, salaries for actors on daytime dramas were rarely increased. As the soaps lost their audiences and their ratings, the network reduced or even eliminated salary increases.

In 2001, I heard the first rumblings that things were not going well at ABC. I received a call from the Business Affairs Department. The representative said, "We want to renew Anna Lee's contract for two more years. We're so excited about having her back." Then a pause, a long pause. "Oh, by the way, we are reducing her guarantee from a show to half a show." What they really meant was that they were cutting her salary in half!

In the soap opera world, actors who are under contract get paid by the show. Soaps film five episodes a week. If an actor works two shows that week, that's what they get paid for. All contract actors, however, have a "guarantee." That means that even if they don't work a particular week, they still get paid based on that guarantee.

In Mom's case, she had a one-show guarantee. Now they wanted to cut that in half.

I said, "It's one thing not to give her a raise, but to cut her salary in half is not acceptable. It would not be possible for her to live on the new figure." I explained that Mom was on a limited income and permanently wheelchair bound. Like many senior citizens, Mother was underinsured. When her house burned down in 1994, her financial situation changed forever. It took a great deal of resourcefulness to make sure she had a roof over her head.

When the Business Affairs person told me that it wasn't just Anna Lee who was being affected, it was others as well, I explained that it was always her dream to be on *General Hospital* until her last breath. And, I continued, "She had a 'gentleman's agreement' with one of the former executive producers."

Gloria Monty had suggested to Mother that she would be Lila Quartermaine until the day she died. Mom never forgot that. A few years later, Executive Producer Wendy Riche echoed those sentiments. But they had both left so they were no longer in a position to carry out their promises to keep Mom on the show.

I told the network person that I felt there was a lack of sensitivity on the part of some at the network. I called everyone connected with the show. Nobody responded.

Finally, ABC phoned again and made another offer: "We'll give your mother her full guarantee, but we'll only sign her for one year." At least that, I thought, would buy us some time. The new contract would be in effect from November 2002 through 2003.

No word from the network until August 2003. "We have decided not to renew Anna Lee's contract," said the network representative. These words were hurriedly added, probably to deflect anything I might say, "She'll still be on the show, but as a recurring character."

I knew this news would distress Mom. I pleaded her cause with the current producer via phone messages and faxed letters, explaining that her dismissal from the show would devastate her when she found out.

Anna Lee was an icon in the soap world! They knew she had little time left, and her salary was far less than many of the other performers, and she had given her best days to the show. Would it be too much to ask that she maintain that status in the twilight of her life?

Not a word in response.

I still hadn't mentioned any of this to Mother.

Next on my list was the then–Chairman and Chief Executive of Disney. (Disney had purchased Capital Cities/ABC, Inc., in 1995.) I wrote that what Anna Lee made on *General Hospital* was pocket change to the network, and suggested that it would be positive public relations for the network. He could save the day and give Anna Lee her job back.

Nothing.

Despite her complaining, "I hate getting up so early," I knew that she loved every moment of the preparation and the production. She loved the attention and adulation from the cast, the crew, and the fans. She loved working.

When it was evident that ABC's decision was final, I came in and sat down on the edge of her bed and told her what had happened. I tried to downplay the rejection and let her know that many people were in her corner, making the news as positive as possible. I also phoned Army Archerd, the long-time columnist for *Daily Variety*, and had Mom speak with him.

He wrote about the situation on October 30, 2003. "Anna Lee sadly tells me she has not received a renewal of her stand on 'General Hospital.' [She] tells me ... 'The show has been a reason for me to go on.'"

Soap Opera Digest ran the story on November 18, 2003, under the headline, "GH'S ANNA LEE OUT!"

ABC issued a rebuttal statement: "Anna Lee has been a beloved cast member of *General Hospital* for many years, and it is our intent to continue to use her in a recurring role as Lila Quartermaine ... as story needs may dictate."

Mom put on a brave face. Even at 90, she was feisty. But she was hurt.

Her spirit had been remarkable—up to that time. Unfortunately, losing her job essentially meant that she lost her will and any purpose to go on. She became increasingly frail and irritable from that moment until the day she died.

I couldn't help but remember how she looked at her 90th birthday party earlier that year: Fantastic! The makeup and the hair, every inch the English Rose.

I don't know how much longer she could have actually worked on *General Hospital*. I do believe that keeping her under contract and working a few times a year would have kept her feeling like she was still part of the "family."

Once her work on the show ended, the only thing that kept her going was working on this book. It was an effort, but she still had all those stories to tell about her life. She worked on it until a few days before she died.

One week after she passed, I accepted the Daytime Emmy Lifetime Achievement Award for her in New York. It was a privilege for me, her youngest son, to accept this on her behalf, and I was received warmly by all her fans, colleagues, and *General Hospital* actors. I'm sad to say that there was no acknowledgement from anyone at the network.

To ABC's credit, a memorial episode aired on *General Hospital* on July 16, 2004. The "family" recounted their love and admiration for Lila. The tears they shed were real.

On July 31, our family held a memorial service for at Mom at Pierce Brothers Westwood Village Mortuary, followed by a reception at her Doheny Drive home. As befitting my mother, English garden party attire was called for. I knew she would have wanted it to be a celebration of her life.

So, there it is: a remarkable career, the last 25 years of it on *General Hospital* with a slightly bittersweet ending.

Anna Lee had a sensational beginning and an enchanting in-between.

This book is her story, the one she wanted to tell.

Los Angeles, California
2006

26

In Memoriam

Anna Lee's colleagues from *General Hospital* remember her with admiration and anecdotes.

Leslie Charleson (Monica Quartermaine, 1977–present): I called her "Mummie," just like the British children call their mothers. I had that privilege and I felt very possessive of her. I saw the frustration as she became progressively beholden to the cane, then the walker, and finally the wheelchair. Sometimes she'd be sitting so that she couldn't see what was going on behind her because she couldn't turn her head. She'd bring a mirror and take it out from her little purse and hold it as her rear view mirror. One day we were taking five on the set. She was in her wheelchair, and she said to no on in particular, "I have one line in this scene, and I don't know what the fuck it is." This came out of her beautiful, angelic mouth. It was so incongruous. I took it very hard when we lost her because I was so close to her. Many of us felt she was in a better place. For someone who had so much energy and determination and spunk, we felt that now she could run and play and be with Robert and wouldn't any longer be confined to a body that didn't work.

Shelley Curtis (Consulting Producer/Director, 1978, 1992–2001): Anna knew how to play a scene honestly. She was the wisdom of the show, the grounding, stabilizing force. It was possible for Anna to play a scene and the audience wouldn't notice she was in a wheelchair. She always looked so beautiful. If you lit her right, you'd never see her age. When I was directing, I'd walk out on the stage, and Anna would always be there, completely ready from toes to hair. She was prepared, prepared, prepared. We never had to wait for her. I always went to Anna's parties at her house. She loved parties and having people visit. She wasn't the actress in the spoiled way but in the classic way. When I visited her, she'd hold my hand and then thank *me* for coming.

Stuart Damon (Alan Quartermaine, 1977–present): Anna and I had incredible respect and love for each other. Underneath her dignity she was what I called a "geriatric slut." She had the most wicked sense of humor. What made it doubly funny was, of course how she looked: the genteel English lady. And the stuff that would come out of her mouth! It was always subtle, never brazen. We had such a good time together. She was my adopted mom. Her deterioration was a very slow process. One little thing would go wrong and then another; then she'd be in the hospital. It was like watching a building fall over in slow motion. But whenever I saw her in the dressing room, the makeup room, the hallway, on the set, I never saw any acknowledgment that everything wasn't just as perfect as it should be. The only acknowledgment was the external one—the cane, the walker, the wheelchair—which became props for the extension of the character. I'll always remember how we laughed and laughed.

Jane Elliot (Tracy Quartermaine, 1977–present): I've never known anybody who dealt with a disability with more grace. There was no self-pity, not a moment of blaming anyone. Anna Lee kept her humor and warmth and passion for her work throughout. She worked with the same commitment on the last day as the first. She loved to come to work and was never happier than when in makeup and costume.

Jo Ann (Josie) Emmerich (Senior Vice President, ABC Daytime, 1986–1991): Anna Lee had a natural ability to embody her character. As Lila, she was so likeable and so lovable and such a contrast to her curmudgeon husband. For someone who had that career in film and then to find that same passion for the day-to-day grind of soap opera is quite wonderful. She had that magnetism and ability to convey emotion with seemingly little effort. And she had a great smile and delightful personality and energy about her. Anna Lee was so animated and her personality was so infectious. The role of Lila was just perfect for her.

Anthony Geary (Luke Spencer: 1978–85; Bill Eckert: 1991–93; Luke Spencer, 1993–present): Anna was on the show when I came on. She was the most elegant person I'd ever known. She was so classy and so sweet to everyone and such a professional. Gloria [Monty] saw how taken

I was with her and said, "Maybe Luke should be as taken with Lila as you are with Anna." So when Luke went work for ELQ, he got to flirt with Lila. I had a ball with that. And Anna loved it. Even the last time I saw her in makeup, I knelt down, kissed her hand, and said, "I'm still waiting for those scenes where we get to consummate our flirting." She laughed and said, "Oh, wouldn't that be wonderful."

John Ingle (Edward Quartermaine, 1993–2004; 2005–present): I frequently called Anna, and I would say to Zoraida, her caregiver, and "Please tell Anna that her Edward the Second is on the phone." If those phone conversations could have been taped, they would sound as if they were right out of a Noël Coward drawing room comedy. We had a very loving relationship in that I protected her. For instance, when I would push her in the wheelchair, I'd ask, "Is it all right if I tap you when your line comes or when we're supposed to turn?" She would say yes. My byword for her was "indestructible." She would be in her makeup chair with her eyes closed while they were doing her eyes. I'd come up behind her and say, "Hello, sweetie." She'd say, "Who is it?" "What the hell do you mean?" I'd say. "Who do you hope it is? Or who do you hope it isn't?" When she would come on the sound stage, I would say, "He-e-e-ere she is. Miss Anna Lee!" Everyone would applaud, and she would wave to her "subjects." She always remained a lady.

Francesca James (Supervising Producer, 1990–1991; 1994–1996): I wish I could say I remember meeting Anna for the first time, but when I was producing, it was always like a runaway train. I do know that I have a tremendous amount of regard for people who have been around, whose careers have sustained themselves, and meeting Anna was meeting one of those people. I remember being startled by her beauty and elegance. The Old World flavor of Anna Lee was something that I loved being around. I loved listening to her speak. She spoke with a kind of grace that is not seen in this day and age. I could have listened to her forever. And she carried herself like a queen, even in the wheelchair. She was totally gracious to everyone, the cast, the crew. There was no prima donna about her... ever. She was a complete team player. Lila's grit was certainly apparent in Anna and vice versa. Even at the end, when she could not raise her head, nothing could keep her from coming to work. Despite the elegant and eloquent exterior, Anna/Lila had to be fierce, emotionally and psychologically.

Anne Jeffreys (Amanda Barrington, 1984–present): I remember my first scene with her quite well. The first time on the set, she was in the wheelchair. I asked, "Do you have a problem with your legs?" She laughed and pulled up her dress and showed me the braces on both legs. She told me how uncomfortable she was. She was very forthcoming about the surgery and its aftereffects. Anna couldn't have been a sweeter, nicer lady. She never complained, and I admired her so much for that. And what a professional! She was a joy to be with. I would say she was spunky, even toward the end. She was certainly not a pussycat. She was always "veddy, veddy" British in that she was not standoffish, but always dignified and the perfect lady. She was a class act.

Wally Kurth (Ned Ashton, 1991–present): I was Lila's favorite grandson. Or at least that's how Anna Lee referred to me in the makeup room. I would give her a hug as she wheeled into the makeup room, and she would say, "Oh, it's my favorite grandson!" I referred to her as "my angel." It was wonderful working with her; she was so gracious and so regal. She took great pride in knowing her lines. She was *always* prepared. She didn't want to forget her lines, but as the years went by, she had to depend on cue cards. Because of her neck problem, she had to sit lower and lower in the chair until she was almost prone. It was difficult for me as an actor to get eye contact with her and have an active moment with her character. It was difficult for us on the receiving end. But it couldn't have been easy for her just trying to have the energy she'd had in the past. I'll always remember her as someone who was dedicated and devoted to the art and craft of acting. She was passionate about her work. Against all odds, she willed herself to continue.

Lenny Marcus (Costumer, 1969; 1991–present): God love her, she never gave up wanting to look beautiful. When her physical demands changed, we wanted to keep her looking beautiful. She had this really fashion-savvy way about herself. She knew what looked good on her and what didn't. At one point, she decided she didn't like the way her neck looked. So we put lots of ruffles around. Once she was permanently in the wheelchair, we put her in caftans. They were originally designed to slip over her head. But that became a problem. We replaced them with ones that buttoned down the back, and then later, those were replaced by ones that snapped down the front. Her favorite caftan was pink and white floral chiffon. She was beautiful to the last.

Brad Maule (Dr. Anthony Jones, 1984–2006): My first impression of her was the same as my last: I was mystified by a translucent quality that was very gentle and seemed from another time. There was a gentle, lavender glow all around her. Whenever I saw her, it was almost like being in the presence of royalty. I'd kneel by her wheelchair and hold her hand. It was a way to get close to her and also a sign of respect. I consider her one of the most professional actors I ever worked with and one of the most honorable. While a lot of actors tear up the scenery, she just did the scene. Since she never tried to upstage anyone, she was able to upstage everybody. She was not like some people who give off a holier-than-thou attitude. She had no attitude at all. She could take the raunchiest joke and somehow turn it around on the teller. People like Anna Lee, who are great communicators, live differently. They glow. We all thought of Anna as someone regal and special to be around.

Donna Messina (Head Makeup Artist, 1978–present): It was always fun to be with Anna Lee. So was so classy, so elegant. Toward the end, when she'd get feisty, I tried to ease her pain and make her laugh by calling her "Anna Banana." I treated her like she was my grandma. She always looked like a million bucks, even when she was using the walker or the wheelchair. Either sitting or standing, mobile or immobile, she was a beauty.

Wendy Riche (Executive Producer, 1991–2001): Anna Lee was the role model for everyone on the show. She had a perspective about life that began with "Have fun." She knew not to take too much too seriously, which didn't mean she wasn't deep and serious. And she was always a lady. That doesn't mean she didn't ask for what she needed…. We interact with people of all ages and having the opportunity of having somebody—like a Lila/Anna—with such a history was, to me, an opportunity for storytelling. I spoke to the writers and asked them to write Lila in as much as possible. As the matriarch of the family—and the show—she could work really well with her children and grandchildren. Here was a wise character who also had a sense of humor about life. It was a joy to see her commitment to acting, and the life she brought with her to Lila was inspiring and inspired everybody who worked with her.

Constance Towers (Helena Cassadine, 1997–present): Anna was totally professional even when, at the end, they were putting up cue cards for her. She had such difficulty remembering her lines. I had complete admiration for her. By then, she couldn't lift her head. She lit up when that camera light went on, no matter what aches and pains she had. She was performing. That's part of what kept her alive. Her professional life was reflected in her dressing room, from the lobby card [*Non-Stop New York*] outside her dressing room to the memorabilia inside, her reality was that make-believe world.

Dale Walsh (Cameraman, 1964–present): I can't say enough about this woman. I've thought many times that a person may have physical beauty, but it's the beauty inside that's important. Anna had both. She radiated inner beauty. And she and the camera had a mutual love affair. How could the camera not love her? She was stunningly beautiful. In her later years, maybe I wouldn't get in as tight on her face or if her hand began to shake, I wouldn't want that to be seen, so I would tighten the shot. I tried to move into an angle that would be beneficial to her. She looked so good right up to the end.

Jacklyn Zeman (Bobbie Spencer, 1978–present): Anna Lee had the glamour, classiness, and refinement that a star should have. I never addressed her other than as "AnnaLee," all one word. The biggest surprise about her was her earthy sense of humor. The language didn't match the beauty and the character of the *grande dame* of the show. Because she played Lila for so long, she felt protective of the character's image as well as her personal image. Those of us who have been on the show for so long have many mutual memories—a birthday party, a divorce, a baby shower—we would all tromp over to someone's house to celebrate and be together, just like a real family. Being Lila Quartermaine was important to "AnnaLee."

Filmography and Selected Television Appearances

(Listed by release date. Includes production company and name of character played by Anna Lee. U=uncredited.)

Filmography

Say It with Music. 1932, Paramount–British. (U)
His Lordship. 1932, Westminster Films, Ltd. (U)
Ebb Tide. 1932, Paramount–British. (U)
Yes, Mr. Brown. 1932, British & Dominion. (scene cut)
Mayfair Girl. 1933, Warner Bros.–First National. (U)
King's Cup. 1933, British & Dominion. (U)
Chelsea Life. 1933, Paramount. Hon. Muriel Maxton.
The Bermondsey Kid. 1933, Warner Bros.–First National. (U)
Bitter Sweet. 1933, British & Dominion. (scene cut)
Mannequin. 1934, Real Art/RKO. Babette.
Faces. 1934, British & Dominion. Madeleine Pelham.
Lucky Loser. 1934, British & Dominion. Ursula Hamilton.
Rolling in Money. 1934, Fox-British. Lady Eggleby.
The Camels Are Coming. 1934, Gainsborough. Anita Rodgers.
Heat Wave. 1935, Gaumont–British. Jane Allison.
The Passing of the Third Floor Back. 1935, Gaumont–British. Vivian.
First a Girl. 1935, Gaumont–British. Princess Mironoff
The Man Who Changed His Mind. 1936, Gainsborough. Dr. Clare Wyatt.

O.H.M.S. (aka: *You're in the Army Now*). 1937, Gaumont–British. Sally Briggs.

King Solomon's Mines. 1937, Gaumont–British. Kathleen O'Brien.

Non-Stop New York. 1937, Gaumont–British. Jennie Carr.

The Four Just Men (aka: *The Secret Four*). 1938, Ealing. Ann Lodge.

Young Man's Fancy. 1940, Ealing. Ada.

Return to Yesterday. 1940, Ealing. Carol Sands.

Seven Sinners (aka: *Café of the Seven Sinners*). 1940, Universal. Dorothy Henderson.

My Life with Caroline. 1941, RKO. Caroline Mason.

How Green Was My Valley. 1941, 20th Century–Fox. Bronwen Morgan.

Flying Tigers. 1942, Republic Pictures Corporation. Brooke Elliott.

Commandos Strike at Dawn. 1942, Columbia Pictures. Judith Bowen.

Forever and a Day. 1943, RKO. Cornelia Trimble-Pomfret.

Hangmen Also Die. 1943, Arnold Pressburger Films. Mascha Novotny.

Flesh and Fantasy. 1943, Universal Pictures. Rowena.

Summer Storm. 1944, Angelus Productions/United Artists. Nadina Kalenin.

Bedlam. 1946, RKO. Nell Bowen.

G.I. War Brides. 1946, Republic Pictures Corp. Linda Powell.

High Conquest. 1947, Monogram Pictures Corp. Marie Correl.

The Ghost and Mrs. Muir. 1947, 20th Century–Fox. Mrs. Miles Fairley.

Fort Apache. 1948, Argosy Pictures/RKO. Emily Collingwood.

Best Man Wins. 1948, Columbia Pictures Corp. Nancy Smiley.

Prison Warden. 1949, Columbia Pictures Corp. Elisa Burnell.

Gideon's Day (aka: *Gideon of Scotland Yard*). 1958, Columbia Pictures Corp. Kate Gideon.

The Last Hurrah. 1958, Columbia Pictures Corp. Gert Minihan.

This Earth Is Mine. 1959, Universal-International Pictures. Charlotte Rambeau.

The Horse Soldiers. 1959, The Mirisch Corp.–United Artists. Mrs. Buford.

The Crimson Kimono. 1959, Globe Enterprises/Columbia Pictures Corp. Mac.

Jet Over the Atlantic. 1960, Benedict Bogeaus Productions/Inter Continent. Ursula Leverett.

The Big Night. 1960, Maycliff Productions/Paramount Pictures. Mrs. Turner.

Two Rode Together. 1961, Columbia Pictures Corp. Mrs. Malaprop.

The Man Who Shot Liberty Valance. 1962, John Ford Productions/Paramount. (U: woman in stagecoach).

Jack the Giant Killer. 1962, Edward Small Prods./United Artists. Lady Constance.

Whatever Happened to Baby Jane? 1962, Seven Arts/Warner Bros. Mrs. Bates.

The Prize. 1963, MGM/Roxbury Productions, Inc. (U: American reporter).

For Those Who Think Young. 1964, Aubrey Schenck Productions–United Artists. Laura Pruitt.

The Sound of Music. 1965, 20th Century–Fox. Sister Margaretta.

7 Women. 1966, MGM. Mrs. Russell.

Picture Mommy Dead (aka: *Color Mommy Dead*). 1966, Bert I. Gordon Productions/Embassy Pictures Corp. Elsie Kornwald.

In Like Flint. 1967, 20th Century–Fox. Elisabeth.

Star! 1968, 20th Century–Fox. (U).

Legend of the Northwest (aka: *Bearheart of the Great Northwest*). 1978, Rand Productions. (Produced in 1962; not released until 1978 due to legal entanglements.)

Beyond the Next Mountain. 1987, released only on DVD 2004.

The Right Hand Man. 1987, UAA Films. Old woman.

Beverly Hills Brats. 1989, Taurus Entertainment Co. Distributors.

Listen to Me. 1989, Weintraub Entertainment Co., 1989. Grandmother.

What Can I Do? (First screened November 18, 1993; now in collection of and distributed by Museum of Modern Art, New York.) Old woman.

Notable Television
Guest Appearances (Partial)

Listing includes name of program, episode title, network, air date(s), and character name, where known.

Robert Montgomery Presents, "The Citadel," ABC, June 19, 1950.

The Clock, "The Checked Suit," NBC, August 11, 1950.

Ford Theatre Hour, "The Marble Faun," CBS, October 10, 1950; Miriam.

The Web, "Mirror of Delusion," CBS, November 1, 1950.

Kraft Television Theatre, "Sixteen," NBC, November 8, 1950.

Somerset Maugham Theatre (aka: *Teller of Tales*), "The String of Beads," CBS, November 29, 1950.

A Date With Judy, ABC, 1951–2; Dora Foster.

Lux Video Theatre, "To the Lovely Margaret," CBS, February 19, 1951.

Ford Theatre Hour, "Peter Ibbetson," CBS, May 18, 1951.

The Web, "Wanted, Someone Innocent," CBS, June 20, 1951.

It's News to Me, CBS, July 2, 1951–August 27, 1954; quiz show panelist.

We Take Your Word, April 1, 1950–March 1, 1951; quiz show panelist.

Pulitzer Prize Playhouse, "Monsieur Beaucaire," ABC, March 12, 1952.

Robert Montgomery Presents, "The Truth About Blayds," NBC, April 28, 1952.

Robert Montgomery Presents, "The Ringmaster," NBC, May 16, 1952.

Kraft Television Theatre, "Indian Summer," NBC, August 20, 1952.

Armstrong Circle Theatre, "Run to the Magic," NBC, February 16, 1954.

Pepsi-Cola Playhouse, "The Loner," ABC, March 27, 1955.

My Friend Flicka, "Black Dust," CBS, January 13, 1956.

The Charles Farrell Show, CBS, July 16, July 23, August 6, 1956, and others; Doris Mayfield.

Perry Mason, "The Case of the Lazy Lover," CBS, May 31, 1958.

Shirley Temple's Storybook, "The Little Lame Prince," NBC, July 15, 1958; Fairy Godmother.

Peter Gunn, "Sister of the Friendless," NBC, December 22, 1958; Sister Thomas Aquinas.

The Further Adventures of Ellery Queen, "Death Likes It Hot," NBC, January 30, 1959.

The Loretta Young Show (aka: *Letter to Loretta*), "Strictly Personal," NBC, April 19, 1959.

Hawaiian Eye, "Beach Boy," ABC, November 18, 1959; Donna Lane.

Alcoa Presents One Step Beyond, "Who Are You?" ABC, February 2, 1960; Helen Mason.

The Loretta Young Show (aka: *Letter to Loretta*), "The Unwanted," NBC, May 1, 1960; Ann Tracy.

The Barbara Stanwyck Show, "The Mink Coat," NBC, September 19, 1960.

Wagon Train, "The Colter Craven Story," NBC, November 23, 1960; Mrs. Craven.

Hawaiian Eye, "Swan Song for a Hero," ABC, December 7, 1960; Holly Morrison.

Maverick, "Diamond Flush," ABC, February 5, 1961; Helen Ferguson.

Perry Mason, "The Case of the Unsuitable Uncle," CBS, November 8, 1962; Crystal Durham.

77 Sunset Strip, "The Diplomatic Caper," ABC, January 26, 1962; Lela Franklin.

McHale's Navy, "The Day They Captured Santa," ABC, December 12, 1962; Pamela Parfrey.

Dr. Kildare, "The Ship's Doctor," NBC, April 18, 1963; Frances Alland.

The Alfred Hitchcock Hour, NBC, "Last Seen Wearing Blue Jeans," April 19, 1963; Roberta Saunders.

Combat!, "The Enemy," ABC, January 5, 1965; Sister Lescaut.

Daniel Boone, "The Ben Franklin Encounter," NBC, March 18, 1965; Clara Merivale.

My Three Sons, "London Memories," CBS, April 12, 1966; Louise Allen.

Gunsmoke, "Rope Fever," CBS, December 4, 1967; Amy Bassett.

Family Affair, "Go Home, Mr. French," CBS, September 25, 1967; Lorna.

Felony Squad, "Time on Trial," ABC, November 1, 1967; Martha Lindley.

Mannix, "Edge of the Knife," CBS, November 9, 1968; Mrs. Harriman.

Hawaii Five-O, CBS, "Yesterday Died and Tomorrow Won't Be Born," CBS, December 19, 1968; Mrs. McGovern.

The Outcasts, "Give Me Tomorrow," ABC, April 21, 1969; Amelia.

Mr. Deeds Goes to Town, (pilot) ABC, September 26, 1969.

Mission: Impossible, "The Martyr," CBS, March 29, 1970; Maria Malik.

The Bold Ones: The Senator, "Power Play," NBC, November 1, 1970; Frances Mallon.

The ABC Saturday Superstar Movie, "Oliver and the Artful Dodger, Part 1, September 9, 1972, and Part 2, October 18, 1972; various voices.

The Streets of San Francisco, "Deadline," ABC, February 15, 1973; Mrs. Claridge.

My Darling Daughters' Anniversary, ABC, November 7, 1973; Judge Barbara Hanline.

The F.B.I., "The Killing Truth," ABC, December 9, 1973; Susan Harper.

Eleanor and Franklin, ABC, January 11, 1976; Laura Delano.

Eleanor and Franklin: The White House Years, ABC, March 13, 1977; Laura Delano.

The Night Rider, ABC, May 11, 1979; Lady Earl.

The Beasts Are in the Streets, NBC, May 18, 1978; Mrs. Jackson.

General Hospital, ABC, 1978–2003; Lila Quartermaine.

B.J. and the Bear, NBC, "The Eyes of Texas," NBC, November 10, 1979; Laura.

Scruples, ABC, February 25, 1980; Aunt Wilhelmina.

Port Charles, ABC, 1997–2003; Lila Quartermaine.

Index

Page numbers in **bold italics** indicate photographs.